DOWN TO EARTH DHARMA

Insight Meditation to Awaken the Heart

REBECCA BRADSHAW

SHAMBHALA

Shambhala Publications, Inc.
2129 13th Street
Boulder, Colorado 80302
www.shambhala.com

Cover art: NAITZTOYA/Adobe Stock
Cover design: Daniel Urban-Brown
Interior design: Kate Huber-Parker

9 8 7 6 5 4 3 2 1

First Edition
Printed in the United States of America

Shambhala Publications makes every effort
to print on acid-free, recycled paper.
Shambhala Publications is distributed worldwide by
Penguin Random House, Inc., and its subsidiaries.

Library of Congress Cataloging-in-Publication Data
Names: Bradshaw, Rebecca, author.
Title: Down to earth dharma: insight meditation to awaken the heart / Rebecca Bradshaw.
Description: Boulder: Shambhala Publications, 2024.
Identifiers: LCCN 2024003495 | ISBN 9781645473213 (trade paperback)
Subjects: LCSH: Vipaśyanā (Buddhism) | Buddhism—Doctrines. |
Buddhism—Essence, genius, nature.
Classification: LCC BQ4570.W6 B73 2024 | DDC 294.3/444082—dc23/eng/20240325
LC record available at https://lccn.loc.gov/2024003495

DEDICATED TO MICHELE

who made the journey possible

Praise for *Down to Earth Dharma*

"*Down to Earth Dharma* is an awakening journey into the reclamation of the eclipsed feminine within Buddhism. Rebecca's gentle, incisive approach, drawing from decades of deep meditation practice, is refreshing, healing, and engaging. Throughout there is a beautifully crafted weaving of a Buddhist worldview and its essential meditative practices with a receptive, intimate approach to life. In a world relentlessly driven by 'getting to the next thing,' this book invites us to take our foot off the accelerator and attune to the simple joy of listening more carefully to the heart. It is a vital contribution to rebalancing the ways patriarchal Buddhism tends to prefer transcendence over being rooted and truly 'Down to Earth.'"

— **THANISSARA**, author of *Time to Stand Up*

"With beautiful prose and an open heart, Rebecca Bradshaw guides us on a timeless and timely journey into the heart of what really matters in Buddhist practice. Her message—that we are made real through love and that we find wisdom through nature, the body, and relationship—is a necessary inspiration for those interested in the deep well-being that comes from waking up here and now."

— **DEVON HASE**, coauthor of *How Not to Be a Hot Mess*

"*Down to Earth Dharma* is a wonderful and engaging exploration of how the feminine archetype can greatly enrich and transform our dharma practice. Rebecca Bradshaw shows with exceptional clarity and warmth how receptivity, intuition, embodiment and relaxation open us more deeply to the classical teachings of the Buddha. She draws on a wealth of experience as a longtime meditator, teacher, therapist, world traveler, and lover of nature as she shares the many stories of her struggles and insights, always highlighting a feminine perspective that has sometimes been lost in the often hard-driving energy here in the West. These are lessons that will be invaluable for us all in these challenging times. Highly recommended."

— **JOSEPH GOLDSTEIN**, cofounder of the Insight Meditation Society and author of *Insight Meditation*

"Bradshaw's emphasis on engagement and our individual connection to the world encourages readers to transmit Buddhist practice through to all aspects of life. She offers healing to the hearts of readers and requests they pass it along to the hearts of others and to the rest of the world."

—SHARON SALZBERG, author of *Lovingkindness* and *Real Life*

"*Down to Earth Dharma* is a clear, illuminating guide that invites us to engage with the world from a place of embodiment. Rebecca's insightful book offers practical wisdom and classical and modern teachings that awaken the heart, making the dharma accessible and relevant to all. It encourages living with authenticity and compassion, guiding both new and seasoned practitioners toward a deeper connection with themselves and the world."

—DEVIN BERRY, meditation teacher, youth worker,
and cofounder of Deep Time Liberation

"Rebecca takes us on a wondrous journey through the landscape of a mind in practice. She uses artistry, storytelling and playfulness to explain age-old practices in detail. If I were new to meditation, I would feel confident in understanding basic principles that would get me on my way with a joy and curiosity that she invites us into. And for a more seasoned meditator, this book helps remind us of the expansive possibilities that an Insight Practice has to offer. It is a very creative yet in-depth exploration."

—JOANNA HARDY, lecturer, meditation teacher,
and cofounder of Meditation Coalition

"*Down to Earth Dharma* is an important book—whether you're just beginning a meditation practice or you've been meditating for decades. Rebecca clearly and beautifully articulates the importance of balancing vigorous effort with the yin, feminine, or receptive qualities of awareness. These qualities are too often undervalued in mainstream mindfulness and Buddhist teachings—let alone mainstream Western culture. Within this frame, Rebecca also seamlessly weaves in wisdom from her deep connection with the natural world. I highly recommend this book!"

—JESSICA MOREY, founder of Inward Bound Mindfulness

CONTENTS

PREFACE

The geese are taking off from the lake in the early morning light, flying south to their winter home. They honk repeatedly, encouraging each other as they begin another long day of journeying.* They navigate using signs we don't understand, but they can feel and intuit, and they will experience many vicissitudes of weather: hot days and cold ones, clear skies with a tailwind and stormy turbulence. There will be obstacles: hunters, pollution, airplanes, and headwinds. It's a vulnerable undertaking for these sensitive beings. Heading out on a long voyage takes courage, yet they don't fly alone.

Each day, we too take off in the morning light, embarking on our spiritual journey, courageously facing the ups and downs of life, embracing the inevitable joys and sorrows. We will navigate from the heart, by feeling and intuition, trusting ourselves to find our way home. There will be obstacles, many changes of circumstances. Yet we don't journey alone; we are supported by many beings and by the universe itself. Take heart, friends. Just as the geese courageously travel through all the obstacles, answering an ancient call from deep in their being, we claim our own age-old calling from the depths of our being to fly to our true home. We can call it freedom, the deepest belonging, the spacious and tender heart. We have a long journey ahead of us. May we meet it with grace, courage, and a willingness to open to this wild human life.

* Canada geese can fly 1,500 miles in a single day, if weather permits.

DOWN TO EARTH DHARMA

INTRODUCTION
PREPARING FOR OUR JOURNEY

Our Heart's Aspiration

What does our heart really want? Do we know? Perhaps the complications and distractions of modern life have kept us so busy that we haven't had time lately to check in. Try it now. Take a minute and ask your heart: *What do you really want?* Ask a few times if you need to. If you're not the type to talk to your heart, just put the question out there and make space for an answer. Wait for a response from somewhere quieter than your cognitive mind, a voice that emerges from lower in the body. This answer is important because it is your homing instinct in your travels and provides fuel for your quest. It is your own inner wisdom, your questing heart, guiding you to freedom from inner bondage.

Perhaps our deepest human aspiration is the unbinding of the heart-mind, the release of the contracted burden of our heart into a wider space of freedom. Related to this, many of us feel the yearning for more aliveness, a deeper connection, more authenticity, and greater joy in this life right here on earth. We sense that something has been lost, some connection is missing, something more real is just out of reach. In modern life we have grown increasingly estranged from our embeddedness in the world. Living primarily in our heads, we've become strangers to our own bodies and sense experience, disconnected from intimate contact with the world around us. We spend more and more time indoors in synthetic environments and on-screen in virtual realms, further and further away from the earth. We've lost our roots and feel unstable and shaky, estranged from our home. Yet even so, all of us have had times of quiet, connection, and belonging, moments of homecoming that we know as a deep sense of place. We're homesick for that place, and our yearning is our guide back.

We try to get home through the only way we know: rational thought. We keep attempting to *think* our way to peace. *How do I become happy? How do I fill this void that I feel every so often when I put down my phone or pause in the hurried schedule of my day? If I just think long enough, I'll be able to find the answer.* But thinking is part of the exile. The answer isn't in thought, the paradigm that we know. The answer is in the embodied heart, that untamed territory of feeling and sensing. What will we find there? Do we have a yearning strong enough to make the journey?

Down-to-earth dharma calls on us to establish a genuine connection with the world around us—to walk with a free heart and mind through this world, feet on the ground, eyes open, alive. Let's engage our Buddhist practice to sing with the wild insecurity of the world, to let our hearts be touched and to respond. Life is calling on us to engage, to come out of our safe cognitive cocoons and sink through the heart down into earth, embodied. The world is getting crazier, and we need to be ready. We should know how to be present, to feel our connectedness and respond, for ourselves, our families, our communities, and our planet.

The list of problems we face—economic inequality, racism, sexism, social injustice, gun violence, polarization of views, authoritarian regimes, war, the climate crisis, and the extinction of species—can feel overwhelming. How are we going to respond? We're not going to be able to think ourselves out of all of this; we're going to have to feel our way. Love is going to get us through now and in the coming times. Wisdom is needed, too, but love is going to keep us alive. This book is an invitation into the feeling heart and body, grounded in the 2,600-year-old path of Buddhism. May it enable us to answer the call of the heart's yearning, healing our homesickness. May it provide understanding of how we got here and how we might evolve. May it open us to authentic connection to the world around us. May it help save us.

The Need for Balance

In our journey, we will be exploring two archetypal energies manifesting within all of us in differing degrees, traditionally known as the *masculine* and *feminine* archetypes. These two paradigms reflect ways of orienting toward and engaging with the world. Regardless of our gender, both orientations are present in us. Both archetypal energies are important for our functioning and needed for balance. When one paradigm becomes overly predominant, things go awry. Knowing how to recognize imbalance and regain balance is an essential skill in our lives and in our meditation practice.

The masculine paradigm or archetype is oriented toward action, focus, individualism, achieving a goal, and transcendence. Relying on the conceptual mind, analysis, and rationality, this archetype highlights intellect and the absolute. We can also call it *mind energy, yang,* or an *active orientation* toward life, terms I will use interchangeably throughout the book. The feminine paradigm, on the other hand, manifests as feeling, embodiment, relaxation, receptivity, and intuition. Being is more important than doing. This archetype recognizes our interdependence and emphasizes our relational embeddedness in life. We can also call it *heart energy, yin,* or a *receptive orientation* toward life. Too much masculine or active energy can result in control, domination, and disconnection from the world around us. Too much feminine or receptive energy, on the other hand, can manifest as passivity and overwhelm. Yin and yang balance each other; they need each other.

Using the terms *masculine paradigm* and *feminine paradigm* in today's social environment is complicated. Gender is fluid within all of us, and polarized terms like *masculine* and *feminine* may feel too hardline binary to some. Others may take issue with the values assigned to one term or the other. After much contemplation and consultation, I have decided to stick with this structure as encompassing the widest package of qualities—but not exclusively. I will also employ the other terms outlined here, especially when they convey the meaning important for the specific context. If the terms *feminine* and *masculine* are uncomfortable for you, feel free to translate them as yin and yang, receptive and active, or heart and mind. We can also remember that these polarities are not hard and fast binaries but rather mutually supporting qualities on a continuum that flows through all of us.

Modern life in many parts of the West, particularly in the United States, reflects a deep imbalance of these qualities: yang energy without sufficient yin energy. Dominant patriarchal culture values and prioritizes the masculine or active energies. As a result, most of us experience our hearts and minds being skewed in this direction, creating an imbalance within ourselves and society at large.[1] I want to be clear: this book is not about disparaging men or masculine paradigm energies. The qualities of initiative, conceptualization, goal orientation, and action are all needed in our lives. However, when these qualities are not balanced with heart and receptivity, they can become toxic and manifest as aggression, manipulation, cruelty, dissociation, and unbridled greed. We know this lack of balance in the ever-increasing emphasis on speed and efficiency, the unsustainable nature of our lifestyles without regard for limitation and human need. It is expressed in the desecration of the natural world, in disregarding sustainability and the rights of animals, plants, and minerals. Our economic systems promote greed and inequality, and our political bodies minimize human services in favor of war. We know this disbalance in the frenzied disconnection of our electronic lives and in the shallowness of our entertainment options. We feel it in the loss of connection to the land around us and in our separation from the plants and animals. Almost all of us—even those who were raised in more balanced cultures—have internalized deeply androcentric conditioning.

In modern culture, masculine paradigm qualities generally subsume the gentler orientation of the feminine archetype. Strategic thinking and intelligence tend to be more highly valued than love and compassion, and individuation is emphasized over community. We assume that thinking and analyzing can solve all problems, and then overlook the intelligence of heart and intuition. Constant productivity and ceaseless striving to excel are normalized. Independence is emphasized, disavowing our deep interdependence.

Our hearts—and bodies—are breaking under the stress and strain of this unbalanced way of living. We yearn for something that perhaps we can't yet articulate but sense underneath the cacophony of modern life. We want time and space to listen to our hearts, to rest and to be. We wish for our minds to quiet and our hearts to be still. We hunger to feel our connection to the world around us, to the people, the trees, and the earth, knowing that we belong here. We are searching for the strength, beauty, and gentleness of the yin archetype within. The dominance of the mind seeks balance in the heart. We wish to reclaim our ability to feel deeply, embody wisdom, and sense the sacredness of this very world.

The qualities of the feminine paradigm are not foreign to any of us; rather they are part of our very being, persevering as undercurrents in dominant Western culture and still flourishing in more balanced cultures both in the United States and around the world. We can reawaken and nourish these down-to-earth heart-based qualities. Buddhism from the feminine archetype supports this yearning of our heart. This journey into yin energy goes against the mainstream of modern industrial culture, yet it honors and trusts profound ways of being that have roots in all of us. Let's be prodigal children, coming home to reclaim our inheritance.

Buddhism and Androcentrism

I wish to express heartfelt appreciation for the monastic orders that have preserved the Buddha's teachings for 2,600 years. Many generations of women and men have dedicated their lives to the practice and transmission of the teachings. It's highly unlikely that we would have the Buddha's dispensation today without their commitment and practice.

Now that Insight Meditation is well established in the United States—although some would claim that we are still in the early years of transmission—it is time to evaluate what we have inherited and what legacy we want to pass on. Which perspectives and ways of presenting Theravada or classical Buddhism have been emphasized and which have been left out? What conditioning have we inherited both in our expression of Buddhist truths and in our practice of meditation? What has been devalued and needs emphasis? How, for example, would the dharma look if it had been preserved primarily by a female monastic lineage?

Because of the diversity of Buddhist communities in the United States and the West, clarifying which communities we are addressing is important in our exploration. There are many Asian Theravada Buddhist temples in the United States (Cambodian, Sri Lankan, Thai, Burmese, Vietnamese, and Malaysian) where Buddhism retains the flavor and influence of the native country. We will be focusing, however, on what are sometimes called Western convert communities, practice centers that were established in the United States when Westerners who practiced meditation in India, Thailand, and Myanmar (Burma) in the 1960s and early '70s returned to the United States and founded retreat centers.[2] The presentation of the teachings through these primarily white middle- and upper-middle-class teachers tended to emphasize what fit in with our modern, industrialized civilization, leaning toward the masculine paradigm. Exploring the meeting of this androcentric transmission of Buddhism over the centuries with our current dominant culture leaning toward the masculine paradigm can highlight some gaps and orient us toward more balance.

Let us turn toward investigating any tendencies in the preservation of the teachings. The most complete rendering of Buddhist teachings— and of any spiritual lineage—emerges from a balanced expression of the masculine and feminine paradigms. Buddhism arose almost 2,600 years ago at a time when religious traditions around the world were growing increasingly dominated and controlled by men. The Buddhist teachings were formally preserved and transmitted for most of their long history through a primarily male monastic tradition. Except for the small volume of poems called the Therigatha (Songs of the Elder Nuns) and one section of the Samyutta-nikaya (one set of Buddhist discourses), the voices of women are either largely absent from the extensive canonical writings and discourses of Early Buddhism or have faded into the background through centuries of androcentric transmission. The absence of female voices has been further exacerbated in Theravada Buddhism by the historical loss of the female monastic order due to a lack of support.[3] Although the truths the Buddha taught are universal and not dependent on culture, the transmission of his teachings has been conditioned by the cultures in which they have been embedded. The nature of this history of transmission has shaped which teachings were preserved and how they were disseminated. Embedded in male monasticism, Early Buddhism has historically tended toward androcentrism at the expense of the feminine archetype.[4]

A current parallel may help us appreciate how this gender imbalance affects the transmission of ideas. The 2018 documentary *This Changes Everything,* which explores gender disparity in Hollywood, observes that the overwhelming majority of film directors have been men. Male directors tend to make films with more male characters and to cater their products to male sensibilities. A female director tells us that it has been a great loss for all of us that we have not had the perspective of more women in the movies. The same is true for Buddhism: the voices and directors have been overwhelmingly male, and it's a great loss for all of us—male, female, and nonbinary—that the feminine voice and paradigm have not had equal representation over the centuries in Buddhism.

In current times, the dominant culture's preference for masculine paradigm energies can join with this historical inheritance to reinforce an unbalanced approach to the teachings and our meditation practice. Institutionalized and internalized sexism in Western Buddhist-convert organizations compounds the preference for the masculine paradigm. At an international vipassana teachers meeting in 2012, participants were invited to list ways institutionalized sexism manifests in our Insight Meditation communities. Teachers of all genders listed twenty-five, including the tendency to worship male teachers, assigning senior teachers to male students more often than women, and the stigmatizing of emotional expression. There is still work to do to address institutionalized sexism and the devaluing of the feminine paradigm in all our Buddhist communities in order to bring beautiful balance into our ways of expressing and living the Buddhist path.

It is important to note that even with a long history of androcentric transmission, the Buddha's teachings have been expressed through the feminine paradigm at many times over the centuries by both monastics and lay teachers. Currently in our Insight Meditation communities, the feminine voice in teachers of all genders is thriving along with a growing recognition that the teachings need to be presented in a balanced manner—both active and receptive, goal-oriented and present moment–oriented, energetic and relaxed, conceptual and heart-embracing, transcendent and relational.

This book endeavors to support this trend toward the cultivation of the feminine paradigm. We will honor and value ways of being that include the heart, feeling, intuition, embodiment, receptivity, interdependence, and relationality. We will weave together this cultivation both internally within this body, heart, and mind, and externally in our connection with the world around us. May this exploration lead to deeper balance within all of us, for ourselves, for each other, and for our planet Earth.

Who Am I?

Who am I? What is my social location and my cultural and familiar conditioning? What life experiences have shaped me? I want to answer these questions because we are entering into a relationship, and these factors influence how I experience the world and how I present it.* Most importantly perhaps for this book, I identify as a cisgendered woman, and my racial background is white. I consider myself heterosexual and have a long-term partner, recently made husband. I grew up in South Minneapolis in a middle-class family with seven siblings. Yes, we were Catholic. After my parents had a disagreement with the Church, we eventually landed with the Unitarian Universalists, but not before my mother tried to teach us Hindu meditation. In college, I majored in Spanish and Ibero-American studies and practiced earth-based spirituality. In my late teens and early twenties, my life was enriched by studying and working abroad in Peru,

---

* Also when I read a book, I always want to know the story of the author, so I google them to see what I can learn. I'll save you the googling.

Spain, Mexico, and Nicaragua. Shortly thereafter I found Buddhist meditation in the Insight Meditation tradition and knew quickly that this was my spiritual home. I studied for many years under both Western lay and Eastern monastic teachers in the Burmese Mahasi lineage, one of the most rigorous and disciplined systems of practice in classical Buddhism. Eventually I trained to be a dharma teacher at the Insight Meditation Society (IMS), where we studied the sutras, discourses, and commentaries of the Pali canon as our primary texts. In more recent times I have practiced the Kwan Yin dharmas in the Chan lineage of Master Hua of the City of Ten Thousand Buddhas. Learning qigong in a water tradition has also been a very important part of my spiritual practice. The woods, lakes, hills, and the earth itself, including all the beings that reside here, teach me, too, in myriad wordless ways. I have worked as a paper girl,* babysitter, fast-food worker, waiter, farmworker, home health aide, English as a Second Language teacher, Spanish teacher, psychotherapist, and dharma teacher. I currently live in the hills of Western Massachusetts with my partner/husband of close to three decades, Bob, our two cats Sparky and Iris Bonita, and all the woodland beings both seen and unseen who call this area their home. All these experiences have contributed to who I am and how I perceive the world. While I aspire to write in a way that feels inclusive to all, I will inevitably default at times to habits and cultural conditioning that stem from these experiences and my social locations. You, too, bring your own influences, social identities, and life experiences to the reading of this book. Let's set out together to explore the wilderness of our embodied heart-mind and the freedom of the Buddha's teachings.

Blessings and Protection

We embark on our journey by first calling on and receiving blessings and support. Oh, did you think you were going to do it all on your own? In the heroic spiritual quest according to the masculine paradigm, the

---

* For you younger people, a paper girl delivers newspapers door-to-door in a neighborhood on foot or by bike.

hero embarks alone on their road, meets many obstacles, and battles their way to the end of their quest. The relational paradigm in the story tends to be overlooked, but the fact is that the hero usually can't complete their quest on their own and receives help and blessings along the way. We are no different: we need nurturing and nourishment on our meditation journey. We begin our practice by connecting with that which supports and blesses as we dive deeply into the delights and challenges of spiritual life.

The word *blessing* is not commonly used in convert Buddhist circles and may even be regarded with some suspicion. For some, *bless* is a charged term that feels too religious, awkward, or foreign. I googled it to see exactly what it means. Two salient definitions are "to receive support and protection" and "to make sacred."

The dominant paradigm in much of Western culture is based in extreme individualism: the idea that we rely almost entirely on ourselves and our own efforts to succeed in life—or to succeed in meditation. Of course, our individual efforts are indispensable. It takes enormous determination to cultivate a spiritual path. Only we can get ourselves to our meditation cushion to engage in formal meditation practice. We ourselves must call forth the intention for mindfulness in our informal practice as we move through our day. Individual commitment and perseverance are required on our path. However, we don't walk this path alone. We recognize our embeddedness in life, our interdependence, and our need for help. In Theravada monastic traditions, many meditations start with chanting homage to the Triple Jewel—the Buddha, the Dharma, and the Sangha. This chant is a blessing that reminds us of the support that we can call on. Consciously bringing these three supports to mind, and even voicing them, can help us feel strong and connected.

The historical Buddha provides us inspiration as an example of the enlightened heart and mind. If the Buddha doesn't inspire you, any noble, uplifting person, historical or current, can serve as this support. Perhaps your own religion provides an example of an awakened being. These beings act as reminders of our own capacity for awakening as we call on our potential for the most profound freedom of heart and mind.

We are also blessed with the Dharma—the truth and the teachings. A rich history of meditation teachings is available to us through the 2,600 years from the time of the Buddha up to the present day. Insight Meditation was not invented ten or twenty years ago, but rather is a tried-and-true spiritual path with the strength of centuries of transmission. These teachings support us with instructions and guidelines for paying attention to our own experience in order to develop understanding that frees our heart-mind. In addition, the Dharma points toward the truth of our own experience, which teaches us everything we need to know. We call on the Dharma to point the way.

The third jewel, the Sangha—the community of both monastics and laypeople, historical and present-day—blesses us with spiritual companionship. Our spiritual ancestors, primarily from Southeast Asia, have held the Insight Meditation tradition for centuries, passing the knowledge from teacher to student and practicing just like we do. We can feel the cumulative support of those who have taken on monastic robes, both monks and nuns, devoting their entire lives to these teachings and ensuring that they are not lost but rather transmitted to the next generation. We are also blessed with centuries of laypeople who have upheld this transmission through their own meditation and generosity. We call on these spiritual ancestors to bless and support us on our path.

Our biological ancestors can be part of our sangha, too. We may relate strongly to one or more of our ancestors and the strengths that we inherited from them. If our ancestors survived traumatic and horrifying circumstances, we can recognize the resilience of our own internal survivor. Perhaps an ancestor had a spiritual leaning, whether recognized externally or not, that we inherited. I connect to my Celtic ancestors, who emphasized the aliveness of all things and the sacredness of everyday life. We call on our biological ancestors to bless our journey and to support us.

Our sangha also includes our family, friends, and fellow practitioners— the people around us who hold us in community. They can inspire and support us. They may even aid our practice by irritating us and showing us where we are still stuck. Both friend and foe teach us how to come out of our self-absorbed cocoons and engage skillfully and kindly in this world. We call on them as an important part of our spiritual support network.

Along with the three refuges, in our Insight communities we also chant the five mindfulness trainings: guidelines to protect us from unskillful and unwholesome actions that lead to suffering. (The short version of these precepts, to be explored more fully in later chapters, stipulates refraining from killing, stealing, sexual misconduct, lying, and misusing intoxicants.)

These precepts safeguard us from the turbulence of a heart-mind filled with remorse, regret, and complication. The precepts encourage us in wholesome, helpful actions that bring happiness to ourselves and the world by reminding us of our intention to live with compassion. They create a protective space for us and for those with whom we come in contact. We call them in as protection from committing actions that harm ourselves or others.

Buddhist lineages also include a host of other protective and blessing chants. Many cultures understand that we can connect with myriad forces in the world for support. Buddhist psychology describes thirty-two realms of existence, most of these heavenly realms occupied by heavenly beings. The Buddhist worldview generally accepts that these unseen beings can provide support.

Reciting an ancient chant is one way to receive the blessings of these beings. We connect with the cumulative spiritual power of centuries of people who have voiced these verses before us. Chanting wakes up the mind and heart and soothes the body. The vibrations both energize and calm us. Chanting nourishes devotion and other heart qualities. Right now, I am on retreat, and every morning I chant the Khandha-Paritta, a Pali protection chant that sends *metta* (lovingkindness) to all beings around me, including the footless, the two-footed, the four-footed, and the many-footed. After sending metta, the chanter requests that the creepy-crawly slithery beings not harm us. In the end we ask them to depart, but with metta! This chant imbues my meditation space with kindness and protection. So far, the footless and the footed ones have indeed left me alone. During my times at the monastery in the Sagaing

Hills of Myanmar, the sound of Pali chanting rolled through the valleys, touching a wordless place deep within imbued with the timelessness of the dharma. We can feel this same force field of the dharma whenever we visit temples or meditation centers and be nourished by its power and protection.

Moving on to the second part of the definition of *blessing*—sacredness—creating a sacred place, a spiritual sense of our home, can help us relax into our practice and feel supported. Our systems settle down and connect best under conditions of safety. What provides this support in our own home? As we settle into practice, we gather props that nurture a feeling of safety, protection, and strength. Pictures in our meditation space or on our altar of our spiritual elders, familial ancestors, mentors, or other loved ones can inspire and protect us. Statues of Kwan Yin—the embodiment of compassion—or the Buddha or other archetypes may support us. If we practice from a secular orientation, an image that reminds us of qualities we want to call forth could serve as a support, such as a photo depicting the vast ocean or a radiant flower blossom. We can take time to feel our resonance with these images, knowing that love, companionship, and support exist in this world.

For many, nature reminds us of sacredness. We may take in the powerful energy of the trees, the earth, and the beings both human and non-human that surround us. Whether we're living in the country or the city, connecting with the beauty and sacredness of the natural world can resonate deeply. Flowers growing in our garden can support our awakening. Plants that we lovingly nurture in the window of our apartment can nourish our hearts. Sitting under a tree, we connect with our roots and the sky. Resting on a rock, we know our own inner stability. Objects from nature in our meditation space can ground and uplift us.

Knowing the environment around us situates us firmly in our place on earth, reminding us that we belong. All the beings in our community are part of our sangha. How well do we know our neighborhoods? Do we walk there and pay attention? Can we connect with the barking dog or greet the person waiting for the bus at the same time as us? What can we learn about the plants and beings around us? Jenny Odell in

How to Do Nothing calls our cultural disconnection from the nonhuman beings in our environment "species loneliness."[5] We can heal this alienation by learning the names of the flowers that we see, including the weeds in the cracks in the sidewalk. We can get to know the animals in our neighborhood, both domestic and wild. Rose-breasted grosbeaks come to our backyard bird feeders in the summer. I know them individually by the pattern they have on their breast, a rose-colored splotch ending in a line. My husband and I have even named them, including one with a very long line whom we called Linus. The plants and animals of our bioregion are part of our sangha and knowing them helps heal a loneliness we may not have even known we were suffering. Getting to know our neighborhood—whether rural, suburban, or urban—we feel embeddedness, safety, and belonging. We relate to the people and other beings around us, the land around us, and our homes as sacred. This orientation encourages quiet, more settled energy.

We can sum up the many blessings and protections we cultivate and receive on the path by citing a well-known Buddhist sutra: the Mangala Sutra, the Discourse of Great Blessings. This teaching discusses thirty-eight blessings in our lives, which we can place in four main categories. First, our ethical conduct is a blessing and protection for us, safeguarding us from actions that cause suffering to ourselves and others. We can reflect on the ways that we have acted ethically and enjoy healthy self-esteem. Second, generosity is a blessing we create when we share of ourselves with others, assuring us of a feeling of abundance. We bring joy and lightness to our heart-mind by contemplating our good deeds and acts of kindness, all the ways that we have given of ourselves. Third, both hearing and studying the dharma and enjoying the fruits of our own practice are beautiful blessings. We can appreciate our good fortune in having opportunities to encounter the teachings. Fourth, the highest blessing is having the conditions in our lives to be able to practice the dharma. We can reflect on what we've learned in our own practice and acknowledge that we have been truly fortunate to have the opportunity and conditions to transform our lives. We can relate to our lives as sacred, the hallowed ground of our spiritual path.

And now it's time to start on our journey. We will study the practice of Insight Meditation, meandering and musing along our way, feeling and intuiting. Our reflections will emphasize the yin perspective of the heart, bringing balance to these profound and sacred teachings. We will also encourage a full flourishing of the path of meditation, valuing heart and mind, embracing both the feminine and masculine paradigms within us all. Let's explore the wilderness of our own lives and life itself.

PART ONE

MINDFULNESS AND THE BODY

MINDFULNESS

What Meditation Is

What is meditation? It is a technique that facilitates directly experiencing our lives as a way to understand deeply the nature of reality, the way things are. Knowing how our world is, we learn to walk through this life with a free heart and mind. We awaken the heart-mind of nonclinging, eventually opening to *nibbana* (nirvana or enlightenment).[1] We could also say meditation is relaxing into ever-deepening intimacy with the mystery of life. They're both true. We open out of the contraction of the small ego-centric self and relax into being life itself. We experience this as freedom.

From the active paradigm, meditation is a technique working toward a goal. We want to free the heart-mind and awaken the deepest wisdom and compassion. This goal is helpful as a structure and gives purpose to our path. We have direction: we are going somewhere, and we are doing something. The masculine paradigm of initiative and energy is activated.

However, when our mind is set on a future goal, we may risk missing the journey itself. Our attention can be fixated on when we're going to get our meditation exactly right. We find ourselves leaning forward out of presence, hurrying into the next moment, which may hold the key, and missing the one we're in. And then we do that again. In its extreme, we devalue the moment we are in as never quite good enough because there must be a better one that we can get to. Our happiness is always just out of reach.

From the overemphasized mind-centered paradigm, we believe that controlling the heart and the mind is the way to peace. We turn to meditation to try to master our heart and mind so that they fit an imagined ideal state. Trying to get somewhere, to produce a perfect state, we find ourselves instead becoming increasingly tense and tangled. The demanding nature of this effort disturbs and contracts the heart-mind. We have taken our goal too far.

While acknowledging the benefit of having purpose and direction in our meditation practice, it's equally true that we are not going anywhere and we're not doing anything. Where can we ever be but here and now? There is no journey to take to arrive at the present moment. We're here! Rather than trying to get somewhere, from the heart paradigm we relax into now and here. Less like a hunter and more like a gatherer, we receive rather than pursue. This kind of attention orients toward a state of openness—each moment fresh, resisting our tendency to adhere to one version of reality. We understand that this life is a vast mystery that cannot be fully understood. We commit ourselves to being comfortable in this unknowing, in this vastness, which manifests in the face of a daisy and the feel of our feet on the floorboards.

This more receptive orientation loves the journey itself. We allow ourselves to be intimate with and touched by this life. This moment is it: perfect and in need of nothing more. And we love it for simply being. The heart opens and lets in the bright red maple leaves, the swampy smell of the bog, the beeping of the truck, and the warmth of the sun. The unwholesome states that block the heart dissolve, allowing room for the beautiful states of heart to shine forth. This journey is softer. We do not "do" this orientation; life does us. As we relax more and more deeply into right here now, life through this intimacy tells us how things are.

As we arrive more fully here, we access a kind of unconditional joy independent of any goal. One young man at a Teen Retreat at the Insight Meditation Society wrote a beautiful piece describing the first time he experienced this kind of joy. He said it wasn't about a video game or new sneakers; it was just the joy of being here right now. It blew his mind! It blows our mind the first time we experience this huge paradigm shift. We come out of the belief that happiness is something we will achieve in the future and land in the unconditional happiness of the heart-mind simply present on this earth, right here, right now.

Mindfulness from the Heart

Mindfulness or *sati* is the heart of Buddhist meditation practice. What exactly is this quality we call *mindfulness*? After nearly three decades of practice, I said to my teacher during a retreat, "I think I'm finally understanding what mindfulness is." She laughed and said, "That shows that you're paying attention." Our understanding of mindfulness deepens over the years. Let's never be too sure that we know what it is so that we don't close down our investigation of this most incredible quality that the Buddha called "the master of all things."

Mindfulness—the ability to pay full attention unobstructed by greed or judgment—is at the root of our ability to change our conditioned patterning and free the heart and mind of bondage. But mindfulness is more than just paying attention or being present: true mindfulness brings wisdom to our attention and frees the heart-mind through feeling and understanding.

In the Pali language, the same word, *citta*, is used for both "mind" and "heart." Ajahn Chah, the Thai forest master, says, "Buddhism is a religion of the heart," and many of his translations use the word *heart*. But in our Western culture, which tends to be fascinated by the ways of the mind and leery of the ways of the heart, *citta* is almost always translated as "mind." Following this pattern of preference for mind over heart, the general translation for *sati* is "mindfulness." What happens when we translate *sati* as "heartfulness"? How does the flavor of our attention change? Mindfulness may feel analytical and detached. Heartfulness tastes of wholehearted presence that brings all of us, mind *and* heart, to this moment.

The Buddhist scholar Bhikkhu Analayo says that sati is a feminine quality. The Pali word is in the feminine gender, pointing toward its receptive nature. We take in experience and let it give birth to an intuitive understanding that can liberate. Suzuki Roshi suggests that with sati we should be ready to see with a soft mind. We call forth both alertness and softness with a receptive, open, and flexible attitude. We cultivate a heart-mind ready to meet the world just as it is.

Mindfulness, or heartfulness, receives the present moment and learns from it. It's nondemanding; no matter what the moment offers, sati receives it. With mindfulness, we let go of arguing with the experience of the present moment. We don't need it to be different or better and improved; it is what it is. Can we meet that? With receptivity, we don't struggle to be free, but rather give up the struggle, relax, and surrender to the moment. We rest in life as it manifests, without resistance. That's freedom.

Mindfulness from the heart recognizes that the core of Buddhist practice is relationship. Life is relationship. We are always relating, whether connecting to our own embodied experience, to other people, or to the world around us. The quality of this relationship determines whether the moment is experienced as suffering or freedom and whether the wake left behind us is one of turbulence or compassion. We tend this relationship to understand it deeply and guide it ever more consistently toward open-hearted peace.

At first, mindfulness can feel like a personal achievement. *I am being mindful,* we think. As we set out, this attitude can help us to clarify the presence and knowing that are characteristics of mindfulness. Identification with mindfulness can help us come out of the complex trance of the thinking and conceptual mind. However, as we relax into greater and greater receptivity, identification with mindfulness lessens, and we increasingly feel that mindfulness is just happening, arising due to causes and conditions. It's not so personal. As we identify less with being the *person* being mindful, our practice takes on a more spacious quality. Relaxing more deeply, this spaciousness settles into wide compassionate awareness.

Mindfulness melds into awareness: a knowing as vast as the universe. Can we grasp awareness? Is there any way that we can make it ours? Awareness is not mine or yours. It just is; it's part of this wide world. This body, heart, and mind are a vehicle for consciousness to express itself. This body is a home for the world to sense, experience, and know itself. Awareness knows this world, receiving it openheartedly and without judgment. Awareness illuminates this life.

Collecting the Heart-Mind

As vipassana, or mindfulness, meditators, we wish to connect with life as it presents itself moment by moment in our body, mind, and heart. If we tell ourselves, *Sit down and pay attention to your life,* we all know how that will go. Therefore, it is usually recommended that we use an anchor, or primary object, to connect and stabilize our attention. Traditionally, focusing on the sensations of breathing is a convenient anchor that is always present while we're alive. We rest our attention with the breath at the abdomen or at the tip of the nostrils or upper lip area, connecting with the sensations we feel as we breathe in and out. When our attention wanders elsewhere, we gently direct it back to the sensations of breathing.

Whether the breath is long or short, smooth or coarse, subtle or gross, we strengthen the ability to connect with the present moment through feeling our breath. We direct our attention to the actual sensations themselves—expansion and contraction, heat and coolness, pressure, tingling, and movement—without controlling or trying to change them. At first, we may find that we *think about* the breath, at some distance from the actual experience. As we rest our attention closer to our body, we notice the difference between thinking about the breath and truly connecting with it, thinking about body sensations and feeling them. We are coming down to earth, to our embodied home on this planet.

Having an anchor or home base helps us connect our attention to the present moment and develops concentration, or *samadhi*. If the breath isn't comfortable for us, however, any somatic experience can serve. Our anchor should be neutral or slightly pleasant so that it is easy to engage. For some meditators, the breath will not be the best anchor if it feels tight or overcontrolled. In this case, alternatives may work better, such as feeling the whole body sitting alternating with the sensations of the hands touching each other or the thighs. Another possible anchor is the experience of hearing sounds coming and going. One anchor is not better than another. What's important is that the anchor feels comfortable and easy to engage.

With our comfortable anchor or home base, we begin to settle down and develop concentration. Stronger concentration leads to increased clarity, giving us a fighting chance to see what is happening in our minds and hearts. We use this clarity to observe for ourselves what leads to suffering and what leads to happiness. This is the true gift of meditation.

When we hear the word *concentration*, however, what comes to mind? We may think of furrowing the brow, determination, and effort. We hear that concentration is important in our meditation practice, so we sit down and try to focus on our breath. We bring that determination and effort to this project. We may even furrow our brow. We may become frustrated, and then we try harder, furrowing our brow more. Maybe we even get a headache. One of the paradoxes of concentration is that the harder we try, the less settled the mind becomes. Perhaps it is better to translate *samadhi* as "nondistractedness" or "unification"—ideas that might help us relax. We're really just trying to settle down.

Many of us approach meditation like a woodpecker pecking on a tree. We try to pound it out. We whack at our meditation object over and over again. We use force and will to try to get what we want. Our practice may also contain elements of the style of the blue jay, determined and bossy. We hope that if we boss our attention, it will obey us. In this way we attempt to concentrate our attention on our breath or other anchor.

What if our meditation were more like the song of the wood thrush? Light, ethereal, and gentle. When we hear the wood thrush sing, we feel blessed, and we relax and quiet. The wood thrush can point us toward a gentler kind of effort, easing our way into concentration. The deepest concentration comes out of relaxation. We might do better being wood thrushes rather than woodpeckers!

If birds aren't our thing, we can imagine a drummer and a flute player. Do we practice like a drum soloist banging away? Or is our effort more like the flute player's, flowing and smooth? We can combine the right drumbeats and the lyrical song of the flute. The drummer and the flutist work together; the drummer contains and gives structure to our musical composition and the flute provides the melody.

Concentration and mindfulness are often described as having two components: an active one of aiming and a receptive one of sustaining. A softer rendering might call them connecting and receiving. First, we aim the awareness toward an object, and then we allow it to rest there and know the experience. Because of our preference for the active paradigm, we can find ourselves repeatedly aiming, just like the woodpecker, and not allowing ourselves to rest with knowing the experience. In our anxiety to get it right, we overshoot the target and feel worn out with the repetition of aiming. Many Westerners need to emphasize the receptive part of concentration, resting and being with the meditation object. Sayadaw U Pandita would describe sustaining as rubbing the experience. When we rub the experience, we are invited into intimacy, like hearing the song of the wood thrush or the flute.

Concentration and mindfulness work in tandem. Concentration gets us to the park and mindfulness smells the roses. We can't smell the roses if we don't get to the park, so concentration helps us arrive. Once we are at the park, we receive the experience of the moment, including the smell of the roses. We settle in; we don't keep looking for the park.

Now that we have arrived at the park, we may smell the roses, and we might also notice the sound of the waterfall and the songs of the birds, the feeling of the breeze on our cheeks, and the contact of our feet with the earth. When we experience successive moments of presence, we are not distracted. This type of concentration, called *momentary concentration*, isn't focusing on a single object but rather successive moments of mindfulness that coalesce as nondistractedness. This more receptive type of concentration not narrowing in on one object receives each moment, whatever is arising, in ongoing presence. The drummer fades into the background and the flute song becomes predominant.

Let's allow the woodpecker and the wood thrush to live in the same neighborhood, coexisting, each one contributing to the soundscape of our meditation. The woodpecker beckons us here, and the thrush encourages us to relax into the experience of presence. The drummer calls us to arrive, and the flutist sings our song.

Intimacy with All Things

The thirteenth-century Zen master Dōgen is known for having taught that without intimacy, there is no awakening; in awakening, there is intimacy with all things and all beings.

Orienting toward the feminine paradigm, intimacy can be described as "close familiarity" or "friendship." Familiarity strengthens over time as we connect repeatedly with our own experience and the world around us. We start by creating this "close familiarity" with our own selves. Who are we? What are we? We scramble endlessly, so very busy, responding on automatic and rarely take time to stop and experience who and what we are. Through a formal meditation practice and informal mindfulness practice during our day, we cultivate this intimacy, this close familiarity, with our own being. We orient toward our embodied experience through our senses, and this leads us inward to our full complexity as a living, breathing, alive human being.

The second part of the definition of intimacy is friendship. Intimacy is possible only when the heart is kind. Judging or critiquing creates a barrier that prevents us from getting truly close to our experience. Practicing kindhearted awareness, we nurture a relationship of love, trust, and openness with our own body and heart. It takes time, just as developing intimacy with another person takes time. Our heart needs to confirm that we are trustworthy, warm, and respectful. Are we going to boss it around, or are we going to listen and be present like a true friend?

This intimacy with our own experience develops as we turn toward what's really happening in our body, heart, and mind and not what we think should be happening, what we want to be happening, nor what a good meditator would be experiencing, but rather what is in reality the truth of our experience. Since we maintain many ideas of who we are and what we aren't, when we sit down and experience mind, heart, and body directly, intimately, we are often surprised by what shows up. I entered my first three-month retreat thinking that I was pretty together and was shocked to discover that I was quite a mess! Emotions that I had kept tightly sequestered—anger, fear, loneliness, and grief—arose in full force in my heart-mind. The German-born meditation matriarch Ruth Denison used to say with her delightful German accent, "Self-knowledge, darlings, is always bad news!"[2] While this statement might be a bit of an exaggeration, it contains a lot of truth. We free the heart-mind by not turning away but instead turning toward the whole catastrophe, experiencing our life with curiosity and warmth.

In case I sound too discouraging, we also discover strengths of which we may have been previously unaware. During that first long retreat I was amazed at my capacity for joy, concentration, relaxation, and spaciousness. We discover that we are larger than we thought, more capable than we knew, and wiser and more loving than we believed possible. This too is part of intimacy with our own experience, familiarity with who and what we are as a living, breathing human being.

This intimacy is a genuine path toward awakening, expressed beautifully in the enlightenment poem of the Japanese nun Izumi Shikibu.

Watching the moon
at midnight,
solitary, mid-sky,
I knew myself completely,
no part left out.[3]

The freedom of her heart-mind, no part left out, is held within the open sky and peaceful moonlight. As intimacy deepens, we too feel that we know ourselves more completely, nothing exiled.

Developing this intimacy within our own selves, we turn toward the world around us and cultivate familiarity with all things, again emphasizing closeness and friendship. How do we become close to the world around us? By letting it in. The environmentalist Paul Shepard wrote, "Ultimately, to be present in the world means making room for the world to be present in you."[4] We receive the experience of being embedded in this world through seeing, hearing, smelling, tasting, and feeling the body and the heart. We let life in through our senses as the portals joining the inner and the outer. Dōgen describes this intimacy thus: "Let your heart go out and abide in things. Let things return and abide in your heart."[5] In intentionally connecting with life around us, nonjudgmental respectful attention facilitates coming closer. With an attitude of friendliness, kindness, and patience, we encourage this intimacy with all things to flourish.

To bring this intimacy to greater fruition, we dissolve what separates and shields us from the world around us. Through meditation practice, we feel the estrangement of greed, hatred, and delusion—the three roots of suffering—and know for ourselves how they separate us from genuinely touching life. We feel in our own hearts how greed occupies space that could be available for connection, smothering any possible intimacy with the desired object. Aversion hopes not to meet the experience at all, turning away, pulling back from connecting. Delusion anesthetizes us, obscuring and dulling any potential intimacy. To truly connect with life necessitates dealing with these three roots of suffering. For true intimacy we dissolve the separation created by greed, hatred, and delusion. We heal our estrangement as a separate defensive self and recognize our undeniable embeddedness and vulnerable interconnectedness.

The eighth-century Chinese poet Li Po offers a reflection capturing the intimacy of this relationship with the world around us.

The birds have vanished into the sky,
Now the last cloud drains away.
We sit together, the mountains and me,
until only the mountain remains.[6]

We become intimate with all manifestations of life—ourselves, other people, trees, birds, snails—and even the supposedly inanimate—tables, clouds, breakfast, rocks. Intimacy with all things! What does it mean to connect intimately with a rock? Rocks are amazing beings, so solid and direct. When we need grounding, they're a great friend. Intimacy with all things leads us into a personal experience of the beingness of many things that are considered not-so-sentient in the dominant materialistic view that objectifies anything that isn't human. This objectification of the natural world is directly responsible for much of the destruction of modern industrial society. When trees are viewed as nonsentient, it doesn't matter if we cut them down. When rocks have no being, it's okay to blow off the top of a mountain. When the earth itself is considered inanimate, it doesn't matter how we treat it. But when we develop intimacy, we know deep in our own hearts that trees feel, mountains have beingness, and life everywhere deserves respect.

In her book *Under a White Sky*, Elizabeth Kolbert writes about the effort to save the endangered pupfish at Devils Hole. The biologist Phil Pister is asked, "What good are pupfish?" and he responds, "What good are you?"[7] From the feminine paradigm, we know that all beings have a right to exist and thrive just because they are.

Through intimacy with all things, we reclaim our feminine archetypal relationship with life: one of receptivity, respect, and mutuality. This relationship feels everything as alive, including other human beings, chickadees, frogs, fish, bears, as well as chairs, brooms, and rocks. Each has their own individuality that intermingles with our own. Everything is in relationship. Today while walking in the snowy landscape, I heard the high-pitched *kee-eeeee-arrr* of a red-tailed hawk. In that moment, I was in relationship with the hawk and she was my friend. We were connected, and I was more whole, more embedded, because of this relationship. The philosopher Thomas Berry said, "We are most ourselves when we are most intimate with the rivers and mountains and woodlands, with the sun and the moon and the stars in the heavens; when we are most intimate with the air we breathe, the Earth that supports us."[8]

Intimacy with the world around us is urgently needed to change the destructive path that our species is bulldozing through it. The rational, logical mind of the materialistic scientific paradigm views plants and minerals as dead objects. The feminine receptive intuitive heart knows they are alive, vibrant, responsive beings. Intimacy opens the heart of compassion, nurturing concern for the trees and the minerals and the earth itself. Out of this compassion emerges the ethical wish to not cause harm. Feeling this direct intimate relationship with all beings may just save this world. We enter into relationship with the earth and her beings with respect and endeavor to live together in a way that is sustainable for everybody and everything.

Active and Receptive Mindfulness

Mindfulness can be experienced in both an active and receptive mode. We can play with these orientations while looking at a flower. What happens when we look actively at a flower, knowing what it is? In contrast, what is the experience of softening and receiving the sight of a flower with no preconceptions? Why, it's downright psychedelic. Flowers are amazing. The novelist Iris Murdoch said, "People from a planet without flowers would think we must be mad with joy the whole time to have such things about us."[9] With active mindfulness we decide quickly what a flower looks like, and we may dismiss any real intimacy with the experience. With receptive mindfulness we soften and let ourselves be touched by these unique vibrant moments of life.

Usually when we are mindful of some sense experience, our attention goes out in an active manner to meet that experience. A sight appears, for example, and our attention goes toward what is being seen. A sound arises, and our attention moves to the origin of the sound. Deeply rooted in our mammalian conditioning, this active attention has as its agenda to understand what the thing is and whether it is friendly or a threat. This orientation is geared for our survival, and it's looking for clarity. This active bearing tends toward efficiency and moves quickly into the conceptual mind to name and analyze, glossing over the true nature of this evolving experience.

Once we've figured out what we need to know, we pay less attention. We proceed according to our expectations, assuming things will act a certain way. When we've confirmed that they are more or less doing so, we no longer look and listen, and the experience loses vibrancy and aliveness. Yesterday, sitting at the lake, I heard what I labeled as an electric saw and felt aversion. I knew what it was and established my stance toward it.

When I relaxed and received the experience, the saw sounded like a cello and it was beautiful. When I knew what the sound was (an electric saw), I limited it to my expectations, but when I received it with the open heart, the sound came alive in a fresh, vibrant way, entirely different from my assumptions.

Receptive mindfulness doesn't go out to get experience but rather lets the expressions of life come to us. From this receptive paradigm, we experience yin mindfulness, a resting quality of effortlessness in our meditation. We soften and let ourselves be touched by sights, sounds, body sensations, smells, and tastes. We relax into not-knowing and allow space for the freshness of this moment. Experience turns out to be more alive, always new, with never a dull moment. The mystery of life comes forth. We can't really nail anything down; we can only experience it.

Try this out with a sense experience: for example, eating a mouthful of rice or any other food. In the active mode, we taste the rice, know it's rice, and may even describe it as somewhat bland. What happens when our attention is receptive and we let the taste of the rice come to us? The flavor and texture of rice change throughout an entire mouthful, with a different experience at the beginning, middle, and end. It's more alive, unconfined by the limitations of concept.

We can experiment with receptive mindfulness with hearing, too. Take, for example, hearing wind in the trees. With more active mindfulness, how is our experience of the wind in the trees? With softer, more receptive mindfulness, what changes? Perhaps we see that what we thought was a single sound is a chorus, with high, middle, and low notes, building to a crescendo and then fading, sometimes a shush, a whisper, a flutter, and a patter. This chorus reflects the true nature of life—constantly moving and changing. Receptive mindfulness moves us closer to the truth of things, to unremitting impermanence.

Mindfulness from a more receptive orientation widens into awareness. At its widest, awareness feels fully receptive. Awareness could be described as listening to experience. As truly good listeners, we are receptive, not fixing or judging or commenting. As we listen, we let experience tell us how it is.

With receptive mindfulness, we are coparticipants with the world rather than managers of life. We are fully embedded, rather than separate and in charge. We rest in belonging. We allow ourselves to be vulnerable and touched by life rather than focused on obtaining our desires.

Control has fewer places to hide in this paradigm. Our attempts to grasp or to push away are recognized clearly in the spaciousness of receptivity. We rest in being rather than activate into doing.

Of course, we need both active and receptive mindfulness. Active mindfulness is very handy for figuring out how to deal with and manage the life around us. When we feel scattered, aiming our attention can help us collect ourselves. Yet let's not miss the beauty of receptive mindfulness, which allows us to see more clearly the nature of life and enjoy the mystery of this world.

The Zen master Dōgen said, "When the self advances to confirm the ten thousand things, that is delusion. When the ten thousand things advance to confirm the self, that is realization."[10] Using mindfulness actively to confirm who we are, that's delusion. Letting experience be received by this sensing heart-mind-body, that's freedom. The more receptive mode clears out the doer and lets the ten thousand things confirm realization.

Internal and External Mindfulness

In the Satipatthana Sutra (the Four Foundations of Mindfulness), the premier sutra for meditation instructions, the Buddha describes four areas upon which to develop mindfulness: the body, feeling tone, mind states, and *dhammas* (phenomena). In the refrain sections of the sutra, with each foundation we are encouraged to contemplate our experience both internally and externally. We contemplate the body internally and externally, feeling tone internally and externally, mind states internally and externally, and dhammas internally and externally. Internally we explore our own experience. Externally we see or deduce the experience of others. Both focuses are necessary for balanced integrated practice.

Internal mindfulness, centering on mindfulness of our own body, heart, and mind, orients toward the five physical senses and the sixth sense of the heart-mind. We connect moment by moment with these experiences in order to understand their true nature and the fundamental characteristics of reality. These internal experiences teach us about how we suffer and how we can unbind, liberating our heart-mind through understanding. Internal mindfulness, exploring our own body, heart, and mind, is clearly important. The Buddha said that in this "fathom-long body," suffering and the end of suffering can be known.

Understanding what is going on within this body, heart, and mind provides all the teachings we need about the nature of reality. However, emphasizing internal mindfulness exclusively can encourage the meditative danger of self-absorption. We get lost within ourselves, captivated by our dramas and forgetting the larger world around us. While internal mindfulness is crucial, we need external mindfulness for balance.

External mindfulness brings us out of our individual focus and into the larger field. Relating to others, we recognize that the rest of the world shares our fundamental predicament of living as a sentient being in an untamable universe. We either see directly or infer that what is happening for ourselves is also true for others. As we breathe, so do others. Their physical form shares the fundamental characteristics of our own. Other humans struggle in heart and mind just as we do. A shift occurs when internal mindfulness is balanced with external mindfulness. External mindfulness draws us out of the self-absorption that strengthens the sense of ourselves as separate individuals solely interested in our own salvation. With external mindfulness, we understand our shared humanity with others. What happens in this body and heart-mind happens in the body and heart-mind of others. These experiences are the nature of sentient life, not our personal success or failure. Seeing the universality of experience loosens identification with it and engenders compassion for all beings.

External mindfulness reminds us that we live not as separate independent beings, but rather in a web of interconnectedness. This teaching encourages us to pay attention to the environment within which we find ourselves, beckoning us to feel into the experience of other beings. Internal mindfulness inclines toward our own liberation. External mindfulness inclines us toward engagement in the world. When internal mindfulness aligns with the individualistic bent of androcentric conditioning, we run the risk of disengaged spirituality, self-absorbed in our own cocoon. Looking outside of ourselves provides necessary balance that opens the heart in compassion and calls on us to alleviate suffering. As we explore our own hearts, bodies, and minds, we know that we are subject to impermanence, subject to illness and aging, subject to *dukkha* (suffering, stress). Participating intimately with life unfolding in our being, we then look out and see that the same is true for other humans, for animals, for trees, for all beings in this realm. How can the heart not respond with compassion? "That's me!" can be our refrain.

Grounding with the Earth

Down-to-earth dharma emphasizes our connection to the earth. Do we know this earth? How does it feel to connect directly with this huge molten globe of energy? How have we become estranged from this most intimate relationship between our bodies and the earth? Learning to connect with the earth can be one of our greatest supports in our meditation practice.

As Westerners, our energy tends to be stuck in our heads or somewhere slightly above and around our heads. Because of our unbalanced ways of being that emphasize the conceptual, thinking mind over the feeling, sensing body, we find ourselves strangers within our own bodies. We feel alienated, not at home, and aren't exactly sure why. We may be so fascinated by our thinking mind that we don't even know that we're exiled from embodied life. We've gotten comfortable in the virtual world of our minds. Yet this mind world is a made-up world; it's not real. It's useful in order to navigate, but it's lonely because it's not in close contact with life itself. So we wander, looking to return home.

With meditation we learn to drop our energy from the head down to the heart and the belly. Allowing the heart to feel, the energy drops down into the body. Focusing on the breath at the abdomen, awareness joins with the body, and we experience a respite from our exile in the fabrications of the mind. Feeling the whole body sitting and the hands touching, we come down to earth. At first, we may be uncomfortable in this strange land, not sure how to land here, experiencing a mix of thinking about our experience and truly feeling it. Gradually we connect more and more directly with the heart, the belly, and the body.

Grounding in our bodies keeps us real. The mind is a slippery thing. When our journey of meditation takes place primarily in our minds, we can create stories that support our ego's version of ourselves. When our awakening occurs only in the mind, it's not yet real, still needing to be processed through the body. The body is more honest. When we feel the hardness of the heart's shielding, we find it difficult to deny that we carry our share of aversion and judgment. Feeling the tension in the body, we must admit that we have more work to do. Sensing the body directly tells us where we're holding on and where we need to let go.

In our journey down to earth, we travel through the heart and the torso, through the legs and feet, into contact with the earth itself. What does the earth feel like, this big mother of ours? How do we rest here? We engage in a process of entraining our energy with the energy of the earth. We don't know this experience like a fact; we know it through feeling and sensing. We take a step and sense this contact. We sit on the earth and feel this relationship. We receive and allow ourselves to be received.

This intimate connection with the earth provides ballast for our journey. A sailboat without proper ballast gets knocked over by the winds, and we tumble into the water. With ballast, however, we have the capacity to steer and to use the wind to move forward. We can also compare grounding with those plastic punching dolls that contain sand at the bottom. They get hit and they bounce back up because of the sand ballast. If the sand were in their heads, when they got hit, they would fall over and stay there. When our energy is located primarily in our heads, we are like big plastic dolls with ballast in the head. We get hit by life, are knocked over, and don't get up so easily. With ballast lower in the body, we bounce back more readily. As we drop our energy into the body, we find a source of resilient power and stability.

Ballast and stability are especially important when opening the heart to experiencing more connection with the world around us. The heart needs to be supported in this process. When we open the heart without grounding further down in the belly and into the earth, the heart is left on its own. This wild world can be too much for the heart to deal with; it can burn out in the craziness of the immense amount of suffering it meets. Aligning the heart with the belly and down into this earth, we feel supported and strengthened enough to open to life's myriad joys and sorrows.

While the process sounds simple enough, the journey is full of surprises and challenges. Dropping down into the heart, oh the heart! What have we exiled and abandoned in order to survive? How has our heart protected itself? What have we not allowed the heart to feel? How do we allow for the ten thousand joys and the ten thousand sorrows? A complicated, fascinating, and rich process of discovery unfolds as we journey downward.

Dropping the energy further into the belly, we unearth our deepest core beliefs about life. Our unconscious conditioning that binds our heart-mind becomes conscious, and this is the beginning of change. On the journey from the head to the earth, we encounter what we have exiled, disowned, or disavowed. We collect these exiled parts of our being and bring them home. Through kind and compassionate awareness, we allow them to be experienced, and the experiencing itself is a reclaiming of our wholeness. Coming down to earth, we gather up what we have lost, and doing so, come home at last.

Elements

The Satipatthana Sutra provides many exercises that help us in this process of getting grounded. First, contemplation of the breath brings us right into the body. Then we are encouraged to be mindful of our posture, being aware of sitting, lying, walking, and standing. We are instructed to bring mindfulness to all our activities as we move through the day, even using the toilet. Clearly, no activity is left out of our awareness. We are encouraged to be mindful of this body in all postures and all activities.

The sutra continues with the practice of investigating this body as the play of earth, wind, fire, and air elements. Elemental practice draws us even more intimately into our embodied presence, feeling our physical sensed experience. Rather than focusing on the conceptual identification of the four elements, we turn toward the physical sensations they point to. We connect with the earth element as pressure, hardness, softness, smoothness, roughness, heaviness, and lightness. The fire element is felt as heat or cold. The wind element flows through our body as movement, tingling, and pulsing. The water element is expressed as dispersion or cohesiveness. We are this play of sensations, an embodied sensate being walking on the earth. We share this elemental nature with all of life. This body recognizes its kinship with the elemental world surrounding it and knows this earth as its home. As Rainer Maria Rilke wrote, "The inner, what is it: if not intensified sky hurled through with birds and deep with the winds of homecoming."[11]

The practice of the elements not only connects us viscerally with our embodied experience, it also loosens identification with the body. While we wish to come home to and live in our bodies, we're encouraged to not overidentify with them. We realize that this body is the play of the elements of the universe coming together and dissolving in different formations, changing all the time. The body is not a thing, but rather a dynamic process—salt water, a summer breeze, ashes, and glowing embers—borrowed from the universe to which it will all return. "It's a rental car," Ram Dass says, given to us for just some time. Knowing this, we ground in our body with lightness, holding the body in spacious awareness.

This elemental nature at play in the world surrounding us speaks to us in an intuitive and nonconceptual way about the qualities we need on our journey. The solid earthy quality of the rock points toward our own steadiness within. The tree tells us of equanimity, deeply rooted and yet open and flexible to the world around us. The song of the brook reminds us to flow joyfully. The sunlight on new winter snow hums with tranquility. The loon's wail resonates with sorrow, and the lilting song of the wood thrush tells us that we can hold it lightly. The musky smell of the rotting tree trunk reminds us that all things end. When we pause, listen, and receive, the wild elemental world around us is always whispering—and sometimes shouting—the lessons of truth.

2

THE BODY

GROUNDING IN SENSE-BASED REALITY

Ways of Knowing

One day I was walking near a salt marsh and saw a group of children participating in an outdoor nature workshop. One little boy seemed confused and asked the teacher what to do. She said, "Take this ruler and this piece of paper and . . ." she hesitated, "just go measure something." Her instructions fit the contemporary view of how we learn: we measure, calculate, systematize, and take apart nature. I yearned for her to tell that young boy to sit down next to the marsh and see, hear, smell, and feel his animal body in the presence of this environment and then come back to tell her what he had learned. This is how we function from the feminine paradigm.

How do we know the truth of things? How do we know what we know? The way most of us frame the knowing of things is through the conceptual mind, the masculine paradigm.

Modern Western culture based in scientific reasoning and androcentric conditioning emphasizes conceptual knowledge. We've been in trouble ever since the French philosopher René Descartes said, "I think, therefore I am." We take for granted that we know things through cognition, intellect, and analysis. We know facts; we analyze, generalize, think through; and we then have a pretty good grip on things. Called by some the religion of science, it's explicit, clear, logical, and it makes sense. Of course, this cognitive way of knowing is a useful and important tool for navigating our world. Science has advanced our lives in countless ways. Can we, however, expand our ways of knowing?

The feminine paradigm approaches knowing through intimacy. We get familiar with life by connecting directly with experience, softening into close contact. This kind of knowing is more implicit and counts on our capacity to feel and be vulnerable to what we meet. It requires being willing to let ourselves be touched by life.

When fixated on the conceptual realm as the only valid way to know the world, we trap ourselves in the disembodied world of the mind. We limit the ways that we perceive the world and, in so doing, limit the freedom of our heart-mind. We lose touch with vast realms of our inner life and our intimate connection with the world around us. We wind up alienated from ourselves and our embeddedness in the vibrant experience of our home, the earth.

Because of having internalized this preference for a mind-centered relationship to the world, we can be inclined to practice meditation by measuring, systematizing, and conceptually understanding life, all at a slight remove from connecting with experience itself. We love to think about and analyze our practice. While this can be useful at times, deeper learning is like sitting next to the marsh and seeing, hearing, smelling, and feeling our animal body. Our meditation practice from a more receptive paradigm lets us reclaim the capacity to learn through immersion and participation in life. The self-described "black, lesbian, mother, warrior, poet" Audre Lorde summed it up thus: "The white fathers told us, I think therefore I am; and the black mother in each of us—the poet—whispers in our dreams, I feel therefore I can be free."[1]

Our Insight Meditation practice teaches us ways of knowing based in the heart, the body, and even the cells. These embodied, intuitive ways of knowing could more accurately be called *ways of being*. More direct than cognitive knowing, they liberate the heart and mind through intimacy and offer healing on a societal and planetary level. We skillfully utilize

Buddhist cognitive frameworks, such as the Four Noble Truths, the Four Foundations of Mindfulness, and the Noble Eightfold Path,[2] to orient us but recognize that cognitive comprehension is not enough to transform the heart and mind. Intellectual understanding does not usually change us much. A more intimate kind of knowing is needed for the heart-mind to unbind.

Cognitive knowing is a step away from direct experience. This mind-based way of knowing is based on past experiences, assumptions, and conditioning, and as such, is not very fresh. Vipassana practice instructs us to connect directly moment by moment with what is happening and thereby develop intuitive wisdom. This knowing is not reasoned or thought out, but rather learned from close familiarity with our own experience. When first teaching Insight Meditation in Spanish, because there is no direct translation of the word *insight*, for *insight meditation* we used *meditación intuitiva*, "intuitive meditation." This points us toward this direct, noncognitive, intimate, deeply feminine way of connecting with life.

In the Spanish language there are two words that describe these different ways of knowing. *Saber* is to know a fact. *Conocer* is to know a person or an experience. When learning Spanish, English speakers get confused about these two terms because we only have the one word, *to know*, in English. To distinguish between these two, we can think of *conocer* as "to become familiar with." When studying Buddhism, we can also become confused. Inclining toward the first way of knowing things, the *saber* way, we try to think our way into freedom. We hope that by intellectually understanding the Buddhist teachings, we will become transformed. We just have to figure it out. Staying in the terrain of knowing facts and lists and intellectually understanding Buddhism, however, we are unlikely to experience deep transformation.

While knowing facts in the *saber* manner is helpful, we need to know life in a *conocer* fashion, to experience the truths of life by rubbing up close to them. By becoming intimate with suffering, intimate with freedom, we access transformation that endures. Feeling our way into impermanence, suffering and stress, and not-self—the three basic truths about life—the heart-mind learns on a visceral level the way things truly are in this world and how to navigate life with freedom.

Our spiritual journey requires faith in this embodied feminine paradigm way of knowing. Having tended toward faith in facts, logic, structure, and reasoning, we learn to trust unmediated contact, feeling, and intuitive knowing. Zen teachers often say, "Not knowing is most intimate." Not knowing in our usual cognitive way, we move closer to this dynamic life and the truth of wild existence, unobstructed by our ideas of things. We dissolve the protective cognitive shield that keeps us separate and allow ourselves to be genuinely touched by the beauty and terror of the world within and around us. This ever-shifting vibrant experience teaches us.

We Buddhist teachers often talk about investigating our experience. Hearing this word *investigate*, we may naturally tend to think, analyze, measure, conceptualize, and deconstruct. Sometimes this is a useful way to investigate, but mindful investigation in our insight practice points to the moment-to-moment experiencing of our lives. This exploration is more direct, and the insight that arises is intuitive, emerging out of aha moments that feel fresh rather than from the churning of the mind arriving at a conclusion. Instead of trying to make sense out of what we experience, we feel it and let it teach us.

This more embodied way of knowing transforms how we see the world. Cognitively, we regard the world as separate from us and something to be managed, controlled, and manipulated. We "other" the things of the world. Body- and heart-centered knowing leads to feeling our interconnectedness in a very alive world. Zen master Dōgen teaches that we become part of a living, breathing, alive world, fully at home. All things become alive, and we become co-alive with all things. Richard Wagamese, an Ojibway novelist and essayist, wrote, "Being spiritual is just opening myself to living and allowing myself to absorb and be absorbed at the same time. . . . The overwhelming awe and wonder we feel teach us more than we can ever glean or come to know of things. In the presence of that wonder, the head has no answers and the heart has no questions."[3]

Meditation practice reacquaints us with these embodied and heart-centered ways of being, engendering compassionate coexistence and great care with the effect of our actions upon other beings and the earth itself. Through a greater sense of belonging and connectedness, we cultivate an ethics of respect, appreciation, and compassion in relationship to all that lives. We counter our strong bias to navigate the world with our minds, with instruments and measuring sticks, by reclaiming our innate navigation methods based in feeling, sensing, and embodiment. We connect over and over again with the body and heart, quieting the cognitive mind. Relaxing into intimacy, we escape the prison of the primacy of the thinking mind and open our being to embodied heartfelt ways of knowing.

Thought-Based Reality

One beautiful spring day my partner and I went canoeing on a remote pond in southern New Hampshire. When we arrived, the tree frogs were trilling loudly, a sound we enjoy as a harbinger of spring. Then a person began shooting a gun in the woods; this experience we didn't enjoy so much. The universe that we created with the sound of the tree frogs was pleasant, and the world we associated with the gunshots was unpleasant. At one point, my partner turned to me and said, "If we didn't know that the sound of the tree frogs was frogs and the sound of the gunshots was someone shooting, would we even have a preference for one over the other?" The sound of tree frogs is shrill, actually not so pleasant, but the idea of tree frogs is pleasant. The sound of the gun is not much more unpleasant than the sound of the tree frogs, but the idea of somebody shooting a gun in the woods is more unpleasant (to us). My partner and I were experiencing the world through our concepts and not through our direct experience. For all of us, many of the problems in our lives are created out of the stories of the conceptual realm.

Where do we live most of the time? In our thoughts, right? We spend most of our lives in thought-based reality, the conceptual worlds that we create through perception, cognition, and emotional response. Thought-based reality is tricky and slippery in its hold on actual reality. Therefore, it is vitally important to understand the thinking mind so we can use it skillfully without getting entrapped and lost in the worlds we fabricate.

Our conceptual worlds are a made-up creation. Life is comprised of moment-by-moment sense contacts, the coming together of a sense experience (like a smell, a thought, a sight) with a sense organ (like the nose, the mind, or the eye) and the knowing of the experience. For example, an experience of seeing consists of the joining together of form and color, the eye, and the knowing of seeing. Perception begins its work here, taking this bare sense experience and then filtering and organizing it; it searches through files in the mind to decide what this experience is and labels it. Then perception interprets what is seen, heard, smelled, felt, tasted, and thought, using memories, associations, conditioned perceptual categories, and deeply rooted beliefs. In this process, perception moves from bare attention to greater conceptualization. We see an orange irregular shape moving downward outside and guess, *It's a leaf.* Then we notice it's a maple leaf. This prompts us to think about how much we like maple syrup and where we might get some. Perception moves on into the realm of karmic formations, the response of the mind to perceptions. Here the mind figures out how this experience should be managed. The basic question the mind considers is: *Do we want to keep this experience, get rid of it, or ignore it?* Further proliferation and entanglement manifest as we attempt to bring reality into accord with our wishes.

The interpretations of perception are a best guess based on prior experience. Perception works like a connect-the-dots game: taking a few reference points, tying them together with lines, and creating a picture of reality. Once I was sitting next to the marsh on a very windy day and watched my mind go through this process. I heard crackling sounds (sense contact), and within a second or two, perception flipped quickly through the files in my mind, trying to decide what it was. After rejecting several alternatives, it decided that the sound was *water flowing over rocks*—not a bad guess, but as it turned out, not correct. The next second a large tree fell down two feet behind me. This being completely unexpected, there was no file, no past association for this reality, so perception didn't consider it. Now I am sure this possible scenario has a chart placed at the front of the file cabinet! Later I was sitting on a bridge with my eyes closed and something touched my hand. Perception decided: *a wild animal*. No, it was the neighbor's dog. Perception just guesses. It makes up stories, filling in a lot of information unconsciously. Our picture of reality is auto-filled. It saves energy but is prone to error.

Concept is a generalization, a rounding off. Although each sense experience itself is completely new and fresh, once perception figures out what something is, we pay less attention to the actual stimuli. Our minds don't like to use any more energy than necessary, so they naturally conserve it through these shortcut methods. Therefore, when something seems familiar, we see our concept of the object, not the object itself. Conceptual reality is useful for navigating the world with efficiency. Every time I walk up to a closed door, I know how to open it because of the conceptual files in my mind. With concepts we can think and plan and analyze. Concepts are a step removed, however, from the kind of intimacy with reality that unbinds the heart and mind. In their tendency to help us round off experience and stabilize reality, they are prone to error and gloss over the deeper truth of impermanence.

Conceptual reality deadens our experience of life, picking up enough information to know what something is and then expending little additional effort to know the event more thoroughly. In this way we engage with life through our conceptual ideas, rather than through the actual experience. This became clear to me one day when working as a therapist with a woman who had recently arrived from Puerto Rico. While we were sitting in my office, she looked out the window and said to me (in Spanish), "Rebecca, there's the most beautiful bird out there!" Being a birder, I looked out the window to identify the bird and commented, "Oh, that's just a blue jay. They're very common here." I realized later that she had seen the blue jay but I had not. I had seen my idea of a blue jay. I began to look at blue jays more closely and realized that they are quite beautiful birds, but because of their familiarity I had stopped seeing them. Now I more often really see a blue jay.

As we move from direct awareness to more and more detailed perception, into conceptualization, and then into mental proliferation, we move further and further from the way things are to the way we construct them to be. As this happens repeatedly, deep neural grooves are created in the mind: views and assumptions about the world, ourselves, and life become ossified. These very assumptions then influence perception, as we tend to see what agrees with our views. Perception is inclined to see what fits "our reality"—the old conditioning—leading to limited flexibility in the heart and mind. It's hard to update the files when we have a lock on them. An old story attributed to Lao-Tzu, the sixth-century philosopher of Daoism, tells of a villager whose ax went missing. The old man was sure that the neighbor's boy had stolen the item: he looked like a thief, acted like a thief, and even spoke like a thief. After the ax turned up in the field one day, this boy then looked and acted like any other boy.

With this imprecise science of creating reality, we fabricate worlds in our minds that we believe and inhabit. Sometimes they accord closely with reality, and many times they are just made up. One person described them as Self-Important Bulletins from the Department of Misinformation. We meander from actual experience into stories that create our world. When we're caught in thought-based reality, we believe these stories with tenacity. How many times have we been stuck in whole fantasies that later turn out to have nothing to do with reality? Once, on a long meditation retreat, I saw a note on the bulletin board that my ex had written to his new girlfriend—I knew his handwriting. I perseverated about the note for a week (and learned many useful ways to be mindful of afflictive emotions), only to have him tell me after the retreat that he hadn't written any notes at all. I had made it all up. As we observe this story-making process, we can build a healthy skepticism toward our views and assumptions. We learn to hold our stories with more lightness, leaving room for change and adaptation.

Getting Lost

It is an unusually warm day in Minnesota in April 1976. The snow is melting in glistening streamlets and chuckling sounds, and the sky shines cerulean blue. With my new driver's license and my mom's old green

Volkswagen Beetle, my friends and I skip school in order to drive around and get lost. We stock up on supplies—Hostess cupcakes, Frito-Lay potato chips, Reese's peanut butter cups, and Coke—and then, with a sense of adventure, drive aimlessly for hours through the streets of Minneapolis. Finding ourselves in unknown districts, everything feels bright and fresh. At times we accidentally wind up back in familiar territory, and the brightness fades until we once again get lost. Our minds sparkle with the joy of fresh seeing.

In meditation we try regularly to not know where we are in order to see life with fresh vision. When we are sure about where we are, we pay less attention, as familiarity breeds laziness of perception. We see enough to know that we've seen this before and we don't have to task ourselves with inquiry or curiosity. We inhabit our past ideas of what is present rather than this unique moment as it is. It's efficient this way. Defamiliarization, an art technique in which familiar objects are presented in an unfamiliar way, allows for a fresh perspective. We are attempting to defamiliarize reality so we can see it in new ways untainted by our past perceptions and conditioning.

Not knowing where we are in unfamiliar territory, the mind is fresh, bright, and curious. The heart pays more attention with fewer preconceptions. This freshness opens us up to deeper intimacy with life around and within us. But it can be difficult to maintain this curious and open-minded attention with experiences that are familiar to us, like breathing or walking. I have a friend who uses the phrase *Hello, moment that I've never met before* as a way to encourage this not-knowing attitude. In meditation, we practice this fresh seeing, over and over again. *Hello, breath that I've never experienced before. Hello, step that I've never taken before.* This livelier engagement awakens the heart-mind to move closer to the truth of this moment with a sense of adventure.

I still like to get lost, often in the woods near my home. I bushwhack for hours through the forest and marshes and hills, navigating by the sun and the terrain. (Warning: Don't try this unless you are sure that you can get yourself unlost.) I enjoy the freshness that comes from being in a place that I don't know, and even the slight edginess of not having familiar landmarks. When I once again know where I am, I'm just a bit disappointed. What was clear and open now becomes comfortable, yes, but lacking the same vitality. I challenge myself to see with fresh eyes, even in places I am already familiar with.

Once we have domesticated our minds and know where we are, we might stop paying close attention and start to rely on past knowledge to navigate. With don't-know mind, however, the world becomes refreshingly alive. In our meditation, we practice relating to the known with the mind that doesn't know, connecting with the truth that each moment is new and has never happened before. This attitude supports seeing things as they really are rather than how we think they are, leading us deeper into the mysteries of reality.

Sense-Based Reality

When I was young, my father regularly took me, my seven siblings, and our friends camping on a parcel of land about an hour and a half north of Minneapolis. We ran through the woods, swam in the river, and made bonfires at night. As a young teen, I liked to go off on my own for my favorite activity: an exercise I called "finding myself." I would sit under a tree in the meadow and explore the feeling of being fully alive and present. I discovered that when I was connected to my sense experience—with hearing, smelling, seeing, and feeling my body—I felt like I had found myself. When I spent my time lost in thought, I knew that I had missed a vital thread. These early experiments were my first conscious explorations of sense-based reality, practicing rudimentary vipassana.

An alternative to thought-based reality is embodiment in sense-based reality. We allow attention to sink fully into this experience of being human through our six sense experiences. We receive the inputs of hearing, seeing, smelling, tasting, and touch through the body. We include the heart-mind as a sixth sense, experiencing it directly rather than through conceptual thought. We repeatedly abandon our thought-created worlds and come back to the sense experience of the present moment.

As we nurture a direct sense connection, we develop increasing intimacy with life as it manifests in this body. We distinguish the difference between the thought of a breath and the actual feeling of a breath, the thought of a sound and the very experience of hearing, the thought of a taste and directly tasting. At first, being so accustomed to experiencing life through the medium of concepts, we aren't exactly sure how to connect more directly. But with time and soft receptivity, we find that life is waiting and willing to come forward to meet us. The blind French resistance fighter Jacques Lusseyran expresses this beautifully in his autobiography *And There Was Light*: "Being blind," he says, "I thought I should have to go out to meet things, but I found that they came to meet me instead. I have never had to go more than halfway."[4]

As moments of mindfulness with sense contact increase, we experience life as more and more alive. A breath that felt neutral and maybe even boring is now rich with changing sensation. The taste of a spoon of oatmeal, which we assumed we knew, takes on different flavors at the beginning, middle, and end of the mouthful eaten. Colors jump out, vibrant and rich. How did we miss that life is so alive? We develop a deep appreciation for the miracle we live in every moment.

Sense contact takes us deep into the inner world of our body and heart and then connects us with the world around us. We touch the world and the world touches us through our senses; they are our portals for intimate connection with life on earth. We escape the tyranny of the disconnected mind and heal our exile. Tuning in to our sense experience, we become coparticipants in the wildness of the world. We sense our kinship with all beings and know that we belong here.

Of course, conceptual reality reasserts itself. Seeing a sunset, we think, *It's so beautiful!* Our experience of the sunset becomes the concept of "beautiful," one step removed, exiled from unmediated connection. Direct contact with the sunset reveals the seeing of yellow, orange, red, mauve, and violet, swirling and evolving—and most importantly, alive! Listening to a familiar piece of music, we may think about how much we love the song, removing us by one step. But when we directly experience the tones and vibrations waxing and waning, the music becomes vibrant. Living through our conceptual filters dulls life; living through our direct experience enlivens.

Moment by moment we have this opportunity to return to this full-bodied presence. The present moment never gives up on us.

Being embodied answers our heart's yearning to come home. Our home on this planet is this very body, and dropping from the dissociated realm of thought into the alive world of our senses, we land fully here: a dynamic human being on this earth. We recognize that we belong here, we are met here, and the invitation always stands to come home.

Sense-based reality not only heals our alienation from the web of life but also teaches us wisdom and compassion. This world of sense experience is ready to tell us how life is. We let body intelligence teach us in a way that the thinking mind can't. The truths of impermanence, stress, and not-self—known as the three characteristics of reality—seep into our heart-mind as we steep in direct contact with our sense experience. We notice that the vibrant sensations are constantly changing, life is always moving, and we can't peg it down and fix it in one place. We see that sense experiences are to a large extent unmanageable and uncontrollable and trying to make them be the way we want causes tension and stress. We shift from experiencing ourselves as concrete beings to knowing that we are an ever-changing river of sense experience. Each sensed moment arises and passes away in relationship; none is independent. Directly encountering these truths, we rework our understanding of reality. We know with increasing clarity that the world is untamable, and we can't find happiness and peace through trying to control this wildness. We consider the alternative of surrender, of letting go, of freedom through accommodation to the truth of things.

The Buddha strongly emphasizes mindfulness of the body as essential for our freedom. He instructed:

There is one thing that when cultivated and regularly practiced leads to deep spiritual intention, to peace, to mindfulness and clear comprehension, to vision and knowledge, to a happy life here and now and to the culmination of wisdom and awakening. And what is that one thing? It is mindfulness centered on the body. (Anguttara Nikaya 1.43)

We take this advice from the Buddha and slowly erode the patriarchal conditioning that the body is a hindrance to our spiritual progress and that "getting out of here" is the answer to life's existential dilemmas. We break through the influence of millennia of messaging deeply ingrained in our collective unconscious, telling us that the body is unspiritual and drags us down to earth while the seat of spirituality is in the transcendent mind. This split of spirituality from the body, reflecting the dominance of the mind over the heart, leads to dissociated spirituality not in contact with the breadth and depth of joy and suffering on this earth. Healing this split within ourselves, we experience transcendence right here and now, fully embodied on this planet.

Active Management of Thinking

Being embodied and accessing greater connection to the heart paradigm require us to learn how to relax the cognitive mind. Sometimes our mind is beset by thought and doesn't want to let go. A Tibetan Buddhist master said, "The epitome of the human condition is to be caught in a huge traffic jam of discursive thought."[5] We are so worn out with our thinking mind, yet we still hope that we can think our way into truth and enlightenment! A Tibetan saying tells us, "You cannot get butter by squeezing the sand." Thinking will not satisfy the deepest yearnings of our heart. We learn to relate to the thinking mind in a way that leaves room for us to connect with the present moment through the spacious heart-mind and embodied intuitive presence.

The overactive thinking mind is the initial and ongoing challenge for any meditator. The first time I formally practiced Insight Meditation, I was living in Nicaragua and read instructions from a book. I sat down, tried to concentrate on my breath, and found I couldn't follow more than half a breath before my mind veered off into thought. After five minutes I gave up, thinking, *This is impossible. Nobody can do this.** We can learn,

---

* Curiously, I then signed up for the three-month retreat at the Insight Meditation Society, seeing that I clearly needed some help.

however, that it is possible to relate to the thinking mind skillfully. Rather than considering thinking a problem, let's consider it a rich area for exploration. We spend a good deal of our time thinking; it's a huge part of our human experience. It's worth getting to know it more intimately.

We can orient toward thinking from both the active and receptive paradigms. From the active paradigm, thinking can be managed and restrained. To do this, we begin by loosening our identification with our thoughts. As untrained humans, when a thought arises, we get hooked by it, believe it, and let it proliferate. In meditation training, when we notice that a thought has arisen, we just let it go. Whether it's fascinating or troublesome, pleasant or unpleasant, we drop it and redirect our attention back to the breath or other primary object. We don't try to hit it with a baseball bat or make a big deal about it. Rather than despair when we repeatedly get lost in the cognitive grip of the mind, we can be happy that presence is always here, always available. Instead of using the wake-up moment as a time to berate ourselves for thinking, we can appreciate it. Each time we remember that we're not here, we're already back here. That's pretty cool.

During my first five-month silent retreat, I made a commitment to never voluntarily follow a thought. In other words, I made the decision to not deliberately choose to think about something. That doesn't mean that I didn't think; I thought a lot. The commitment to letting go of thinking, however, was enormously helpful in breaking my attachment to my thoughts. Anytime I noticed I was thinking, I just dropped it, making everything simple: just let go. This bare bones practice of just letting go can teach us that we don't have to believe our thoughts or get involved in them. Our attachment to thoughts and to thinking itself loosens.

In this letting-go training, we want to avoid creating an adversarial relationship with our thoughts. Fighting our thoughts leads to . . . more thinking! Thinking is a helpful part of our human life. There is no problem with thinking. If the mind insists on thinking, we can notice thinking as our present reality. We can connect with a simple note, "Oh, yes, just thinking." Pema Chödrön tells the story of a rancher from Texas who used the phrase "Thinking, good buddy." This wording reflects a friendly and compassionate relationship that doesn't exile any of our experience, including thinking.

This active management of thoughts becomes problematic when it morphs into control. In the effort to restrict thinking, we become increasingly tense. Early in my first long retreat, I mistakenly thought that I was supposed to be able to control thinking. Day after day, I struggled, trying to force my attention to remain with the sensations of breathing. Finally, thoroughly exasperated, I complained in a meeting with my teacher Sharon that I was a failure as a meditator because I couldn't keep my attention on my breath. My teacher said something that I never forgot. "You can't control if your attention stays on the breath. The only moment of choice is the moment you wake up from being lost in thought. You can then decide whether to indulge the thought or return to the breath. That's all the control you have." I thought, *I can do that. I can commit to returning to the breath.* This instruction was a great relief to me. A task that had seemed impossible now felt manageable. When we have the mistaken belief that we are supposed to stop thinking, and the task proves impossible. To let go of the thought and come back to the breath or some other home base is something we can do.

When we become stuck in our thoughts, we identify with and believe them. As our ability to let go of thoughts increases, our attachment to them decreases. They become less sticky, and we find that we become aware of the thought earlier, rather than when the train has left the station and is way down the track. It occurs to us that maybe we don't need to believe our thoughts.* We take them less seriously, and they become more transparent, less thick and dense. We can see through them and even start to play with them.

According to Professor Fred Luskin of Stanford University, we have over sixty thousand thoughts a day, and the vast majority of them are the same as the thoughts we had yesterday. On one retreat I walked the same circuit every afternoon, seeing the same stimuli repeatedly, and I had the same thoughts day after day: some thoughts of appreciation, but mostly judgmental thoughts. Fascinated by this, I started to play with my own

---

* We really should start teaching this in kindergarten.

mind. When I saw the same thought just starting to form, I lightheart-edly said to myself, *We've already had this thought. Maybe we can skip it today.* This playful technique was enough to let it go.

Having the ability to actively manage thinking is very helpful when our thoughts are unwholesome and likely to lead to unskillful actions. The mind is the originator of all actions of body and speech. If we can restrain the tendencies toward greed or hatred at the thought stage, we are more likely to act ethically in the world. Lessening our attachment to and identification with our thoughts gives us some choice about think-ing. The moment of awareness of thought is a powerful one because it gives us some space to decide if a thought is worth thinking. We can dif-ferentiate between wholesome or helpful thoughts and unwholesome or harmful thoughts. We can choose not to feed the unwholesome thoughts by letting them go and nourish the wholesome ones by knowing them with mindfulness. Understanding my own tendencies around getting caught in unwholesome thoughts later in the day, I employ a general rule not to believe my thoughts after 8:00 p.m. and let them go. When I must make a decision, I'll tell myself, *Not now. We'll think about this tomorrow morning.* This active management of thought arises out of the wisdom of understanding which kinds of thoughts are useful and which kinds are destructive and should be abandoned.

Receptive Exploration of Thought

Whereas an active relationship toward thought involves management and initiative, the receptive orientation treats thoughts as any other sense object: something to be known and investigated. Once we have some dex-terity with managing thoughts, giving us a bit more space, we can be-come interested in what thought is. *How do we experience thinking? What happens to a thought when we become aware of it? Does it go away? Does it continue? Does it slowly peter out? How do we experience the difference between being aware of thinking and being lost in a thought? How powerful is a thought when we're aware of it as opposed to when we're unaware of it? What's going on when a thought is particularly sticky?*

For eighteen years I led the Teen Retreat at the Insight Meditation Society, enjoying the curiosity and energy of younger people. During one retreat, a young woman told me that she was not very good at meditation. She then explained the different kinds of thoughts that arose in her meditations. She said that there were light thoughts that would come and go. Some thoughts were very sticky, and it was hard for her to extricate herself from them. Other thoughts ran in the background, and she was only vaguely aware of them. Thoughts that commented on all the actions she took arose often—the voice of what I call "the sportscaster." Contrary to her assessment, she was an excellent meditator, as she was clearly seeing what was going on in her mind and developing understanding about the thinking mind.

The nature of thought is a fascinating area for direct investigation. A thought is such an insubstantial thing, and yet when we're unaware, it becomes extremely powerful, running our entire life and propelling us into speech and actions. Just consider some actions we have committed in our lives that started with a single thought. Yet awareness changes the nature of the thought itself. When we notice that we are thinking, sometimes the thought vanishes immediately; other times it slowly dissipates; and sometimes it's sticky and seduces us right back into the story. We see that thought is only as powerful as we let it be. Over time, thought loses its opaque quality and becomes more transparent. We can see through it rather than feel lost within it. Thinking is a problem only when we get entangled in our thoughts and controlled by them. Awareness disempowers thought from its tyranny by loosening attachment and giving us options.

As we explore thoughts as events that arise and pass away, our attachment loosens and nonidentification becomes possible. During one early retreat I found myself repeatedly judging other meditators. These very unpleasant thoughts felt relentless. *Why is he walking so noisily? Doesn't he know that you're supposed to walk quietly? Why are they slouching so much while sitting? Meditators should sit up straighter. Who is she trying to be, dressed so pretty?* I felt dismayed at the meanness of my own mind and judged myself to be a bad person. I just wanted these judgmental thoughts to stop, but they wouldn't. In a meeting with my teacher

Joseph, I described this onslaught of critical thoughts and shared my assessment of my low self-worth. He listened politely, paused, and then simply said, "It's just a thought." I experienced a shock as I recognized the truth of these words. The judgmental thoughts were just thoughts and nothing more. When we identify with them, yes, they can be a problem. Wars start this way. When I identified with and believed these judgmental thoughts, I separated myself from others and made up stories about what kind of person I was. But when I didn't identify with them, when I saw them as just thoughts, there was no problem. They were experiences that arose and passed away, ephemeral with no real substance. With this understanding, my relationship to the judgmental thoughts changed. These thoughts still arose, but they didn't bother me so much. I recognized them and didn't take them so seriously. They were no longer a problem.

Particularly sticky thoughts may point toward the need for further investigation. Many times, we are caught in the grip of thinking because we're trying to avoid feeling what's going on for us. In fact, when thoughts feel quite sticky, very often emotion is fueling them. The obsessive-thinking nature of an emotion distracts us from directly feeling the emotion. To further our understanding, we can ask ourselves, *What am I feeling right now?* We check for an embodied experience of a hidden or unacknowledged emotion. Anger may present itself as obsessive thoughts about revenge or self-righteousness, distracting us from our visceral experience. When we soften into the physicality of tightness in the heart center and our muscles, we more fully feel the anger. Thoughts related to an emotion are trying to call our attention to meet what we are feeling. When we allow our emotions to be present and feel them in the body, the mind can quiet.

As part of our investigation, we can get curious about why we are thinking. I like to walk in the woods, and although my preference is to be present, some days my mind just wants to think. Sometimes I have a problem that I'm trying to solve. Other times the mind just wishes to create solidity, to establish a self that exists and has a past and a future. In the quiet spaciousness of little thought, the ego part of ourselves can get a bit nervous and worried that it isn't doing its job of keeping everything together. We think to create ourselves, to establish a narrative, to make sure that we are real and that our lives are under control. Spaciousness can be an acquired taste—one that we become accustomed to as we lose our fear of the space between thoughts.

We are attached to thinking because it creates a cohesive narrative for our world; it feels secure. All our thinking is primarily centered around how we can make life go our way. Check it out for yourself. We like this thought-centered orientation because we feel protected from vulnerability. It gives us the illusion of control. Once while I was on retreat in the Northwest, I heard a sound in the distance. My first thought was, *Oh, that's a cow mooing.* I felt happy because I like cows. Then I thought, *No, that's a chain saw cutting down the forest.* I was then unhappy because I like trees. My mind felt determined to know, *Is it a cow or is it a chain saw?* There was no real reason why it was important for me to know, but my mind perseverated, wanting to ascertain which scenario was true in order to determine which kind of world I was living in and whether there was any threat. To try to establish security, I kept thinking.

Ultimately, we develop no preference around thinking or not thinking. With spacious equanimity we allow thoughts to come and go. Thinking is okay. Sometimes it's even useful. Can we be okay with spacing out? Do we demand of ourselves that we are always present? Perhaps we need a "thought vacation." We can take such a break without ever leaving our meditation cushion. Sometimes we've had enough of grounded reality, so we create a virtual reality in our minds. It's okay. Don't freak out about it. One time a student complained to Suzuki Roshi about unstoppable thinking, and Suzuki Roshi just said, "Is there some problem with thinking?"[6]

As we learn the nature of thought, we disempower the primacy of the cognitive mind. Instead of placing our trust in the strategizing thinking mind, we lean into presence and our ability to deal with life. As we have increased confidence in our capacity, we can relax the controlling of the cognitive mind; we know we can manage what comes toward us in this wild life. We soften into presence, leaving behind the sharpness of the cognitive mind.

Both the active and receptive orientations toward thought are useful. The active mode helps us when it is important to restrain certain kinds of thoughts, especially unskillful ones that can lead to trouble. In order to lessen clinging and give us more choice, we practice actively letting thoughts go. The receptive mode, on the other hand, allows us to become intimate with thought and to explore its nature more deeply. Knowing the nature of thought and how it expresses itself leads to deeper understanding and more spaciousness of heart and mind.

Relaxing the Cognitive Grip

We all know that we humans live primarily in the world of our thoughts. We can call the stickiness of this conditioning "the cognitive grip." How do we relax the grip of our thoughts? What facilitates dropping into more direct unmediated contact with the present moment? Let's explore some ways to let go of the thought world and drop into alive presence.

When we find ourselves lost in the thought world, we have the option to orient toward our sense experience. We connect with an experience in the body that feels comfortable and easy to be with, giving the mind somewhere to rest outside of thought. Traditional meditation objects like the breath are one such point of contact. We can also hear sounds arising and passing away, and notice seeing, smelling, and tasting. Our bodies provide a rich sensual connection to the reality of this moment. Learning to rest more in our embodied connection with the earth, life, and each other, we relax the mind.

As part of our proclivity to live in our thinking minds, we are a nature-deprived society. Many of us suffer from nature-deficit disorder, leading to diminished connection with our sense experience and a corresponding increased tendency to be lost in the stories of our mind. We tend to live virtual lives, rather than ones connected to our bodies and our environment. Connecting with the earth strengthens our ability to rest our weary minds, as the earth is about as far from our thinking mind as we can get. Spending time outdoors and in nature, what the Japanese refer to as *forest bathing*, supports relaxation of the cognitive grip. Sitting under a tree, we can absorb the rootedness and spaciousness of tree energy. We can go for a walk in the woods, with the intention to notice the diverse sense experiences arising. We receive the rich palette of smells, sights, sounds, and body sensations. We can take sense walks in the park or down the street in the city too, where we also encounter a vibrant variety of sights, sounds, and smells. The trees and other plants are our support, reminding us how to be here simply.

Noticing and taking in the ever-present beauty surrounding us can drop us out of thinking and into presence. The sunlight striking the Kwan Yin statue, the last of the wood asters blooming in the side yard, the frost on the early morning grass . . . beauty opens us to awe and wonder—heart qualities that connect us with here and now. One summer my partner and I visited Banff National Park in Canada, an ecosystem with active glaciers. Walking the trails in the mountains, we would come to a turn and be struck with an immense, awe-inspiring glacier in front of us. The beauty was so impactful that it would shock me into deep presence. We can train to find this same beauty anywhere; we can see it in the shaft of afternoon sunlight bathing the room and hear it in the babbling of a nearby creek.

To notice beauty, we may need to slow down. The artist Georgia O'Keeffe said, "Nobody sees a flower—really—it is so small it takes time—we haven't time—and to see takes time, like to have a friend takes time."[7] As we slow down and soften our gaze, we see the flower, and increasingly we feel the flower as a friend. We notice how often we are surrounded by striking beauty but miss it because we are in a hurry, entangled in the dramas in our mind. The reflection in the puddle, the sun shining off the window of the high-rise, the chickadee in the abandoned lot, the purple-pink clover blossom blooming through the cracks in the sidewalk—in the countryside and in the city, beauty reaches out to us when we take the time to slow down and receive it.

As a way to help us drop from our heads and come into embodied presence, some people like to complement meditation practice with a body-based practice, such as yoga, tai chi, or qi gong, that teaches us how to become embodied and grounded. Karate might help us engage with the physicality of emotions like anger. Dancing and singing also connect us with our physical being. Meditation isn't a cure-all; sometimes complementary modalities help us establish a grounded, well-rounded, and balanced practice.

Sensing and Knowing

We have learned how to land in this sensing being of our body. We have explored how to relax the cognitive grip, emerging from the fabricated universes of our minds and coming back to reality in our sense-based experience. Let's investigate further our experience of our senses. When a sense experience arises—hearing, for example—it has both a physical and a mental component. The physical component of hearing includes the vibration of sound waves impacting the ear. The mental component is the knowing of this experience. They arise together, the sensation and the knowing of it. We have focused on connecting with the physicality of the sense experience as this is the grosser and the most grounding level. It's not too subtle, not so hard to find. Connecting with the physical helps us arrive very concretely in the here and now.

The mental component of the knowing of experience is subtler, but real. Here we are not talking about the knowing of the cognitive mind that thinks about what is happening. We are pointing toward sense experience simply known by consciousness without elaboration, like a reflection in the mirror or shining a light on an object. Resting in the knowing of the sense experience can bring an element of lightness into embodiment. When we focus on the sensation, we may inadvertently strengthen a sense of identification, of clinging to it as "me" or "mine." When we include the spaciousness of the knowing mind, attachment to what is known can lessen. Resting in the knowing erases our interference with the arising experiences, letting them be known in their vibrant nature as the play of the universe.

Take the experience of eating dark chocolate, for example. We connect directly with the sense experience of tasting. *We are so happy; it's so good; how can we get more?* We are identifying with this occurrence and wanting to control it. From a different perspective, the act of tasting itself is a magical experience. We can describe the food meeting the tongue with its taste receptors, but the process is more mysterious than that. Resting in the knowing mind, we can encounter this tasting as alive, magical, vibrant, and clearly not our personal property. We see things from a larger perspective.

The truth that sense experiences are both personal and impersonal is a conundrum like a Zen koan. They're personal in that they are happening within our body and to that extent are our responsibility. The sensations of stabbing and aching in the knee are taking place in my body. On this level, we connect, feel, and explore our relationship to what is happening. We work with reactivity and increase our capacity to hold all sensations, both pleasant and unpleasant, with some grace and poise. In addition, we respond appropriately and wisely and take good care of our bodies.

On the level of the knowing of sense experiences, they are not so personal. We rest back into awareness and let the display unfold. The sensations bubble out of the universe and die back into it. Sounds appear and fade away. Magic happens moment by moment, resulting in this display that we call "my body," with hearing, seeing, tasting, smelling, and sensing held in a vaster space. Connecting with the knowing mind, we appreciate the capacity of our heart-mind to open to this expansive spaciousness.

These two ways of relating to sense experience—through connecting with the object and the knowing of it—balance each other. Focusing too heavily on the sense object, we risk inadvertently identifying with it as who we are, thereby strengthening clinging and attachment. Focusing on the knowing widens spaciousness and understanding. Concentrating too much on the knowing, however, risks spacing out in dissociation and disengagement. We can miss investigating the fundamental impermanent nature of all arising experiences and the nitty-gritty untangling of our reactivity in the face of change. Directing attention toward the sense object brings us here and down to earth. We see more clearly that these sense experiences are always changing, they arise because of causes and conditions, and when these conditions change, they end. We investigate our wish to exert control over these changes, and learn to relax into harmony with this world of impermanence.

In our meditation practice, at times we may focus more on the sensation and at other times we rest in the subtler experience of the knowing mind. In the first case, we bring our attention to our immediate contact with feeling the body, seeing, hearing, smelling, tasting, and emotions in their embodied manifestation. We investigate deeply the nature of things and our relationship to them. On the other hand, we can widen the attentional field of the heart-mind and then rest back into knowing consciousness, experiencing the vastness of our own heart-mind. Accessing both sensing and knowing, we land down to earth with a boundless heart-mind.

EFFORT FROM THE HEART

The Sweet Point of Effort

In the Flood-Crossing Sutra (Samyutta Nikaya 1.1), a *deva* (heavenly beings who like to listen to the dharma) asks the Buddha about skillful effort. Wanting to know how the Buddha attained liberation, she employs the metaphor of crossing a flood.

"How, dear sir, did you cross the flood?"

"By not halting, friend, and by not straining I crossed the flood."

"But how is it, dear sir, that by not halting and by not straining you crossed the flood?"

"When I came to a standstill, friend, then I sank; but when I struggled, then I got swept away. It is in this way, friend, that by not halting and by not straining I crossed the flood."

The devatā:
"After a long time at last I see
A brahmin who is fully quenched,
Who by not halting, not straining,
Has crossed over attachment to the world." [1]

While the deva was delighted with this reply and praised the Buddha's attainments, you may have noticed that the Buddha did not answer the question. He didn't provide us exact instructions for how to make effort in a skillful manner, but rather extremes to avoid. Halting is too much yin energy and straining is too much yang. Right effort is everything else, somewhere in the middle, determined by what is appropriate in the current context. We call on flexibility and discernment. When we're going too far to the left, we veer right. If we're going too far to the right, we veer left.

Skillful effort, one part of the Noble Eightfold Path the Buddha described for the spiritual life, is central to our spiritual practice. Exploring how to make appropriate and balanced effort remains with us throughout our journey. Looking at effort through the lens of masculine and feminine paradigms gives us a deeper understanding about how to navigate this territory.

From the masculine paradigm, effort involves initiative, determination, and persistence. This kind of effort gets us to our meditation cushion and helps us to stay. It brings intentionality to how we live and apply our meditation practice in our daily life. Initiative gets us to do something. When we don't make some kind of effort, our habitual conditioning will run our lives and we will sink.

Initially, enormous determined effort is often necessary in our meditation practice. For example, during my first long retreat at the beginning of my meditation journey, I was focused and strict. I didn't miss any sitting meditation periods or take any naps. I slept only when necessary and ate only two meals a day. I was ruthless in my commitment to not voluntarily encourage thoughts, and I followed exactly the instructions of my meditation teachers. This uncompromising determination and commitment helped crack my hard shell (I was a tough cookie) and develop concentration and mindfulness. It was the right kind of effort for that time in my practice. Many Buddhist sutras point toward this kind of tenacity and perseverance.

This kind of effort, however, often needs balance because it can easily veer into *striving*: the attempt to control our heart-mind and make it conform to an ideal. Orienting our efforts from an unbalanced masculine worldview, believing that our minds, hearts, and bodies are to be subjugated to our will, we strain. We are going to fix ourselves and make our mind and body do what we wish. We may not be conscious of the underlying level of aggression we carry toward ourselves, pushing, pushing, pushing. *You're not doing enough. You're not doing it well enough. You have to try harder! Something different should be happening; something better.* Control leads to tension and frustration as we see that we cannot dominate our hearts and minds through willpower. While some use of willpower and determination has benefits, ultimately this strategy turns out to be limited and ineffective, and this really messes with our minds. We come smack-dab up against the limitations of will, and we do not like it.

The unfettered active paradigm depletes and uses up, with no regard for limits. The dominant paradigm tells us that we are limitless, we can have it all, and so we drain our own inner resources trying to live up to this fallacy. The heart recognizes this mistaken view, and we learn to nourish and replenish. Practice entails continually relaxing back from trying to get anything from it. When we ease back from this unbalanced effort, our nervous system relaxes, opens, and begins to trust us. We build a relationship with our own selves based on cooperation rather than aggression.

Sustainable effort doesn't burn us out. Because sustainability isn't culturally celebrated, we may need to cultivate it. What helps us to feel enthusiastic about meditating? At one point, my practice felt dry and brittle, so I joined a gospel choir. This brought joy and energy to my life, and my practice grew richer and more alive too. From the heart paradigm, we engage in our own resource management.

Because of this pushing energy, many of us need more rest and nourishment. We have become depleted by the doing, striving, and perfectionism. We've worked at an unsustainable pace. The heart acknowledges the need for sustainability. Good self-care maintains an adequate balance in our energetic bank account. Every time we nourish ourselves by getting enough sleep, moving our bodies, relaxing outdoors, and eating well, we invest in our energetic bank account. When we need energy, then it's there for us.

The Buddha compared skillful effort to holding a bird in the hand. Trying to hold the bird gently is an ongoing balancing act. We learn to avoid the extreme of control: holding the bird too tightly, which can strangle it. On the other hand, we should steer clear of laziness: too much looseness, which allows the bird to escape. The unbalanced application of either the masculine or feminine archetype leads to unhelpful effort. The right combination of the two—both firmness and gentleness—is the best way to hold the bird. Practice takes both more and less effort than we imagine. It requires tenacity and steadfastness, yet we also need relaxation and gentleness. Sometimes we need to apply more energy, and sometimes we need to settle back. Wise discernment helps us know whether we are veering too far left or too far right, and we can make appropriate adjustments.

Many Buddhist stories chronicle practitioners making very ardent effort over a long period of time, and then in a moment of relaxation, they become enlightened. Patacara was one of the early nuns whose awakenings were celebrated in the volume called the Therigatha, the Songs of the Elder Nuns. Patacara became a nun after a pretty rough patch, losing both her children, her husband, and her parents and extended family due to various tragedies (eagle attack, drowning, snakebite, and house collapse) all within a twenty-four-hour period. She (not surprisingly) lost her mind, finally recovering when she met the Buddha. Her enlightenment poem describes how hard she worked for years at her meditation. She tells us that she followed the advice of her teacher and wasn't lazy. Between the lines we sense a frustration that we ourselves may share. She asks, "Why haven't I found peace?" Then one night as she goes to her bed to rest, she puts out the lamp and her mind is freed. Her awakening occurs not while she is straining and pushing but rather when she lets go at the end of the day. The years of hard work were not wasted, as they prepared her mind for this moment. Yet the freedom of release emerges from within the feminine paradigm of relaxation and letting go. Not straining through control and striving. Not standing still and sinking. What is in between? An ongoing journey of discovery.

Effortlessness

As we explore balanced effort in our meditation practice, many of us, because of cultural conditioning, need to lean toward relaxation and gentleness. This plan sounds pleasant enough, yet it can be emotionally challenging as we face deeply ingrained personal and cultural beliefs. Fear can arise that we're not going to get anything out of the practice—forgetting, of course, that we're not supposed to get anything, that we're practicing letting go. We are afraid that we are wasting our time, and doing that, from the perspective of the Western emphasis on doing and productivity, is a horrible crime. Meditation without striving, connecting to ordinary life, can seem to us like not doing anything at all. The writer Oscar Wilde said, "To do nothing at all is the most difficult thing in the world."[2] We Westerners always want the quickest and fastest route. One Tibetan Buddhist master suggested that perhaps a little change every decade is enough.

When I first started studying qi gong, I was informed that a central principle of our lineage was the 70 percent rule. We were instructed to stretch to only 70 percent of our capacity, which seemed outrageous to me. I wasn't a 70 percent type of gal; I was a 105 percent type of gal. Obviously this rule applied to everybody else but not to me. However, I began to see that when I was making "full" effort, I was often trying to bypass what I was feeling. When I pulled back to 70 percent effort, my practice became more integrated, including all of what was happening in my body and energetic field.

We can explore the same principle in our meditation practice regarding our connection with what is happening—whether it's a breath, fear, or a pain in the knee. When we find ourselves "efforting," we can ask, *What's really going on here?* Are we trying to bypass an emotion or unpleasant sensation? What shifts when we make 70 percent effort? We explore the courage to be a 70 percent kind of person and meet the world that unfolds minus our efforts to control it.

One qi gong teacher, Dan, tells a story about being a student learning a tai chi form and finding himself getting tenser and tenser. His teacher instructed him to make half as much effort. Dan did this and things felt a little better. Then the teacher said, "Make half as much effort again." He made this adjustment several times until his body truly began to relax. Finally, when he was practically doing nothing, the teacher allowed him to add in a little bit more effort. The teacher took relaxation to an extreme to help Dan come back to a balanced place.

Effort from a feminine paradigm recognizes that there's nothing to get and there's nowhere to go. How could we possibly need to do something to arrive here and now? Here and now is always here and now. We soften into and receive life, rather than control and subjugate it. From this paradigm, we're encouraged to relax and receive. Our practice moves toward effortlessness, allowing the meditation to unfold on its own. As our practice matures, we tend toward this willing and effortless connection to what is true in the moment.

Effortlessness means that we stop demanding that reality suit our needs and start allowing it to be as it is. Eventually we soften into the uncontrollability of life. The eighth-century Indian Buddhist monk Shantideva is attributed with saying, "We are not here to change the world. The world is here to change us." We can call it *surrender*—not resignation—a wholehearted acceptance of things as they are. Without demands, we see that our meditation requires almost no effort because life does itself. We let go of subjugating the heart-mind and body and let them rest as they are, surrounded with awareness. Our process unfolds in a natural way without force. We find within us this joyful energy of curiosity and wonder that isn't interested in getting anywhere but rather rests in the now, free of anxiety and expectation. The Sufi mystic Rumi says, "This mystery gives peace to your longing and makes the road home home."[3]

Eventually, all our effort leads us to effortlessness and relaxation into the present moment without the slightest resistance. All our doing leads to nondoing—what a paradox! There is nothing to get rid of, and there is nothing to gain. Rather than using willpower to meditate, we let awareness itself do the work. Resting in nondoing, this mind/body/heart process rolls on effortlessly.

Striving

At the Teen Retreats at the Insight Meditation Society, in addition to sixty or so teenagers, we had a support staff of about twenty volunteers. One of them, Dave Smith—who is now a meditation teacher in his own right—was a young white man, large, tattooed, with buzz-cut hair. Dave looked tough but had the sweetest heart. One time he said to me, "You know the bulletin board outside of the meditation hall? Have you ever walked by, wishing that there was a note for you?" I nodded. Almost all meditators, in the silence and solitude of retreat, wish for this. "Well," he confessed, "sometimes I would leave notes for myself." "What did the notes say?" I asked. "One of the notes said, 'You're trying hard enough.'"

In our practice, at times we need to call forth great determination and perseverance. It is easy, however, for this effort to turn into striving. We take a goal or idea of where we should be going and try to make our practice fit this ideal. We think if we try harder, we will get "there." One retreat, I noticed that I was judging every breath I took, trying to get it just right. *Was that breath okay? Was I with that breath well enough? Am I doing okay?* Striving bubbles up from anxiety and fear about our own adequacy and completeness.

The foundation of striving energy is the wish for love, acceptance, and survival. We evolved as tribal animals who needed to be included in the group to survive. We still believe that when we do everything just right, we will get what we need. We demand of ourselves that we not make any mistakes so we won't be kicked out of the tribe, which would mean we die. Striving energy can be so persistent and strong because at its core lies our fear of death. We want to be accepted, lovable, included—and therefore not die. In an individualistic culture without strong community or extended family ties, striving gets magnified. Because we don't feel assured of belonging, we must earn it.

In the early years the Burmese master Sayadaw U Pandita taught in the United States, he frequently instructed his Western students to "Try harder!"[4] Given our tendency as Westerners to apply lots of willful energy, we would get tied up in knots. Apparently in Myanmar this was helpful advice, but it didn't work so well in the West. U Pandita caught on and used this exhortation less frequently as time went on. Trying harder can result in a more agitated heart and mind, further from genuine connection with the present moment. We lean into our practice so much that we completely overshoot the moment.

Sometimes striving is obvious, and we see ourselves getting increasingly frustrated and tangled. Other times it's subtler and goes unnoticed because it feels so familiar, just business as usual. Once we recognize that we are striving and pushing forward, we can explore this energy. Rather than trying to avoid it, we can become interested in connecting with it. The heart asks, *What is this energy? How do I recognize it?* We may notice ourselves leaning forward, either physically or energetically. Or we may find ourselves hunkered down, pulling in with determination and becoming increasingly contracted and frustrated. Striving may manifest as a theme of failed expectations. The words *should* and *shouldn't* can indicate to us that striving is present. We think, *My practice should be going differently than it is. This moment should be different than it is.* Sometimes we find ourselves pushing in meditation for an outcome in order to prove we are worthy. Striving can arise when we fear we are a failure because our practice hasn't been going the way we think it ought to. If we push a bit harder, perhaps we will get it right and then we will be worthy of praise, love, and admiration. If we can stay with the breath a little longer . . . If we can think less . . . If we can force our heart to feel peace . . . If we can get rid of this anger . . . We're going to get it just right, but it's going to take effort. Finally, the aggression of striving can get very subtle: perhaps just this tiny wish to be out of this moment or a background vague dissatisfaction with our progress.

As we explore striving, we can connect with the underlying wanting energy that is fueling this unbalanced effort. Connecting directly with the feelings present, we can begin to unbind the emotional patterning that causes us to strive. What is going on in our heart? Can we meet that directly? Often under striving a well of unacknowledged emotion is driving us. Sometimes my voice recognition software wisely translates "striving" as "secrets driving." What are the secrets driving our practice? When striving is present, wishes and wants are driving our practice, often unconsciously. As we feel striving viscerally and get familiar with its tone, we may recognize the aggressive, and even violent, nature of this energy. *I'm going to make you do what I want you to do. I don't care what you want; I'm running the show here.* Check it out. Our heart and nervous system receive this aggression as a threat and become defensive. In this way, striving is counterproductive. Rather than facilitating more opening of the heart-mind, striving encourages our system to close and protect itself.

When we practice Buddhist insight meditation, many of us are hoping that it will make us very "Zen." We will be full of light and love, calm, imperturbable, wise, and then, of course, everybody's going to like us. The idea that meditation is going to make us into the perfect person is the trap of spiritual idealism, which morphs into spiritual ambition: trying to make ourselves look like and conform to an ideal. We imagine that spiritual perfection will give us what we need and want in life, including love and admiration. Spiritual idealism is a tremendous amount of work, requiring us to build strong walls separating us from the qualities and experiences we perceive to be unspiritual. In the process, we separate ourselves from life. It's lonely behind our wall, and we have to be constantly vigilant lest some gap appears where the denied parts of our being can break through. When this idealism colludes with striving energy, we ignore the reality of what is actually happening. We forget that the purpose of practice is to be with what is true, not to attain an imaginary ideal.

Spiritual idealism can lead us into the dangerous territory of spiritual bypassing. We block off experiences that do not seem spiritual to us and ignore their presence. As far as we are concerned, anger, fear, lust, worry, and woundedness—none of that is who we are. We are above all of that, beyond all of that, and we don't need to engage with this messiness. We feel very good about ourselves because we're spiritually evolved. The pain of spiritual bypassing, often unseen, is disconnection from the heart of compassion, the disparagement of our very human needs and challenges, and the expenditure of an enormous amount of effort maintaining the denial of our full humanity. Spiritual bypassing is a dead end. If we're fortunate, something will kick us out of it, maybe a good teacher or a helpful disaster in our lives. Sometimes it takes something radical to break us open, like the death of a loved one, the loss of a job, the end of our relationship, a three-month meditation retreat, or the diagnosis of a serious illness. The force of suffering becomes strong enough to push through the wall of denial, and we meet our lives in their fullness.

Practice is meant to break our will, leaving us just enough to act with kindness and common sense in this world. In my early years of practice, I thought I had to free myself with will (read: control). Only when it became clear that willpower was not going to bring me peace did I consider alternatives. What a surprise to find that we move forward through love. An antidote for striving comes from the heart. Love and compassion allow us to soften into what is happening, rather than trying to make something else happen. Metta combines strength and gentleness, providing the fortitude for the heart to be with life as it is and the flexibility to relax control. The inclusive nature of lovingkindness embraces whatever is present. We grow in meditation not through will but through softening into the truth of life with gentleheartedness. Leaning back and loving what is present, we counteract the tendency to push for perfection.

Practice calls for existential honesty. We want to make the unconscious conscious. By returning repeatedly to our actual experience, we are led deeper into ourselves. Not focused on being perfect, we connect with what is true at this moment and find freedom in the easing of spiritual ambition. When I entered a five-month retreat at the age of twenty-four, I was convinced that I more or less had it together. What I came to realize, however, was that what I had thought was "having it together" was strong rigidity hiding the fear, anger, sorrow, terror, and anxiety that were closer to the truth of my experience much of the time. Contrary to feeling disappointed in these revelations, I experienced great relief. Rather than have my back up against a dam, struggling to hold back the water, I could now relax on the riverbank and accept what was rushing by.

Allowing ourselves to be imperfectly human, to experience the full range of expressions of a normal human life, is a refreshing release. We can take a deep breath, soften, and relax from the anxiety of maintaining appearances both internal and external. Our job is simply to meet who we are rather than to try to create something that we are not. It's so much easier. The transformation will come from this honest engagement with our very lives.

When we find ourselves striving to be a certain way, we know that we've missed the mark. Striving tries to escape the moment that is. The resolution involves sitting back and asking ourselves, *What is true right now? What is happening right now? What am I feeling right now?* We drop from the imaginary realm of the mind into the visceral reality of the heart and body and sit in that fire. We physically relax and settle our energy downward, encouraging ourselves to land right here right now. Then life peeks through the cracks and reveals itself on its own terms. We take down the wall brick by brick. Behind the wall we discover not only darkness, but also the light of our own hearts. We are whole.

The Buddha's Journey

The Buddha's journey, initiated from the masculine paradigm, ends in surrender to the feminine upon his awakening. We may see our own path reflected in this: starting out with enthusiasm and determination, moving into attempts to subjugate and control, and finally learning to let life in and surrender to the way things are.

The Buddha's path begins with his enthusiastic energy and resolve to get to the root of human suffering. Even at the beginning we see hints of the unbalanced masculine paradigm. The Buddha undertakes his spiritual path by separating from his family, including his wife and infant child. Having established his independence, he searches for freedom through controlling the mind. He explores transcendent states of concentration as a path to the deepest yearnings of his heart, resting in the bliss of the concentrated mind. While he excels in these meditative techniques, they don't resolve his basic human dilemma. He comes out of meditation and is still here on this planet, suffering.

Next he turns to controlling the body, engaging in self-mortification and extreme asceticism. He tries to subdue and conquer his body by practicing austerities to overcome his physical needs, including eating almost nothing and never lying down. He deprives himself of food, shelter, and clothing, thinking, as was not uncommon during his time, that this will lead him to a higher state. He finds that this spiritual path also doesn't lead to peace but rather to increasing debility.

Having explored controlling the heart, mind, and body, the Buddha finally considers surrender. His meditation practice turns around when he realizes that softening is the key. When he remembers as a child sitting under a tree during a farming festival, feeling joy and simplicity, his practice shifts. In an archetypal moment, he accepts the nourishment of rice milk pudding from a young woman named Sujata. The feminine enters his path as he nourishes himself and opens to receptive energy. He maintains a strong determination, but it is now infused with kindness as he explores a middle way between asceticism and getting lost in sensual pleasures. His ascetic companions think he has wimped out—a not uncommon perspective when one tries to seek balance—but he regains his energy and continues his journey.

On the night of his enlightenment, as he sits with resolve to attain full awakening, he is attacked by the armies of Mara—the Buddhist personification of obstacles to enlightenment—in the form of violent monsters, seductive maidens, and even mockery about his capacity. We are told that he holds firm against them; the hero valiantly faces the obstacles. From an alternative perspective, we can say he surrenders to his full humanity, letting in what he had repressed and tried to hold back. The Buddha embarks on a healing journey, recovering all the parts of himself that he has tried to transcend, avoid, or conquer. Opening to anger, fear, violence, discontent, hunger and thirst, doubt, longing for gain or fame, and restlessness, the Buddha meets the complete truth of this human life. Now strong enough not to get lost in the catastrophe, he maintains stability as he becomes an integrated human being. The earthy elements of wind, rain, rocks, mud, and darkness accompany this final portion of his journey.

Finally, Mara attacks him by questioning his worthiness. "What right do you have to be here? To make this claim for full awakening?" The Buddha faces self-esteem issues! The final symbolism from the feminine occurs when, in reply, he touches the earth. He has surrendered, come down to earth, and the earth is his witness. During the night that follows, the Buddha continues his integrative experience, reviewing his past lives and bringing home all the fragments of his being.

While our own spiritual journey may not have the same drama and intensity as the Buddha's, many of us travel a similar trajectory. We start with enthusiasm and determination, hoping for transcendence; getting out of here will be the key. Finding ourselves in the messiness of our lives, we attempt to resolve our human suffering through control and subjugation. Finally, as a last alternative, we realize that we need to soften and surrender. At this point our spiritual journey takes on depth as we open to the fullness of who and what we are. Determination and aspiration combined with nourishment, kindness, and receptivity release our heart from suffering. With a balance of the masculine and feminine paradigms, the Buddha completed his journey. Perhaps we, too, will go through these same struggles as the Buddha; we, too, are feeling our way to balance and freedom.

A Line or a Circle?

One morning many years ago, I formally took the five Buddhist precepts with Thich Nhat Hanh. I left home at 4:30 a.m. to arrive by the 6:30 starting time. Cutting it close, I was rushing up the hill to make sure I wasn't late when I caught sight of Thay (as he was affectionately known) approaching the hall with his retinue. He walked with such absolute presence that I stopped, completely stunned. I had never seen anybody walk like that, without the slightest leaning into the future, totally committed to each step in the moment. For me, this sight of Thich Nhat Hanh manifesting "circle energy" was the greatest teaching of the day.

Another way to discuss balanced effort uses the metaphors of a line and a circle. Is our meditation practice dominated by line energy or circle energy? Or is it a balance of line and circle energy? Line energy is associated with yang or mind orientation, and circle energy corresponds to yin and the heart. Line energy orients toward doing, getting somewhere. It is goal-oriented, assertive, and determined. We get all our ducks lined up in a row and embark toward our destination. Circle energy, on the other hand, is represented by being, coming back around to right where we are, connecting with presence here and now. We're not trying to get anywhere, and we're not trying to change anything. Understanding how to balance line and circle energy is essential to our practice of skillful effort.

We need a mix of these orientations in our practice, and yet we often find that our meditation practice is controlled by line energy. Some line energy is absolutely necessary on the path. Harnessing this energy helps us undertake the journey and continue to practice. Especially in the early years, we need discipline to establish our meditation routine. Healthy line energy has aspiration and direction and gets us moving.

Most of us, however, come to practice with an excess of line energy. It gets out of control. We approach meditation like a checklist. Check that moment off . . . and that one. When line energy becomes unbalanced, it tends toward manipulation and control, and we use our practice to try to dominate our experience rather than explore how it is. At its strongest and most unbalanced, line energy can manifest as our own internal dictator, trying to force life to conform to how we think it should be.

We can see overactive line energy manifest when we approach ourselves and our practice as a project to be fixed. We take ideas about how our meditation should be and try to force our experience to conform to these ideals. This spiritual idealism is a setup for frustration. When our practice doesn't measure up to our high standards, we can turn this anger inward, thinking there is something wrong with us or the way we are practicing. We burn out as we fight the wildness of life trying to make it conform to our demands because life is essentially wild and uncontrollable. We come to the end of how far dominance of our own mind and heart can take us.

We can balance by bringing in more circle energy. We curve the line ever so slightly toward presence, toward resting in the now and connecting with our environment. We land right here and look around with no idea of trying to get somewhere else. What is the landscape of this body, mind, and heart? In what environment is this being relating? What is it like to be here without the intention to fix anything? We cultivate our intention to love, to include, to become deeply intimate with our experience as it is—to love the breath, the step, the back pain, the loneliness, the joy, the feel of the wind on the cheek, the taste of oatmeal. To turn a huge ship only takes one degree of change in orientation. With a shift in our compass settings toward love, the line curves eventually into a circle large and wide enough to include everything. In the circle, we seek happiness not as some future goal but as present in the current moment.

Circle energy, however, can also become unbalanced, manifesting as too much passivity or lack of energy. Perhaps our meditation is going around in the same old loop, stuck and lacking freshness, and we feel trapped in our old patterning. Maybe we think we're being spacious, but we're really just spacing out. Sometimes circle energy, too, needs balancing. We can break the circle open, do something unexpected, anything different, to energize and create room for onward movement. For example, when we frequently experience a strong emotion that keeps us entangled in an unhelpful kind of circle, we can explore what moves we can take to move out of that trap. One student, talking about a very old pattern, started to see that she could act outside of that. She said to herself, *You're not trapped in that. You're never trapped in that.*

On one retreat a few years ago, I shoveled several walkways after it snowed. I cleared one in a straight line and then thought, *Why do the sidewalks have to be a straight line?* I shoveled the other walkways in a curvy design and people reacted with delight. The next time we go out, perhaps we don't walk a straight path to our car or the bus. Maybe we will wander to the edge of the yard, taking time to look up at the stars and feel the cool breeze on our cheek. We can enjoy circle energy, landing right here in this amazing world.

Time and Timelessness

Living in the paradigm of time assumes that we came from someplace and are going somewhere. Timelessness challenges this belief. Time inhabits the active paradigm of the mind, and timelessness abides in the receptivity of the heart. Time is linear with a past, present, and future, helping us make sense out of the world and strategize what we want from it. Timelessness, on the other hand, is circular, landing only here, with no future or past. With no agenda, timelessness leaves us open to receiving unfolding reality.

We Westerners are increasingly bound by time and unbalanced in our relationship to it. As the paradigm of the mind has strengthened over the last millennia, time has become increasingly measured, conceptualized, and regimented. We are bound to the clock and ruled by it. Standardized time is useful, as it keeps us on track to get things done. However, we seem to have lost our minds. A technique called time blocking plans out a day in five-minute segments making sure that every moment is productively scheduled. The website Timeular enthusiastically explains, "Time blocking forces you to fill up free time with pre-commitments and a plan of action. Doing so prevents you from wasting precious time on a task that could be finished quicker.... There is no room for random interruptions— there are no blocks of time left unscheduled." Is anybody else having trouble breathing right now? The Komi reindeer herders of the Siberian tundra measure time in a very different way. The flow of their lives comes from the seasons of the year, including two annual migrations for both humans and reindeer from the forests to the mountains and back. They have a saying: "Let the reindeer decide," expressing profound surrender to time based on nature and rhythm. Can we breathe a little better now?

Time blocking demonstrates the dominant societal orientation toward control. Trapped in the world of time, we separate ourselves out of the web of life and regiment our lives so that we can master the world around us. "Letting the reindeer decide" reflects cooperation within the greater web. Connecting with timelessness, we land wholly in the present moment where we can establish a genuine heartfelt relationship to the beings and the land around us.

We folks living in modern industrialized societies have become increasingly estranged from the restfulness and openness of timelessness. The dominance of mind energy moves us further away from an earthy sensual connection to life where we can find the portals to timelessness. Our hearts are bereft, yearning for the timeless. We all remember moments out of time—perhaps an instance of awe, beauty, or delighted surprise—that kicks us out of our scheming minds and rests us deep in the heart. We sense the timeless in the gap between thoughts. We hear it in the loon's wail, the crickets creaking at twilight in the fall, the soft breaths of our daughter sleeping. We see it in the red glow of the setting sun, the cool face of the full moon, the vibrant depths of the tulip blossom. We smell it in the lilacs' offering and the mossy redolence of the woods.

As we rest back into the deep receptivity of timelessness, we are not always sure that we trust this much openness. Timelessness lives outside of our comfortable conceptual world in a don't-know space. We like to *know*, thank you. Timelessness lacks a past or future, with no space for strategizing and control. We feel so damn vulnerable, and so we bounce back into our comfortable world of time. In order to abide here and now, we must acclimate to surrendering our usual game plan of pegging down the things of the world in order to pursue security. This price is high, but we get magic in return and the spaciousness of the untroubled mind and heart content with the mysterious unfolding of things.

T. S. Eliot describes the required surrender and resultant magic of timelessness in his poem "Little Gidding,"

We shall not cease from exploration
And the end of all our exploring
Will be to arrive where we started
And know the place for the first time.
Not known, because not looked for
But heard, half heard, in the stillness
Between two waves of the sea.

Quick now, here, now, always—
A condition of complete simplicity
(Costing not less than everything)
And all shall be well . . .[5]

Experiencing timelessness is rest from the tyranny of time. We give up the linear mind busy with planning, contriving, and controlling this life. This relinquishing is the price we pay to open ourselves to the beauty of the timeless present. In any moment, freeing ourselves from the confinement and pressure of the clock, we become simple, undefended, and vulnerable enough to be touched by the mysteries of the world.

In this simplicity, we let our energy settle back and down toward the earth. We pause and allow ourselves to just be, sipping from the cup of the timeless and being nourished by its openheartedness. Then when we need to function in the world of time, we can pick time up and use it, imbued with the spaciousness and restfulness of timelessness.

Useless Gazing

About ten days into one six-week retreat, my intensive practice of sitting and walking meditation was causing an imbalance in my nervous system. My teacher, Michele McDonald, recommended that I back off and do less sitting meditation. Being stubborn and arrogant, I didn't listen to her. I was good at formal sitting practice, an excellent "yogi," and I was not inclined to drop what I was good at doing. As the imbalance intensified, Michele became emphatic. "Rebecca, you have to stop sitting! You can do one formal sitting a day and that's all." I was horrified and terrified. "But what will I do all day?" I asked. She said, "You'll have to work that out. If you want to, you can practice useless gazing."

Michele explained that useless gazing involves sitting at a window with a cup of tea and looking out. That's it. Nothing to produce, nothing to get, no concentration to build, no intention to be mindful. It's useless; it's undoing. I was terrified of these instructions. I knew how to practice formal meditation, but I had no idea how to do nothing. I looked with great envy at the other yogis following the intensive schedule of sitting and walking meditation. I so wanted—indeed needed—to join them and I couldn't.

Every morning, I woke up and attended the morning meditation before breakfast, my one allowed formal sitting meditation. After breakfast,

I wandered in the woods for several hours, occasionally stopping for a few minutes to sit by a marsh or on a rock, gazing uselessly. I had no plan, no destination, no structure. I felt my way moment by moment into what came next. I came back for lunch, rested, and headed back out into the woods until teatime. Sometimes I curled up in the sun under a tree, inhaling the scent of autumn leaves. I learned all the trails in the area and made a few of my own. After a light dinner, I did my service job, practiced some useless gazing, and listened to the dharma talk.

The first week, I burned with the desire to produce something—to attain a deep state of concentration or have an amazing insight. I felt alternately guilty, worthless, angry, frightened, yearning, tearful, sad, and ashamed. It was so unfair! Why couldn't I be like the other yogis and just practice sitting and walking meditation? I was wasting my time. Was I worthy of existence on this planet if I didn't produce something of value? What would others think of me? I was doing everything that "bad" meditators did. Every day, I walked through a fire of centuries of patriarchal conditioning that insisted I needed to achieve something productive.

Then something shifted. I let go of the need to produce and be a certain way. I surrendered it all. Without this pressure, I could explore fully the receptive heart paradigm of being and resting. A world of intimacy opened with all that was manifesting in and around me. No longer needing reality to manifest in a manner congruent with my own agenda, I was able to connect with reality as it was. Because I didn't need my experience to be a certain way, I fully belonged to the world as it was. Any sense of separation melted and peace deepened. I was in love with the world, and the world was in love with me.

In cultures dominated by the active paradigm, being productive is paramount. When we aren't producing something, we don't feel worthy of living. This cultural attitude can infiltrate our meditation practice as we demand that it leads to something, preferably something of great value. We try to do, do, do something that makes our practice spectacular and validates our worth. When we don't see obvious results, we can feel worthless and dejected. From the receptive paradigm, however, life isn't oriented toward production, but rather toward being—nothing to prove, nothing to produce, nothing to do, no one to be. Life is experienced resting in the infinite space of now.

When our practice conforms to the dominant paradigm of goal orientation and energetic striving, we feel assured and confident that we are accomplishing something. We may build concentration, have exciting experiences, or attain a deep intellectual understanding of the teachings. When we engage from the yin paradigm, however, we may doubt that what we are doing is of worth. Most of us have internalized the perspective on life that mistrusts intuition, relaxation, play, and emotion. We see this conditioning more clearly when we turn our canoe around and face into the stream of internalized grind culture.

When we practice from the receptive nondoing paradigm, this doubt may tell us that we are wasting our time. We aren't making enough effort. We have nothing to show for our time. We should be trying harder and have some concrete evidence of our progress.* The opening of our heart may not be viewed as worthy of our attention, but rather something we should get through as quickly as possible so we can get onto the real business of enlightenment. We may doubt our intuition that feels so simple and spontaneous. We are skeptical about the vulnerability that we increasingly feel, assuming that greater strength and individuation are the goal of our path.

Learning to trust the feminine paradigm within, whether we are male, female, or gender fluid, is a process entailing the courage to drop out of the dominant paradigm and explore parts of our own being that may be underdeveloped. We must be willing to risk producing nothing that will be honored or respected from the dominant culture perspective. We call on our adventurous heart that doesn't want to be limited by access to only part of who we are. Over time, our verified faith in the feminine orientation in our own practice gives us inner confidence and inspiration to continue to deepen. We see that we are more present, kinder, and less reactive. We know from within that we are headed in the right direction.

---

* I often tell students that if you aren't worried you are not making enough effort, you're probably trying too hard.

To understand and integrate the heart paradigm of being and resting, we may have to dare to be nonproductive, to waste time. Give time a rest! We may have to *not* meditate in order to understand meditation from a viewpoint outside of our deeply conditioned requirement to prove ourselves worthy. Incorporating the receptive paradigm, learning about nondoing and resting, we reclaim the intimacy, belonging, and peace that come from letting go of our need to produce. We still do our jobs and take care of our own and our family's needs, yet we also include time to gaze uselessly at this world around us, taking it in, and finding our home right under our feet.

Are We Having Fun Yet?

If our practice isn't fun, at least some of the time, perhaps we're caught in seriousness. Yes, of course, practicing for our freedom from suffering is absolutely serious! And yet the end result of practice is an increased lightness of being. Why wait? We can practice that spaciousness right now by asking the mind to step back and allow the heart to lead.

Playing with our heart-mind, we're not trapped by our old conditioning. We become flexible and enjoy seeing in new and creative ways free of rigid patterning. Putting aside our usual reference points, the world is a miracle. Yesterday, I saw the leaves fall into the sky. In our more serious reality, they were falling into water *reflecting* the sky, but the spacious heart saw leaves falling down into the sky. That was fun.

Playing facilitates relaxation and letting go of our firm hold on the body, mind, and heart. We feel encouraged to not take ourselves so seriously, to loosen hard and fixed patterning within. Out of relaxation emerges the spacious heart that understands that life is wild, unfathomable, and mostly out of our control. We more willingly surrender into life as it presents itself, able to meet the truth of the streaming moments of existence.

We can encourage fun in our practice by taking an aspect of life to explore and finding entertaining ways to engage it. For example, when I want to be more present in my daily life, I might commit to noticing flowers ten times a day. Noticing flowers ten times a day will increase mindfulness in general. If I am lost in fear, let's time it. How long until the fear passes? Let's see if I can improve my time today. When I'm having catastrophizing thoughts about a health concern, I might count how many times today they arise. If I want to be more mindful while eating, I can play a game with myself: How slowly can I eat the first five bites of food? What is the number of bites that I can eat slowly that still feels fun? When we meditate, we can become overly concerned about whether we're getting it exactly right. We don't have to be perfectly mindful; we don't have to always follow the rules. It's okay to play, relaxing our ongoing vigilance about doing the practice correctly. Playing means we're not imprisoned. When we play, we highlight the absolute irony and craziness of this world. It's a weird place, isn't it? We're used to continually managing it and forget that we can have some fun. How do we play with life rather than oppose it? In Myanmar, for example, when the music being blasted over loudspeakers caused aversion to arise, sometimes I would dance with the aversion, moving to the beat of American country music with Burmese lyrics.

Patriarchal conditioning doesn't tend to value play, the joys of discovery, and expressiveness. We're supposed to be accomplishing something to justify our existence. Countering this tendency, we play with abandon. We play because it feels good. We play because it's fun. We enjoy the beautiful quality of mindfulness that allows us to connect with life's manifestations with freshness: the tall grasses waving in the wind, our child's smile, the sound of the crow's caw, the smell of autumn leaves, the ache of loneliness. Mindfulness can reenchant our world, bringing it alive in surprising and delightful ways and reminding us that we live in a wonder-filled world.

Advanced engagement might include playing with heartbreak. Can we play with the pain in the knee? How do we play with our own judgmental mind? *Oh, look at that mean thought! That was a real doozy!* Okay, just for fun, let's see if we can be kind to this frustrating customer service representative from the beginning of the call all the way until the end.

Charlotte Joko Beck says that freedom is "an ordinary wonder."[6] Life is always manifesting in new and surprising ways—sometimes delightful, sometimes painful, yet always fresh. This human existence is unfathomable and unknowable, a mystery that bubbles into being moment by moment. From the mind paradigm, we try to peg it down and understand it. From the heart, we enjoy playing with it.

4

EXPLORING OUR RELATIONSHIP TO FEELING TONE

Pleasant Feeling Tone

During one retreat in the Sagaing Hills region in Myanmar, I studied in detail the pleasantness of my morning cup of Burmese sweet tea, *laphet yay cho*. I love laphet yay cho. Going on retreat, laphet yay cho is the experience that I hang on to when I need something to look forward to. (Those of you who have been on intensive retreat will recognize the go-to that we anticipate when we're struggling. *There's always my afternoon cookie!*) On this occasion, I looked forward to the tea for months before my retreat. Finally, I arrived at the monastery and the next morning showed up at breakfast filled with anticipation. And I cried all the way through breakfast. The laphet yay cho was sweet and delicious, but the enjoyment didn't last. Each sip of tea was pleasant and then it ended. Pleasant, gone. Pleasant, gone. Each moment was ephemeral. I was so disappointed; I had (unconsciously) expected so much more.

Each morning I drank my sweet tea with mindfulness of pleasant feeling tone (*vedana*). I watched the feeling arise, and I watched it pass away. I felt my relationship to this continual ending, passing through disappointment, anger, betrayal, and grief. At times I was so angry at the tea for not delivering what I wanted, and other times I felt betrayed by the tea's inability to satisfy my craving. Finally, one morning as I was mindful of the sweetness of the tea and the pleasantness of the feeling, I experienced pleasantness, ending of pleasantness, and peace. No more struggle with the truth of the impermanence of pleasantness, just a sweet equanimity that was more gratifying than the pleasantness of the tea itself. Life teaches us when we are willing to pay attention and feel our way through experience to the freedom of the heart.

Now that we have landed in sense-based reality, we see that we have issues with this ever-changing world, responses and reactions to what is happening. Buddhist psychology states that each moment of sense contact arises with an affective quality. This first impression upon our system feels either pleasant, unpleasant, or neutral. At first this would seem like not such a big deal. Yet vedana is one of only four foundations of mindfulness listed in the Satipatthana Sutra. Early in my practice I wondered why feeling tone would be so highly elevated. With investigation, I came to understand that our relationship to feeling tone is the keystone to the reactivity that robs us of the spaciousness of the receptive paradigm. It is the foundation of suffering and our opportunity for freedom.

Pleasant feeling tone occurs when an experience of hearing, seeing, smelling, tasting, body sensation, or mind event impacts us in a pleasing manner. When we're not mindful or don't have understanding, this pleasantness causes us to grasp at this experience, just as I grasped at Burmese sweet tea. Grasping leads to craving and self-absorption, and suffering follows. Lack of mindfulness of pleasantness starts the whole ball rolling. This grasping relationship to pleasant experience is deeply conditioned in us humans through millennia of evolutionary reinforcement. It may have survival benefits, yet this mechanism keeps the heart bound in self-centered concern. Given the depth of this conditioning, how do we find our way to freedom?

Buddhism and other patriarchal religions have at times taught overcoming this attachment conditioning by denying oneself, as much as possible, pleasant experiences. Ascetic practices follow this orientation. The Buddha spent years eating very little, not laying down to sleep, and practicing other denials until he decided that this severe asceticism was not the road to freedom. However, many Buddhist discourses reflect an ascetic flavor that cautions us to restrain ourselves from pleasant experiences. Some renunciation of pleasant experiences can be useful in highlighting craving or grasping that may be unconscious and shining a light on our conditioning. Through abstention, we can see more clearly where we are stuck and where true happiness lies. (Spoiler alert: it's not in pleasant experiences.) Sometimes when I am walking downtown past the café that sells my favorite cookies, I purposely don't buy one in order to explore renunciation and the freedom of letting go.

From a more inclusive paradigm, rather than trying to abstain from pleasant experience, we incorporate mindfulness of pleasantness into practice. We know danger of attachment exists based in the deluded view that pleasant sense experiences will satisfy our wish for happiness, yet it's also true that pleasant sense contact calms, soothes, and nourishes us. Pleasantness triggers the parasympathetic nervous system, grounding and relaxing us. Due to the pace and stress of modern life, the nervous systems of many of us are stretched to the limit. Trying to raise children in a single parent or nuclear family system, working a job that pays barely enough to cover the bills or one where we're expected to be on 24/7, living in a world threatened with climate catastrophe, handling a pandemic either living alone or in close quarters with others, keeping up with the pace and endless details of modern life, subject to noise, confusion, and electronic stimulation—this all contributes to nervous systems that are overstimulated and in need of nourishment.

Fully contacting pleasant sense experience can replenish body and heart. We might slow down enough to hear the pigeons cooing as we walk to the subway. We can take in the bobbing face of the black-eyed Susan by the side of the road. We can absorb the warmth of the sun on our face. We can savor our morning cup of tea. With conscious intention we discover that the opportunities for pleasant sense contact are vast. We feel the relaxing reverberations through our body as we mindfully receive these gifts of beauty and comfort from this world. Life repeatedly offers nourishing and comforting sense experience.

As we get closer to a pleasant sense experience and allow ourselves to feel it fully, we also develop understanding about reality. The conceptual frameworks of Buddhist psychology point toward where to pay attention, and transformation comes from learning through mindful sense contact experience. We know directly through mindfully being with these pleasant sense experiences that although they are nourishing, they do not last, so they can't provide us the ultimate reliable happiness that we are looking for. We feel ourselves get attached and try to hold on, and then experience the tension and stress that result. We see craving separate us and block our ability to be in intimate contact. We realize letting go of craving and attachment brings peace. And we know that these realizations aren't just about tea, they apply equally to all of wild reality. These profound understandings of the truths of life can result from our willingness to directly engage with pleasant feeling tone.

In a series of short sutras titled the Gratification, the Danger, and the Escape, the Buddha recognizes that there is gratification in pleasant sense contact.[1] He explains that "The pleasure and joy that arise in dependence on [the world]: this is the gratification of the world." The danger, of course, is that because of the gratification, we become attached to things that are bound to change. "That [the world] is impermanent, suffering, and subject to change this is the danger of the world." We get obsessed with getting pleasant experience and holding on to that which is impermanent. He concludes that "the abandonment of grasping and attachment for the world is the escape." The escape from suffering is letting go of holding on, the peace of this heart-mind right in the middle of the ephemeral nature of pleasant experience. The Buddha said when he directly understood for himself the gratification, the danger, and the escape, his mind and heart were freed.

Yes, please enjoy the many pleasures of this human realm: pleasant body sensations, succulent tastes, beautiful sights, lovely music, happy moods, and so on. But don't put all your happiness eggs in that basket.

Learn how to connect with pleasantness with a light heart-mind that enjoys yet also knows how to let go into the deeper pleasure of peace.

Unpleasant Feeling Tone

I am sitting in the meditation hall at Insight Meditation Society, enjoying a lovely concentrated meditation, when a staff member starts mowing the lawn outside and I get upset. My mind complains, *Why do they have to mow the lawn during sitting periods? Why don't they mow the lawn during walking periods? Don't they know that they are ruining our (read: my) meditation? That's so inconsiderate and not very mindful.* When I emerge from this thought stream enough to realize that I am caught in aversion, I get interested in the unfolding of my response to this unpleasant stimulus. I hear the lawn mower; the sound is experienced as unpleasant; and the response is aversion. Connecting with the sound and resting directly in the unpleasantness of it, I have an epiphany. I don't need to react to this unpleasantness with the whole drama of aversion. I can end with "it's just unpleasant." This first experiential understanding that unpleasantness and aversion do not have to be married, that feeling tone does not have to be followed with reactivity, allows my mind to rest in spacious acceptance.

Without mindfulness and understanding, an unpleasant sense impression is immediately followed by aversion. We hate it and try to push it away so that it won't bother us. At first, unpleasantness and aversion feel bound together with no gap between them. (The same is true for pleasantness and grasping.) With mindful understanding of this chain of conditioning, we can introduce some space, letting go of all the drama in our minds in response to what's unpleasant and just acknowledging the unpleasantness. This saves us a lot of suffering!

It isn't the sense object itself that is unpleasant, but rather the coming together of conditions in this moment and how they impact this heart-body-mind. As my friend Greg likes to say, "The thing itself is innocent." Feeling tone is very dynamic. I love the sound of hermit thrushes and enjoy their singing immensely. One day a couple of summers ago a hermit thrush convention took place in our yard with a number of them singing all day long. As their singing continued for hours into the afternoon, I finally said to my partner, "I do believe I am experiencing the hermit thrush song as unpleasant!" The song wasn't inherently pleasant or unpleasant; the feeling tone came out of the totality of the experience in the moment.

The conceptual mind also contributes to our reaction to feeling tone. Very early this morning on retreat I was enjoying my cup of tea outside when a car passed by. The idea arose that it was unpleasant that a car was passing on the road, but when I listened without preconceptions, the sound—a whispering humming comforting sound—was pleasant. The idea of a car passing by and disturbing my meditation was unpleasant, but the actual sense experience was pleasant. I had created an unpleasant world through my conceptual mind. Later, the landscaping crew backed up their truck with the *beep beep beep* sound which I generally find very unpleasant and to which I usually respond with aversion and judgment. Yet this morning, listening to the sound itself, it wasn't so bad. I experienced equanimity instead of aversion. Equanimity is the heart's response when not trapped in the deep conditioning of reactivity to feeling tone.

When we experience reactivity to a sense experience, we can explore three aspects. First, we can feel the direct experience of hearing, seeing, smelling, tasting, body sensations, or the mind experience of thought and emotion. Then we can rest in the feeling tone of the moment, how the moment impacts us, whether pleasant or unpleasant. Finally, we can explore the response: aversion reacting to unpleasantness or grasping hanging on to pleasantness, or equanimity when not caught in reactivity. Moving our attention between these three experiences of the sense experience, the feeling tone, and the response, we see if the close marriage of feeling tone and reactivity can loosen up and allow a gap of spaciousness. There's no right answer. We're not trying to make ourselves be equanimous. We want to connect with what's truly happening in order to develop heart-mind flexibility that can allow a fresh response. When our experience is aversion, we connect with that. What is it like to hate our experience? How does it feel to grasp after pleasantness? How does this conditioning unfold, and where might it loosen? Rather than telling ourselves how it should be, we move with intimacy through these three aspects of the experience, letting them teach us about suffering and release.

Physical pain provides an excellent opportunity to explore unpleasant feeling tone. What happens when we have a headache? Naturally, we wish for it to go away. The unpleasantness of the sensations conditions the reactivity of aversion. Can we move closer? Can we settle the heart-mind with the sensations, just as they are? If not, can we rest with the unpleasantness, fully acknowledging it? Does this change our experience? If the mind is reactive, hating the experience, what is it like to be averse to this experience? How do we feel when we exile and refuse what is happening? Is this a satisfactory way to live? Is there an alternative? In all this investigating, have any moments of nonreactivity, of equanimity, arisen? How do they feel? One time a student explained to me, "I have this physical pain that I am trying to accept, but I can't seem to make progress with it." I replied, "You hate it, right? That's the truth." She admitted that it was. I surprised her by recommending that she go ahead and hate it, thoroughly, with mindfulness. We start right where we are.

Of course, the sound of a lawn mower falls under Exploring Unpleasantness 101. We start easy. As humans we experience many kinds of unpleasantness from the subtle to the very intense, including chronic pain, aging, illness, sorrow, fear, and loneliness. In our exploration of unpleasantness, we expand the boundaries of what we find acceptable in our human life. When we begin practice, perhaps 95 percent of life is unacceptable. (Or that was my experience.) Let's see if we can increase the amount of life that we are willing to hold. As our limits grow larger, we find ourselves less restless and more at peace. We do not need to expend our energy trying to avoid unpleasantness. Yes, we can take a pain reliever to alleviate the headache. If we need antidepressants, we should take them. Yet we don't peg our ultimate happiness on avoiding unpleasantness. We explore our relationship to unpleasantness in our formal meditation practice, and we also investigate binding and letting go in all the ordinary reactions of our daily life. Our life is our teacher, and there is no shortage of opportunities to learn.

Neutral Feeling Tone

The Buddha sometimes spoke about two feeling tones of pleasant and unpleasant. Other times he referred to three feelings: pleasant, unpleasant, and neutral. We spend the most time exploring pleasant and unpleasant feeling tones because these two fuel the chain of reactivity that leads to aversion and attachment, creating the suffering of the solid separate self. The third feeling tone of neutral, classically described as neither-pleasant-nor-unpleasant, doesn't condition reactivity, but rather spacing out and delusion. When experiences are neutral in flavor, we tend to lose interest. When we don't pay much attention, our usual delusions about life continue to unfold. Delusion is the bedrock upon which develops reactivity, so we don't want to give it room to flourish.

Living as goal-oriented humans, neutral experiences are not considered important. They're not going to get us what we want. Neutral happenings don't matter, so let's just pass by this unengaging experience and get to the real juice. One man calculated how much time it took to tie his shoes and decided that it was too much, so he only bought shoes with Velcro closures. Tying his shoes was too ordinary to be worth his attention. Considering how much of life is ordinary, we miss a lot because we don't value it as worthy of our presence.

When we live in the embedded world of now, every moment is worthy of our attention. Every moment of life is an opportunity to be connected and alive, whether that moment is pleasant, unpleasant, or neutral. We cultivate an appreciation of even that which doesn't have a charge for us. We start with a breath—a fairly neutral experience. Can we connect wholeheartedly with a breath? Or a step. As we connect with heartfelt attention with neutral experiences, they may even become pleasant. The pleasantness of wholehearted presence transforms the experience.

As we relate to this world with kindhearted attention, our appreciation for the ordinary experiences of life flourishes. We no longer demand that life be exciting, stimulating, new and improved in order to deserve our attention. We don't need an iPhone 15; the iPhone 10 is plenty. Or no iPhone at all is fine. Given that our economic system runs on the new and upgraded, the stimulating and flashy, we become cultural revolutionaries as we turn toward appreciating the familiar and mundane.

On our journey, we learn to appreciate subtlety. When concentration and mindfulness are strong, even subtle experiences are felt intensely: The red, orange, and yellow of the autumn leaves in the path. The raucous caw of the woodpecker. The coolness of the breeze on our cheeks. The pungent odor of the earth after rain. Simply received, the world is rich with all the stimulation that we need when we learn how to pay attention. We relate to the ordinary as sacred, with a sense of wholeheartedness we could call reverence.

In meditation practice, we explore with curiosity our relationship to what is neutral. Do we respond with disinterest, and if so, how is this experience? We may even find ourselves bored. What does boredom feel like? For most of us, boredom is a highly disliked state. Can we pay attention to boredom? Boredom often hides some form of wanting or not wanting; we don't want what we have or want something different. What we have is not good enough, not worthy of engagement, and so we disconnect. We may have to learn to travel through the terrain of boredom on our way to the peace of wholehearted presence.

Boredom can be a gateway into the freedom possible through connecting with neutral experience. Passing through boredom and engaging with neutral experience give us glimpses of the flavor of peace. Because neutral experience doesn't easily call forth reactivity, it presents less complicated access to a mind free of grasping and aversion, a heart-mind that settles with just this experience, ordinary and commonplace. Contentment, settling in with no desire for anything else, can flourish. The Zen teacher Susan Murphy says, "We accept all offers."[2] Life is full and rich, and we don't need anything else.

Meditating in the Wild

A number of years ago I undertook a wilderness retreat in the Adirondack Mountains of upstate New York. My retreat was planned for June, and as the date approached, it became clear that it was going to be cold and rainy for the first days, with temperatures not rising out of the forties. I considered canceling but decided that this would be perfect equanimity practice. My partner helped me set up camp on an island and then departed. I was left blissfully alone. Every morning I woke up and, looking out of the tent, confirmed once again that it was cold and rainy. Committed to connecting with all of my experience, I allowed myself a few minutes to complain: *This is my wilderness retreat! I didn't want this! It's not fair! It's so dreary!* And then I asked myself: *How am I going to be happy today?* And I *was* happy. Things are the way they are. After four or five days, the weather turned warm and sunny. Then the biting blackflies came out, and people arrived on the lake. Buddhism teaches us that there is no perfect situation. There's only what we have in front of us right now and the question, *How am I going to be happy now?* The uncompromising wilderness helps us learn the answer.

Meditating outside increases our capacity to embrace life as it is with a nondemanding heart. Nature teaches us that we live in a wild world, and life does not respond to our demands. Sitting outdoors day after day in all kinds of weather, we experience heat, cold, wind, stillness, sun, clouds, humidity, and dryness. They come and go, all without a single wish or command from ourselves. We explore how we relate to both pleasant and unpleasant sensations and ask ourselves if it's possible to meet it all with a wide and spacious heart-mind. Can we accept all offers? We notice when we brace ourselves against the reality of the present moment, wishing for something different, and stretch ourselves to relax into all manifestations of this wild life.

We can consider our nature meditation seat as a power spot, a place where we sow strength and feel completely at home. The Spanish word *querencia* describes a place in a bull ring where the bull feels safe and protected and therefore powerful. This word's etymological root is the verb *querer*, to want or to love, so we could say that this power spot is our place of longing and love. Wherever I've lived I've found such places where I return over and over—in the woods, by the lakes, and next to the streams. When I was a young child, I sat under the huge pine tree in our yard. As a teenager, I settled on a tree leaning over Lake Harriet. During my junior year abroad in Madrid, I sat on a green patch of grass surrounded by busy streets. At my current home I bushwhack to a rock in the middle of the forest or sit on a bench by the side of the marsh. We get to know these places, and they know us. As we develop familiarity with these power spots and the beings who live nearby, we establish a rapport. Power develops out of the friendliness of this growing relationship; the feeling of belonging and support allows us to rest more deeply into our meditation practice, protected by goodwill. I often leave a gift of a few nuts, or at least a few thoughts of gratitude, as I end my meditation and head home. I thank the trees, the water, the rocks, the chipmunks, and the birds for sharing their space with me.

When I am home in western Massachusetts, I meditate outside almost every day, enjoying all kinds of weather.* A slightly adapted Zen story tells us that Banzan, a serious practitioner in search of enlightenment, visits a market where he overhears a conversation between a fruit seller and her customer. The customer asks for the best and juiciest mango. The seller replies that every mango is the best mango, at which point Banzan gets enlightened. Every type of weather is the best weather! A blizzard with snowflakes zinging the face and wind howling through the trees is the best weather. A sunny day with warmth seeping into our cells and soft air entering our nostrils is the best weather. A crisp autumn day with a brisk breeze and the scent of drying leaves is the best weather. Sunny days, blizzards, thunderstorms. It's a wild, wild world. Might as well get used to it.

* I do have hearty Minnesotan blood.

PART TWO

THE HEART

INTRODUCTION TO EMOTIONS

Meeting Emotions with Mindfulness

With mindfulness we connect with our alive embodied experience, traveling down from our usual home in our heads and settling into sense-based life on earth. Descending from the mind down to earth, we now connect with the feminine paradigm of the heart. We meet the heart in all its manifestations, both afflictive and beautiful. The heart is a complex creature! Navigating this terrain calls for care, mindfulness, and willingness to engage both the pleasant and the unpleasant. In the coming chapters, we explore how transformation of the heart develops, beginning with meeting challenging heart-mind states.

In Buddhist psychology, emotions are included under what are called mind states—dispositions of heart and mind that filter and flavor how we view and relate to the world. How we meet or don't meet these states determines our heart's freedom. When the Dalai Lama gave a presentation at Smith College, a student asked him, "What's the most important thing in life?" The Dalai Lama was very open-minded, saying it depended on who you were. "If you are a serious dharma practitioner," he said, "the most important thing is learning how to deal with afflictive emotions."

Connecting skillfully with emotional states is a spiritual task. Learning how to hold both pleasant and unpleasant emotions in loving spaciousness is key for our freedom. Turbulent mind states in particular bind and entangle the heart-mind, limiting its spaciousness. We want to unbind and disentangle them.

Mindfulness practice engenders emotional honesty; we see more clearly what is truly happening in our hearts. When we start meditating, we may feel like we experience more afflictive emotions. Students say, "I was never angry before, and now I'm angry all the time." Well, we likely were angry before, but repressed it or sublimated it into other emotions. Busy running around with a myriad of things to contend with, we easily miss what is true for us. When we sit down and connect directly with body, heart, and mind we can feel our emotional life and heal, integrate, and free the heart.

Without mindfulness, our conditioned response to afflictive emotions is to either repress or drown in them. When we repress, we disavow the emotion and hide the truth of it from ourselves. Unfortunately, repressed emotion tends to emerge anyway in often destructive ways. On the other hand, we may drown in the emotion, encouraging the story and amplifying the feeling. We get completely lost in the drama, not understanding that we have created a limited, fabricated version of reality. We may act out of the story and cause harm to ourselves and our relationships. Mindfulness offers a middle way (between disavowing and drowning) of allowing the experience, seeing it clearly, and relating to it skillfully.

We may come to our Buddhist practice with internalized patriarchal conditioning that views emotions with strong skepticism. During my first long retreat, on about the tenth day I found myself overwhelmed with emotions that I had kept carefully sequestered. I went into my meeting with Joseph and launched into quite a monologue about how I was feeling lonely, afraid, angry, despairing, sad, and several other afflictive emotions. He listened kindly and then simply said, "What's the problem?" I was stunned. *You mean there isn't a problem?* He assured me I would be okay and advised me to just go take a walk. I had unconsciously held the view that it wasn't OK to feel deeply. Meditation can open up our emotional world, freeing places where we are shut down and contracted. Meeting our emotions with mindfulness, we do not need to repress or drown in them. We learn to relate to them with wisdom and great warmth, not exiling any part of our experience.

Meditating with afflictive emotions requires skillful application of mindfulness and a strong dose of lovingkindness and compassion. Because emotions can be so challenging, it is helpful to have a plan. Supported with a structure for our exploration, we can confidently turn our attention toward developing intimacy with our emotional life. Joko Beck suggests that we "suffer intelligently." While turning toward painful emotions is, well, painful, as we learn skillful engagement, we clear our hearts of clutter and the burden of self-centered entanglement. We make room for the beautiful emotions to shine forth. We can describe this process as weeding an overgrown garden. When my husband and I moved to our current house, I discovered a neglected rock garden out back among the ferns and blackberries. As I have carefully and patiently cleared out the brambles and pulled up the weeds, many wonderful discoveries have unfolded. Over the years previously hidden beautiful plants have emerged: wild blueberries, foxglove, Siberian iris, goatsbeard, and miniature juniper bushes. As we clear out the brambles in our hearts, we, too, can uncover beautiful surprises.

We may start our engagement with challenging emotions by actively managing these states. In situations where an emotion threatens to overwhelm us and we may do or say something harmful, we take active steps to lessen the intensity of the emotion. Perhaps we inhale deep breaths to calm our nervous system, or we connect with the sensations of our feet touching the earth. We may ask for a pause in the conversation. We might go for a walk or run or call a friend. We develop our own repertoire of actions that help us exit the afflictive emotional state and regain stability. Early in my practice when I dealt with a lot of fear, I kept a list of activities to engage in when I needed to move away from the intensity of the experience, including calling a friend, watching a movie, or—my favorite—cleaning the house. (With this last method, not only do we fend off our afflictive mind state; we also wind up with a clean living space.)

When we feel enough stability and confidence, we can adopt a receptive stance with emotions. From the orientation of the feminine paradigm, we let them in, meet them, and develop intimacy with this huge part of our humanity. The instructions below, based on the Burmese Mahasi lineage with some adaptations, provide guidelines for how to engage wisely and compassionately with our emotional experience. Although we will focus on afflictive emotions here, the outline is also applicable to positive emotions.

First, when an emotion comes to our awareness, naming it can be helpful. *This is fear; this is loneliness; this is craving.* (Or: *this is calm; this is joy.*) Emotions pull us into a trance in which our thoughts coalesce around a story or narrative that we unconsciously believe. We become hypnotized by our own minds. Making a mental note of the emotion helps us to pull out of the trance of the story, beginning the process of dehypnotizing ourselves.

Next, we connect with our direct experience of the emotion. Emotions manifest as thoughts and body sensations. Grounding in our visceral experience is the best way to disconnect from the storyline and land in presence. What body sensations, obvious or subtle, correspond with this emotion? Anger may feel like clenching in the solar plexus. Loneliness may manifest as heaviness in the heart. Fear can be felt as fluttering in the belly or tingling in the hands. We rest our attention in this embodied expression. The body keeps us honest. The mind has many slippery tricks, but the sensations in the body tell us the truth. From this embodied place, at times a quiet intuitive voice will convey to us the deeper truths this emotion wants us to know.

When the sensations feel intense and overwhelming, we may touch them briefly and then return to a more neutral experience, such as our primary anchor or the feeling of our feet on the floor. Sometimes we will touch and move away repeatedly, titrating the contact so that we can experience the emotion without being overwhelmed. In this way we build confidence in our capacity to open to what's difficult. We know how to exit if necessary, engendering the safety needed to explore more deeply.

Anchoring primarily in the body, we explore how the emotion changes as we engage with it. Does it increase in intensity? Decrease? Go away? Change to another emotion? We see for ourselves through direct participation that emotions are impermanent. The primary underlying delusion of emotions convinces us the feeling is going to last forever. In our meditation, we notice how, in the grips of a strong emotion, we believe it's going to last the rest of our life. Of course, on a rational level we know that's crazy, but that's how it feels. *I feel afraid and I'm going to feel afraid the rest of my life. Wow, this bliss is great and it's just going to keep on going.* When the emotion changes or ends, we observe that even though it felt permanent, it wasn't. Consciously paying attention to the ending of an emotion, we dehypnotize ourselves. Intimacy pokes holes in the delusional misrepresentation of emotions as permanent.

We also observe the manifestation of this emotion in the mind. What is the texture of the mind? Is it dull or alert, tranquil or turbulent? Does the mind feel spacious or confined? What kind of thoughts are present? We're not so interested in the particulars of the story, as we don't want to feed the drama by fixating on the content. It can be helpful, however, to notice what kind of thoughts arise so that we can be more mindful of them. For example, anger may bring thoughts of vengeance or self-righteousness; they're part of the anger package. When loneliness is present, thoughts that nobody loves us may arise. Naming the category of thought without getting involved in the story cultivates deeper understanding of our emotional patterning.

Powerful emotions function by entrancing us in the story. We are hijacked into a made-up world, and we lose perspective of the larger picture. Remember the last time you were angry at someone close to you? You were completely convinced they were a jerk, but the larger story is of course much more nuanced. They are also a dear person. When emotions are strong, the stories are convincing and the attachment can be quite strong. To loosen things up, we can ask, *What if the story isn't true?* and feel our visceral reaction to this suggestion. We often like our stories, even if they are stories of suffering, because they protect us and give us the illusion of control. What if we let go of the story? Once when I was angry at my brother, I sat mindfully with the process. I contemplated what a jerk he was and felt the anger in my body. I asked myself, *What if I let go of the story?* When I released the narrative, a more nuanced scenario emerged. I felt my brother's pain and realized that I had been trying to avoid it. The entire story changed; my perspective shifted and compassion arose. Mindfulness transformed the afflictive emotion and opened my heart to a wider picture. Remembering, when caught in a strong emotion, that our thoughts are filtered through a distorting lens helps us dis-identify with the storyline and emerge from the trance into a fuller perspective.

Investigating our relationship to the emotion is the next important step. How are we holding the emotion? When it's unpleasant, are we hating it? Do we hope by hating it we can make it go away? If so, that is our current truth, and we explore how hating the emotion influences it. (Spoiler alert: It tends to strengthen the emotion.) When the emotion is pleasant, are we trying to make it stay? Are we hoping by hanging on we can make it last? How does attachment feel? How does grasping affect the experience of the emotion? (Spoiler alert: It diminishes the pleasantness.) In other words, we investigate whether we are reacting to this emotion with aversion or grasping. Alternatively, acceptance and equanimity may be present, allowing the emotion to be as it is. When so, we also mindfully connect with this experience, familiarizing ourselves with the peace of nonreactivity.

These suggestions, while wordy, point toward directly engaging with an emotion, rather than thinking about it and trying to figure out what's going on. We are interested in the unfolding process of an emotion rather than the narrative. Thinking serves to separate and move us away from feeling. While there are times when it can be useful to unpack the narrative of an emotion and explore its roots, in meditation practice we meet it more directly and let it teach us. If we find ourselves asking, *Why [is this happening]?* we are likely trying to figure out the emotion in order to get rid of it. The questions that interest us are *what?* and *how?* as in *What is happening?* and *How is the process unfolding?* We explore what an emotion is, how it changes, and how to dehypnotize our heart from its trance. We find our way through by mindfully engaging what is truly happening, not what we think should be happening. Can we feel how simple that is? Like magic, awareness does the work; awareness oversees the transformation.

Befriending Fear

In my early practice, fear was a frequent visitor in my life. At one point I made a list of all the types of fear I had engaged, starting with thirteen varieties and ending up with twenty-four. Several years ago, I added another one. I have become a connoisseur of fear. (The spiritual teacher Ram Dass said that meditation helps us become connoisseurs of our neuroses.) Through this engagement spanning years, I have become less identified with fear and more willing to let it be. In this process, its power to cause me suffering has greatly diminished.

Let me tell you about my journey over years in my early practice with an emotion I called "the dark hole." This fear manifested as a combination of terror, loneliness, and dissociation. My first task entailed recognizing that the fear was present, as it was often covered by strong anxiety. My second task called for knowing how to get out of it when I was caught and spiraling. When exploring painful emotions, it is essential that we first know how to exit them. Emotions are powerful energy that hypnotizes us into a trance, causing us to see the whole world through a filter. When we are caught and hijacked, we take a wild ride because we think we're seeing the world as it really is. Knowing how to break the trance, we can emerge from the vortex. I used the techniques listed in the previous section of this chapter to stabilize and ground myself in present-time reality.

When I had gained some confidence in my exit strategy, I became more interested in exploring this emotion. *What is this place?* What was my direct experience of it? Because it was a dissociated kind of fear, I didn't experience many body sensations. The terror felt endless, like being in dark outer space with no anchors and no one to save me. I was afraid of this fear and intensely disliked it. When it arose, I felt agitated and anxious. With gentle curiosity, however, my capacity to engage it increased. I became more comfortable in this space, and my resistance to it began to melt. Slowly, I found myself able to care about this fear rather than reject it. With compassion I developed a willingness to touch the pain and a softness in response to it.

One day I was going about my business when I saw this fear approaching. I turned toward it and said, truly meaning it, *Hello, my old friend.* The fear stopped dead in its tracks. What was this? This was not what it expected. And it disappeared. I can't say that I never experienced this fear again, but its capacity to seduce me into a trance of enormous suffering lessened. The fear lost its power through mindful awareness and compassionate engagement.

We learn to meet painful emotions like a dear old friend, recognizing them as tender places that need wise attention and soft compassion. We bring them home with kindness-infused mindfulness. While part of our human experience, they don't need to dominate and overwhelm our heart-mind. We know how to engage and feel them in a very simple and direct way. The spaciousness of heart and mind increases as we can accommodate, and no longer need to avoid, our very human emotional responses to life. We can stop running from ourselves and rest more at ease in this precious human life on earth.

The Spaciousness of Nonidentification

An acronym often used to describe meeting emotions with balance is RAIN: recognize, allow/accept, interest/investigate, and nature/nonidentification.[*] In the instructions outlined above we discussed the first three aspects of how to recognize emotions, accept their presence, and investigate their true nature. Engaging these three can run the risk of encouraging attachment to our emotional experience. By developing intimacy through recognizing (or naming), allowing, and investigating, we can inadvertently become too fascinated, using the narratives to consolidate our sense of self. *This is who I am.* Rather than freeing ourselves, we

---

[*] Although this acronym has been adopted and changed by some teachers, it was originally coined by Michele McDonald.

thicken the skin of self. In meditation practice, we want to open to our emotions but not further strengthen our attachment to them. The fourth step, nonidentification, points us toward the impersonal nature of emotions, allowing us to hold them with more spaciousness.

The risk of jumping too quickly to dis-identify with our suffering as "not me, not mine," on the other hand, is a disconnected spirituality lacking in compassion. We may hope to avoid feeling by spiritually bypassing our experience. When we move too quickly to a wisdom perspective of dis-identification, we miss the chance to develop compassion engendered by an honest engagement with our emotional life. We may distance from the emotion without making genuine peace with it. We haven't softened. Our search for integrated peace involves moving through suffering rather than around it.

The Buddha taught that suffering comes from identifying with or owning experience and then feeling that it needs to be controlled. Therefore, understanding identification and nonidentification is crucial for developing freedom with afflictive emotions. We can notice identification when an arising experience feels particularly like "mine." Anger appears, and suddenly we are an angry person and we must fix ourselves. A pain in the shoulders shows up and we glom on to it—it's ours and we have to fix it; we tell ourselves we're probably going to turn into a hunchback as we imagine a future where this pain always exists. *My anger, my pain, my breath.* When we identify with an emotion (or other experience), we take it personally. Identification binds the heart by making the emotion more real and solid. When identified with an emotion, we wind up out of touch with reality, scrambling around in our thought-based world, believing the life that we have created.

The following experiment can give us a feel for the nature of identification and nonidentification. First say to yourself, *I am angry* (or some other afflictive emotion you readily feel). How does this feel in body and mind? Give it a minute or two. Then say, *I feel angry.* How does this feel? Lastly, say to yourself, *Anger is happening,* and feel the result. What is the difference between these three experiences? Feel free to play with them. The first sentence, *I am angry,* is encouraging identification. The second leans toward a bit more spaciousness. The third way (*Anger is happening*) encourages nonidentification: this is an arising human experience, not me or who I am. Yes, we still need to deal with it, yet we can do so with more expanse in the heart.

In truth, experiencing an emotion is both personal and not personal. On the one hand, it is happening to us and it's our responsibility to deal with it. Thich Nhat Hanh said that there's a screaming baby in the room and that baby is yours; you need to take care of it whether you want to or not. That's the personal part. The impersonal aspect is that this emotion is just a manifestation of life in this moment, causes and conditions arising and passing away. We're not to blame for any of it. We're sitting here minding our own business, and suddenly somebody starts up their leaf blower and anger arises. Causes and conditions came together to produce anger. It's not our fault.

Identification involves glomming on to the experience as ours. This attachment develops into management, including resistance to the fact that pleasant things end and unpleasant things arise, that all things change and cannot ultimately be controlled. Wanting to have a good grip on things, we take impermanent experiences seriously, as ours alone, and then try to control life so that these experiences are always pleasant and never unpleasant. We hope for permanence and dependability. Clenching our heart-mind to control and micromanage life takes an enormous amount of energy. It's a full-time job, demanding most of our precious life force. For survival, it's not a bad evolutionary strategy, but it doesn't deliver the happiness we seek.

Nonidentification allows us to access freedom in the midst of feeling an emotion. It's a great energy saver. We don't go through the whole process of creating a reality and then trying to manage it. When we don't identify with an emotion, we hold it with more spaciousness. Emotions are more like a verb than a noun; they arise when causes and conditions come together in a certain way and end when those conditions change. They are not who we are, but rather part of nature. Emotions are universal; all humans feel them. None of it is truly ours; it's life manifesting. The presence of emotions just means we are alive.

Practicing nonidentification, we connect with our shared humanity with all people. The perspective that all human beings experience the same emotions we do can bring spaciousness and compassion to the heart-mind. One time I was sitting in the meditation hall at IMS feeling lonely and full of self-pity. Then I realized that all over the world at that moment people were feeling lonely. No one gets through human life without feeling lonely at times. These realizations opened me up to our shared humanity, loosening the identification and allowing compassion to arise. And then I didn't feel so lonely.

We develop nonidentification by bringing mindfulness to the process of identifying. We learn the freedom of nonidentification by being willing to traverse the process of identification with awareness. We get close to our experience of identification, familiarizing ourselves with the tension that signals our closing down around experience. Are we seeing the emotion as permanent or can we hold it as an arising event that will pass away? Are we identifying with it by taking it personally as saying something about who we are? Or are we understanding that it is a natural experience of being human that arises because certain conditions come together? What happens when awareness meets the experience of contracting around an emotion? Can the heart-mind grow big enough to accommodate our emotional truth with spaciousness?

With nonidentification we loosen our grip, whether subtle or exaggerated, on the arising phenomena in this world, letting things be as they are. This frees up everybody. In this way, we access increasing spaciousness around emotions when they arise. The amount of time spent lost in the stories decreases, and their power to seduce us abates. Emotions arise, are felt, and become transformed by awareness. The heart-mind, as it unbinds, feels wider, more flexible, unbarricaded, and more alive.

Karmic Knots

As we allow ourselves to land in the realm of the feeling heart, we encounter our most tender wounding. All of us carry deeply conditioned beliefs from early childhood that helped us make sense of the world.

These beliefs reflect a survival strategy we learned to manage the world and try to get what we needed and not get hurt. When our childhood was less safe and affirming, these beliefs tend to be more tenacious; we held (and still hold) on to them for our very survival. We adhere to these core beliefs fiercely and with complete dedication. This conditioning can be so central to our worldview that we don't even see it or consciously know its strategies for dealing with the world. When we sit with this body, heart, and mind for very long, however, we find out. We hear our core beliefs.

Many people carry the core belief of *I'm not good enough. I'm not lovable or worthy of love. I'm not okay. There's something wrong with me.* Other core beliefs might be *I won't be able to get what I need* or *What other people need is more important.* Out of this core belief we develop a whole range of emotions and strategies to deal, manifesting as what my teacher Michele calls a *karmic knot.* This knot is not so much a thing but rather a pattern of conditioning consisting of strands of thoughts, beliefs, and emotions tightly and painfully wound together. Tsoknyi Rinpoche names them "beautiful monsters," pointing to both their power and their underlying wish to protect us.[1] When a karmic knot gets triggered, we get pulled into a vortex, unable to see out, and we may remain there for a minute, hours, days, or our whole lifetime. We know we've hit a karmic knot when we think, *Oh not this again!* or *I've been meditating for ten, fifteen years, shouldn't I be through with this one?* We're embarrassed and wouldn't want anybody to know that we feel this way.

Karmic knots are at root a spiritual problem. We most strongly create our sense of self around these conditioned patterns. Strangely, even though they are our greatest source of suffering, we love them because they make sense out of the world in their twisted way. They create a cohesive self, and the very tightness of the tangle points to the powerful amount of attachment and identification involved. Any way we can loosen the knot, whether through psychotherapy or mindfulness practice, introduces more space and freedom in the heart-mind. Breaking up our identification with these knots, our sense of self gets more spacious and flexible. We unbind the heart-mind.

Untangling these knots goes through a predictable pattern of evolution as mindfulness strengthens and wisdom develops. We engage in a process of dehypnotizing ourselves, deconditioning through awareness and love, and with these "sticky" tangles, it takes time. My teacher Michele says to expect ten years to a lifetime. We don't have to wait ten years to experience any freedom; yet we do need to call on buckets of gentle patience as we navigate these waters. Let's look at the evolution of this process using some examples from the karmic knot of *I'm not good enough*.

At first, the karmic pattern operates in our lives under the radar. We're not yet conscious of it; it's just the way the world is. Its power is felt, however, from the subconscious, heavily influencing how we see the world and live in it. Like a fish that thinks the ocean is the only reality there is, we live within our karmic knot conditioning without realizing that there is another way to relate to the world. Our perception serves to confirm our core tangle, as it filters out contrary information and particularly notices information that is congruent with its own beliefs. We notice happenings, for example, that confirm that we're not good enough and completely miss seeing experiences that might suggest that we are actually okay. Our view is narrowed to a slice of life that conforms to our core belief. Like a horse with blinders, we're unable to see the bigger picture. This process keeps us unaware of the tangle even as it profoundly shapes our lives and causes suffering to ourselves and, at times, to those with whom we interact.

Over time, we become aware of the karmic knot in its aftermath. Mindfulness, when not yet strong, will often catch hijacking after it happens. We look back and see that we were caught in a deeply habituated pattern of thoughts and emotions. We begin to understand the patterning as patterning, recognizable as one possible way of seeing the universe rather than the only way. We reflect on how we were seduced into the trance of our old conditioning in order to prime ourselves to catch it earlier in the future.

Eventually we begin to become aware of the karmic knot as it is happening. What we have been avoiding comes into our conscious view, and we allow ourselves to feel it. The pattern has come into present time awareness, yet we are still heavily identified with it. We take it to be true, believe it, and are attached to it. We have enough mindfulness at this point to see what is happening as it happens, but not enough to cut through our deeply conditioned identification. This is painful! The Zen writer Natalie Goldberg says, "The terrible truth, which is rarely mentioned, is that meditation doesn't directly lead us to some vaporous, glazed-eyed peace. It drops us right into the personal meat of human suffering. . . . With practice, we settle right down into the barbed-wire nest, and this changes us."[2]

With "not good enough" patterning, for example, we become more willing to directly experience the edginess of anxiety, the relentlessness of perfectionism, and the vulnerability of social interaction. That's the bad news. For change to happen, we must feel the pain and perceive how we create our life around it. We break through our walls of delusion, self-deception, and dissociation, and that's powerful, even if not pleasant. We are sticking with ourselves, developing emotional honesty. We stop using our energy to resist and avoid these tangles, freeing it up toward interest and investigation of what is happening. Contradicting our usual conditioning to run the other way, we call on our innate curiosity to fuel our commitment to stick with ourselves.

In turning toward suffering, we cultivate the heart that holds the truth with tenderness. We understand that these deeply conditioned patterns are really based in love. They develop from a child trying to learn how to survive in the best ways possible. While the patterning may feel harsh and cruel, the core is love. The anxiety of perfectionism and fear of unworthiness served a function. As we shift from aversion to care, we develop steadfastness in our commitment to not exiling any part of experience.

One challenge of this phase involves becoming interested in this suffering without further entrenching it. We want to open to it but not further tighten our attachment. Our investigation can carry the risk of becoming too fascinating, using the narratives to consolidate our sense of self. *This is who I am.* Rather than freeing ourselves, we thicken the skin of self. The risk of not engaging this phase, however, of jumping too quickly to dis-identify with our suffering as "not me, not mine" is a disconnected spirituality lacking in compassion. We may control the pattern without making genuine peace with it. We haven't softened, and rigidity will remain. Our search for integrated peace involves moving through the experience of the tangle rather than around it.

We taste more freedom as mindfulness strengthens. We see the conditioned knot arise and we realize: there's another way. We taste the freedom of nonidentification, as we see the thoughts and emotions arise due to conditions and pass away. The thoughts become less sticky as we realize they're just thoughts and we don't have to believe them or take them so personally. They are a story that we have told ourselves repeatedly, and we don't have to get caught up in them or play them out.

We now find that we become more able to respond to situations in new and fresh ways. Sometimes a moment appears when a crack in our worldview reveals that we don't have to be stuck in the old conditioned way. We have stopped, at least for a moment, identifying with the thought or emotion. *Wow, I can make mistakes and people still love me!* We can feel the power in this realization. A pattern of conditioning has just broken out of the deep trench in which it was stuck. This opening feels like grace, and yet it is the payoff from many moments of mindfulness. The accumulation of mindful moments gives us the power to break out of old conditioning and have choice. Life becomes more fluid, and our rigid views lose their opaqueness and become transparent. We can see through them, and we can observe life more clearly. We don't have to follow through with the old pattern; why would we want to cause ourselves this suffering? We can choose different ways of being and acting.

As we feel even more stability in our capacity to work with our karmic knots, the thoughts and emotions may still arise, but there's not enough attachment for them to gather steam. As we don't get caught up in these tangles, their karmic force lessens. Strands release and the tangle starts to fall apart. Leonard Cohen said in a *Lion's Roar* interview, "You run through your top ten erotic fantasies, ambition fantasies, revenge fantasies, global ratification fantasies. You run through them all until you bore yourself to death . . . after you run through them for a number of years, they cease to have charge. They bore themselves into non-existence."[3]

We've traveled through these patterns mindfully so many times that they just aren't so interesting or engaging anymore. They've lost their juice. We don't take the bait, so we don't suffer. Sometimes we can see the tangle approaching and we just say, *No thanks. I've done this enough times, I know where it goes, and I'm not so interested in going there.* Different from our original "no thanks" that wasn't able to face the experience, this "no thanks" is based in compassion and equanimity. Why would we want to suffer this again? The sense of not being good enough may still arise, but it doesn't hijack us like before. We *know* it's just a deeply conditioned pattern that we can attend to with mindfulness and care.

As contraction around these tangles diminishes, we experience increased stability and confidence in our ability to meet suffering with grace, and we enjoy growing spaciousness of heart and mind. Before we were running on an old outdated version of the computer program, and it wasn't functioning so well. We have now updated the hard drive to the present and can be flexible to respond to current circumstances with freshness, rather than based on decades-old conditioning. While navigating these phases and developing steady confidence in our ability to work with karmic knots take time and patience, eventually we relax the goal of finally getting it all together and instead enjoy the unfolding process of increasing freedom.

6

CHALLENGING
HEART-MIND STATES

Aversion

Many years ago, I traveled to Myanmar for my first three-week meditation retreat in the Sagaing Hills, the Buddhist heart of the country. Practice in the United States had started to feel too easy, and I wanted to stretch. Having a sensitive body easily impacted by the environment, I traveled with some trepidation. I arrived at the monastery, located on the banks of the Irrawaddy River, and was escorted to my own individual hut, or *kuti*. I immediately noticed that it smelled like mothballs, to which I am allergic. The mothballs were in a very large cabinet, which we moved to the porch. Lifting the cabinet, however, I threw my back out. In addition, during this process, the abbot's deaf nephew stood by watching and making the universal sign for "crazy." Then in the new meditation hall, I discovered that the floors had just been painted with oil-based cement paint, to which I'm also allergic. The smell of smoke fires wafted up from the village below, exacerbating my asthma. Our first night there the entire village celebrated a group monastic ordination, and as is common for Burmese events, music and speeches blasted from loudspeakers all night long so that everybody could enjoy the festivities. I panicked, thinking,

117

I'm not going to live through this experience. In addition, at that time cell and internet service were not widely available in Myanmar. My return home involved five plane trips, making it almost impossible to change plans. With no alternative, I faced this pain, saying to myself, *If this entire three-week experience is about learning how to deal with panic, sign me up.* I got interested in panic. I found it manifested physically in waves and I could surf them up and down. My mind fabricated catastrophic stories over and over until mindful awareness wore them out. A large part of panic is unpleasant stimuli; I increased my tolerance for holding this unpleasantness. Infusing mindfulness with kindness and care, I could "do" panic. As my capacity to meet panic increased, its power to overtake me lessened. By befriending panic, I did not have to avoid it. My capacity to embrace all of life increased.

In Buddhist teachings, aversion, greed, and delusion are known as the three roots of suffering. These mind states obscure reality and entangle the heart-mind. The Buddhist commentaries state that most of us specialize in one of these three roots. (Some of us might have a double major or a major and a minor.) This specialization is our go-to strategy for dealing with the wild nature of the world and our primary teacher in our meditation practice. Greed types want, aversive types don't want, and confused types aren't sure. A short test can help us determine our type. If our primary response to the world is "Yes, I want more!" we are likely a greed or desire type. If our knee-jerk reaction to new information is "No!" we probably specialize in aversion. If our response is usually "Maybe . . . but . . .," we are likely a deluded or confused type. Yes, no, and maybe.

It's worth noting that these three primary strategies for dealing with this world of change also have their positive aspects. Greed types tend toward devotion and enthusiasm. Aversive types can be strong in clear understanding. And confused types lean toward equanimity. Of course, we all manifest all three roots of suffering, and we all possess the seeds of their more positive aspects. Knowing our primary strategy is not a call to strengthen our sense of self, as in *Oh, I'm such an aversive person!* Identifying our primary root can, however, help us to pay closer attention to it and receive it as our teacher. (Hint: If you are still wondering which is your primary strategy, you are probably a confused type. The other two types already know.)

I specialize in aversion and know it well. Aversion can arise in the face of unpleasant experiences and presents in many forms: fury, fear, terror, panic, hatred, ill will, disgust, judgment, anger, annoyance, and sadness, to name just a few. Aversion pushes away or avoids what is happening. Aversion tells us we can't tolerate our experience, so we must get rid of it. An aversive mind state convinces us that this unbearable experience is going to last forever, so therefore we must eliminate it. Aversion, like all afflictive mind states, is wholeheartedly self-centered; its job is to take care of *me*. Aversive mind states separate us from what's happening, objectifying the experience so that we can figure out how to get rid of it. Aversion upholds the fantasy that we can control the world around and within us. I call it a protective strategy; it attempts to shield us from the truth that we can't control things, that unpleasant experiences arise whether or not we want them to and at times we have to bear them.

When aversion is going to cause us to commit harmful actions, we call forth the energy of the active paradigm. We ruthlessly cut off the aversion with the sword of mindfulness. We learn how to move away from it, come out of the trance of the compelling stories, and place our attention elsewhere. We hit the pause button long enough to decide what is skillful in dealing with the situation in front of us. In this way, we save ourselves and others from our harmful actions.

Other times we have the energy and capacity to turn toward aversion with receptivity and intimacy. How does this energy present in the body and the mind? What stories are we telling ourselves? How do we get ensnared by aversion and how do we emerge from its trance? With warm mindfulness, we soften into the experience and allow it spacious room in our body. Kindness teaches us that we can allow and hold the unpleasant experiences of life, letting them arise and pass away without turbulence. Aversion is just a mind state that arises due to conditions and will eventually pass. We can let the stories go, not feeding this energy through *papancha,* the tendency toward mental proliferation. As we befriend aversion, we fall less easily under its spell and find a greater capacity to be with all of life, including all the unpleasant experiences that come our way. The energy taken up trying to make life suit our preferences can convert into aliveness, curiosity, love, and engagement. Gaining the capacity to rest in the truth of ceaseless change, we do not need aversion to protect us.

As we become increasingly comfortable with the wide array of aversive mind states, we realize we can even play with them. During my 7:30 chanting meditation this morning, a leaf blower started up outside. Knowing how much I dislike this sound and the likelihood that aversion would follow, I played aikido with this unpleasant sense experience. In this martial art we join with the opponent's energy and then move in a skillful way. I connected with the sound of the leaf blower and discovered that its tone could harmonize with my chanting. We don't have to oppose what we don't like. We can cooperate wholeheartedly with what the universe sends our way.

We know our practice is mature when we stop complaining about life. Perhaps we can adopt the perspective that freedom is the end of whining.* Most of us control how much whining we do to other people, but what about the whining in our own minds and hearts? What would it be like to quit whining? Take in this freedom. A Zen Buddhist story describes a disciple who, seeking peace, approaches a master named Sono. She instructs him, whatever happens, to say, "Thanks for everything. I have no complaints whatsoever." As we tame aversive mind states, we increasingly live from the receptive space of no complaints whatsoever.

Greed

Years ago, I taught regularly at a retreat center out west. I arrived a day early to adjust to the time change, and the staff and I enjoyed a ritual of baking brownies during my rest day. Not just regular brownies, these were exquisite Ghirardelli dark chocolate brownies, and I was addicted to them. One time I decided to take a brownie back to my cottage, plan-

* I thank Anam Thubten for this perspective.

ning to eat it later. But the brownie didn't make it; I wound up eating it on the path. I was amazed. I had been bested by a brownie. I decided that the next day, I was going to bring a brownie back to the cottage with me, but this time I was going to make the trip with playfulness and mindfulness.

The next afternoon, I walked toward my cottage with my delicious brownie. I felt the desire to eat the brownie arise as intense energy, a burning sensation and tightening in the solar plexus. I was certain that I must eat the brownie. If I didn't eat the brownie, I might die, and if I ate the brownie, I would be happy and satisfied, probably for the rest of my life. As I was mindful of this energy, it increased and then peaked and dissipated. Craving arose and passed away a number of times, and each time I attended to it with mindfulness. I didn't eat the brownie; mindfulness of sense desire gave me choice. I felt empowered because this time I was not bested by the brownie.

Navigating greed is a central task for meditators. Buddhism uses a spectrum of words to describe wanting, each one stronger and more entangled. We start with *preference*, then *wanting* or *desire*, *craving*, *grasping* or *clinging*, and finally *attachment*. We are also talking about *lust*, *coveting*, and all the nuances of the ways that we lean toward pleasant experiences and try to obtain and keep them. I asked a scholar monk whether it was important to be precise about which word to use. He replied, "No, what's important is the amount of suffering present."

We can understand desire as a protection from accepting the true nature of reality. Desire always arises with delusion, the belief that things have permanence and can satisfy us. Sense desire, by holding out hope that this next thing or experience will do it, distracts us from the truths of impermanence and dukkha. We get seduced and entranced by the pleasantness of the object and its alleged ability to satisfy us, and we become oblivious to the drawbacks. We keep wanting and wanting and then trying to satisfy our wanting. Endlessly restless, we continually look for the next thing that will make us happy and satisfied. The Buddha described sense desire as being stuck in debt and never able to pay it off, a metaphor still apt after all the centuries. Joko Beck states the truth simply, "Practice has to be a process of endless disappointment. We have to see that everything we demand (and even get) eventually disappoints us. This discovery is our teacher."[1]

In the sutras, the energy of meeting sense desire is usually yang, or active, in tone. We battle with sense desire, focusing on "getting free from and being independent of it" (Dhammacakkappavattana Sutra). Cut it off with a sword! With out-of-control addictions, this strong renouncing energy is helpful; we don't want to give craving any room to get a grip on us. Applying yang energy can prevent desire from overwhelming us and causing us to act in harmful ways. To support our commitment, we may even remove the desired object(s) from our presence. I don't keep dark chocolate–covered almonds in the house because I can't resist them. If they're not around, then I can't eat them. Monastic communities are often designed around simplicity and renunciation in order to limit the presence of pleasant sense objects and lessen craving.

From a more yin paradigm, we bring softer, more receptive energy. Rather than battle with sense desire, we get to know it intimately and thoroughly, transforming its power through mindfulness. When we have energy and capacity, we turn toward desire with mindfulness and get acquainted with it. How do we experience wanting in the body, mind, and heart? What underlying beliefs and delusions are present? We can notice that wanting is selective in its focus, fixating on what is pleasant and ignoring other information. Can we feel the trance, the seductive energy, that occurs when wanting is present? Can we bear wanting? Do we have to follow its dictates? We sit through the arising and passing away of wanting, investigating its impermanent nature. As we meet this energy and live through it without acting on it, it loses power. We see its game, its false promises and trickery. Through this intimacy with wanting, we get familiar with its ploys and disempower its energy. When desire arises, knowing it so well, we can say, *Hello, my old friend*, and relate to it with wisdom. Instead of being caught in the grip of sense desire, we experience flexibility and freedom to respond skillfully. Getting to know desire intimately, we free the heart and mind of its grip.

In Buddhist sutras, Mara is a being like a coyote trickster who loves to mess with dharma practitioners.* In many stories, Mara approaches a monk or a nun practicing seriously and says some version of "What are you doing? This is crazy, you should be having some fun. Go after sense pleasures. This isn't leading anywhere." (We may have heard the same voice.) The game changes when the monk or nun says, "Mara, I see you." The practitioner is familiar with Mara, intimate with his ways, and they know him so well that he can't fool them. When they say, "Mara I see you," they are stating, "Mara, I really know you and I know your trickery." Mara then either vanishes on the spot or sits dejected, playing in the dirt with a stick. He doesn't know what to do. Because he's been seen, he's lost his power.

We tend to get mighty serious when wanting is present, yet we can learn to take this energy lightly and play with it. In her book *A Heart as Wide as the World,* Sharon Salzberg describes the Dalai Lama's visit to Gethsemani Monastery in Kentucky. The monks sell cheese and fruit-cakes, so they offered the Dalai Lama some cheese. Laughing, he said that what he really wanted was cake. He repeated how unfortunate it was that nobody had offered him cake. His laughter and willingness to mention his preferences in front of a television audience proved that he held his desires lightly and was okay with either cake or cheese.

As we play with sense desire, we can laugh at the craziness of our own heart-mind. One time, decades ago, I took my goddaughter out for a shared hot fudge sundae. When the sundae arrived, I dove in with gusto, pushing away my goddaughter's spoon so that I could get more hot fudge. We laughed and laughed. (She still mentions it sometimes.) The heart-mind can be shameless, and we can hold it like a misguided child.

Greed estranges us from that which we love. Greed occupies space in the heart that could be available for connection, smothering unmediated heartfelt relationship. When we are wanting the Ghirardelli brownie, we no longer taste it. Our attention is captivated by wanting, disconnected from the sense experience itself. As wanting loses its power, intimacy

* In many indigenous American cultures—such as the Navajo—the coyote is an allegorical creature known for trickiness and mischief.

increases. When wanting is absent, we fully enjoy the brownie while grounded in the reality of impermanence.

Meeting wanting directly dilutes its power. We know it as a heart-mind state that arises and passes away. We are not tricked by the delusion that this thing or experience will ultimately satisfy us. Yes, pleasant experiences do bring some temporary satisfaction, and we can enjoy them even knowing they end. With the space created by mindfulness, we make better decisions about which desires we follow. Some desires are skillful wishes toward which we direct our energy. Other desires are unskillful, leading to suffering for ourselves or others, and need to be avoided. When we can live through the energy of desire, we have a choice. Bringing mindfulness to our experience when wanting is present, we are empowered. Poor Mara sits, dejected, playing with a stick in the dirt.

Delusion

Of the three roots of suffering (greed, aversion, and delusion), delusion is the most foundational. Delusion is fundamental ignorance about the nature of this world, and it fuels the reactivity of aversion and greed. Delusion functions by dulling the heart and muddling the mind so that we can't see clearly. This mind state of confusion and endless skeptical thought can manifest as Mara the trickster endlessly twisting facts to spin them as we like.

Delusion became clear to me recently regarding climate change and living in northeastern United States. I secretly carried the hope and belief that perhaps we in the Northeast might not suffer too much from climate change. It's not too hot, we have water, and we haven't had trouble with wildfires. But after several periods of intense toxic smoke from Canadian wildfires and local flooding from increasingly frequent fierce downpours, the truth of reality poked through. I have since heard from many others admitting to the same delusion. Our belief was convenient, but it wasn't in touch with reality.

In the Vipallasa Sutra, the Buddha describes several fundamental delusions or misperceptions about the nature of reality. We see permanence where impermanence is the core nature of all things. We perceive satisfaction and reliability in this world where unsatisfactoriness and unreliability are a truer reality. We feel ourselves to be permanent and controllable when the underlying truth is that the self is fluid and interdependent. These "perversions of perception" entangle us in the endless rounds of reactivity and separation. Clearing up these fundamental delusions is the spiritual task of our meditation practice.

Delusion is a slippery little fella. We don't know what we don't know, and that leaves us in a bit of a pickle. The point of our meditative investigation is to move closer to the way things really are, to gain more clarity, and to cut through our tendency to perceive reality out of old conditioning and desires. The mind is crafty and prone to delusion, so being grounded in the body helps us on our journey. The body doesn't lie. The body doesn't make up stories about the way things may be. The body shows us the truths of impermanence, unsatisfactoriness, and not-self, allowing us to move closer to the way things truly are.

The poet T. S. Eliot said, "Human kind cannot bear very much reality."[2] It's true! Reality is hard to deal with. Life is not a picnic; it's wild, unpredictable, and uncontrollable. Pema Chödrön said, "The truth is inconvenient,"[3] and we would prefer convenience. Delusion is our willful attempt to control the narrative right in our own hearts and minds. We like delusion; it gives us the comfort of living in a convenient bubble. But there's a price. Although delusion operates behind the scenes, its machinations take effort, as reality has a way of continually asserting itself. This effort secretly saps our vitality, and getting more in touch with the way things really are revitalizes us.

The spiritual path is long and arduous for most as we slowly increase our reality tolerance. We build the spiritual strengths needed to face the truth—qualities such as love, equanimity, patience, and commitment—and we chip away at the stone walls and endless mazes in our heart-mind. As our capacity to manage and even thrive in this wild world increases, we no longer need the protection of dullness and confusion. The heart-mind is strong and flexible enough to remain in touch and engaged amid the vicissitudes of everyday life.

How do we cut through delusion and develop insight into the truth? Where do we begin? Relaxing our obsessive faith in our thinking mind, we learn to rest in our embodied experience. We trust not-knowing and let curiosity lead the way. Desire for the freedom of truth supersedes our habitual wish for security and convenience. The quiet space of not-thinking, the gaps in our usual narratives even for a few moments, allow insight a chance to show itself. Starting as intuitive knowing from the gut, insight then manifests in the mind as cognitive understanding. As understanding passes through the heart, we attend to the emotional ramifications that unfold from realizing the truth. Insight is a full experience of body, heart, and mind.

Negotiating Trauma in Our Meditation

Two months into my first three-month retreat, three flashbacks arise in my meditation—freeze-frames without context that suggest early childhood trauma. Having no previous knowledge of personal trauma, I'm absolutely shocked and react strongly, my mind screaming, *No! No!* After twenty minutes, an iron door shuts and it's over, leaving me with lots of questions and no answers. My mind has decided that I am not equipped at this time to deal with this information. Eight years later, after much healing work through psychotherapy and embodied practices such as karate and gospel singing, at the end of a two-month retreat focused on cultivating metta, the more complete story unfolds. It is a shattering experience, accompanied by the indescribable vulnerability of opening to previously unknown trauma. This time my heart is strong enough to hold the intensity.

We cannot talk about down-to-earth dharma—that is, embodied meditation practice—without exploring trauma. Just to be human is traumatic; living in this unpredictable uncontrollable world is harrowing enough. Many of us, in addition, have suffered particularly catastrophic events in our childhood, perhaps as severe as physical, sexual, or emotional abuse, loss of a family member, mental illness in a parent, extreme poverty, or forced migration. We may have suffered trauma stemming from experiences of racism, sexism, homophobia, or gender identity violence. Ancestral trauma in the form of genocide, war, or slavery may have been passed down to us through genetic inheritance and/or intergenerational conditioning. Those born with a particularly sensitive nature, impacted more strongly by the unpredictable stimuli of the outside world, may also manifest trauma patterning.

The deep pain of trauma can be an awakener that fuels our journey. The Buddha was a trauma survivor. His mother died seven days after he was born. Very attuned after nine months in the womb to his mother's sounds, smells, and body, the Buddha would have been deeply affected by this sudden and early loss. Although his mother's sister raised him with much love, this early experience may have caused a deep wound that would set him off on his search in his adulthood.

The legacy of trauma can become vividly apparent as we undertake a meditation practice of embodiment. Trauma can result in deeply conditioned patterns encoded in the mind, heart, physical body, and energy body. As we drop awareness into the body, this patterning may become apparent in challenging ways. The opening of our physical and energetic bodies that occurs in meditation practice may release stored patterns of intense emotion, energetic binding, and physical stress. Memories of previously known and unknown trauma can surface. The practitioner can feel destabilized, fragile, vulnerable, and disoriented. In addition, sometimes trauma piggybacks on meditative insight, distorting the truth in frightening ways. For example, an experience of emptiness may appear like a bleak and terrifying void rather than freeing spaciousness.

Counterbalancing these challenges, however, by opening to what's been hidden and bringing the pieces home, we access unity, wholeness, and even joy. The dissociated or exiled parts of our being weigh on us and demand a steep price in the loss of vitality and energy. Integrating trauma releases this weight, energizing and enlivening us. Knowing all of ourselves more deeply and completely is our journey home.

Because trauma can cause challenging suffering of heart and mind, we may turn to meditation to heal. Meditation, by teaching us how to connect with our experience in a balanced way, can be tremendously therapeutic. Due to the delicate and volatile nature of trauma wounding, however, we may need to learn to meditate in a manner that supports healing rather than inadvertently exacerbates suffering. Some tips can give us discerning guidance as we explore our embodied experience.

The overriding guideline for working with trauma is to respect the pacing of our own heart. I had to wait eight years for fleshed-out narratives associated with those three freeze-frames. While it was happening, this felt much too slow, but in retrospect the timing was wise. Earlier, I would not have been able to deal with the intensity of the process; it would have overwhelmed my nervous system. After two months of metta meditation, my heart and mind were strong, flexible, and deeply caring, the perfect conditions for holding intense trauma.

Because trauma is so painful, practitioners seeking relief from that pain tend to want to push and explore more deeply and quickly than may be wise. For example, we may entertain the secret hope that going deep into the most intense emotional pain will purge it and get rid of it forever. This wish can cause us to override the limits of our nervous system. Pushing is counterproductive, as it causes a defensive reaction. When we force our way into our past trauma, we activate our defenses. We must learn how to ease back, understanding that sometimes less is more. As we respect our heart and body and listen to what is needed rather than demand a particular outcome, we develop a relationship of trust with our own system. As our system knows that we will not approach with aggression, we build the safety that allows our heart-mind to relax and open.

Our meditation practice may not look like what we read about and hear in group instructions. Those healing from trauma need to trust our own experience and let our practice lead us, rather than try to fit into some ideal. For example, hearing that having a daily sitting practice for forty-five minutes is a good idea, we decide to do that. Maybe for us, however, forty-five minutes isn't the most helpful because it opens us up too much and fifteen minutes is better for our system. We experiment to find out what's truly serving us. What happens when we meditate for forty-five minutes? What happens when we sit fifteen? We check out how we feel during the rest of the day, not how we feel while meditating. We may feel great while meditating for forty-five minutes, and then find that this amount of opening produces anxiety during our day. Experimenting, we determine what is right for us. Meditation is like medicine: we all react differently. Some of us need more and some of us need less for the optimum result.

In the same vein, we experiment to find an anchor that is comfortable and calming for us. Bringing awareness to the body can at first feel overstimulating if trauma has conditioned us to live dissociated from our felt experience. Given that being human is traumatizing, all of us experience this dissociation to a certain degree, but trauma and abuse accentuate this tendency. Becoming embodied is a measured, respectful process. Moving closer to our felt experience, we start with the safest anchors. When the breath is activating and does not provide calm and stability, we trust what works for us. We may choose the feeling of the feet on the floor or the sensations in the hands—any experience that is a safe place to land. If the body in its entirety feels unsafe, we may connect with the experience of hearing as a way to start entering our sense experience. We learn to trust our own experience in this terrain of sense embodiment, allowing ourselves to ease our way home.

Those who have experienced significant trauma, particularly those who are survivors of childhood abuse, often manifest strong concentration in their meditation practice. The survivor can develop concentration as a child in order to dissociate to manage the emotional effects of trauma. Concentration is a beautiful quality that feels good when we are sitting in meditation, yet it also opens deeper levels of feeling. It's powerful medicine, and if we take too much, it's like overdosing: we can feel overwhelmed and anxious. We may need to emphasize meditation practices that are less concentrated, such as walking and movement meditations and everyday life mindfulness. We want to get the right dosage of this potent medicine, one that allows us to open at a pace we can integrate and assimilate.

Those who have survived trauma can also possess strong will and determination, manifesting as both a strength and a potential liability.

When we use willfulness to push through defenses, we lack respect for the needs of our particular system. If we determinedly dive into the deepest, most difficult emotional material, we risk reactivating trauma. We may feel like we're making progress, but we're not learning to transform our relationship to our pain. The will must be tempered and used in a balanced way. We study how to touch the edges of suffering and move away, so that we can slowly increase the capacity of our heart to hold pain. We remember we're not trying to get rid of anything, but rather learning how to hold our experience with spaciousness and kindness.

Meditation practice for trauma survivors (and for all of us) needs a strong container of love and kindness to hold the difficulties that come up. Metta practice, while bringing its own challenges, can be deeply healing. Learning to express this lovingkindness to ourselves can help us soften into our experience rather than try to blast through it by force of will. This meditative process is an act of love and reclamation of our own dignity. We strengthen and nourish the heart, body, and mind through meditation and through other healing modalities. Meditation is not always enough on its own. We may need to embrace practices that ground our energy, such as yoga or qi gong. We nourish our hearts with activities like choral singing or forest bathing. Psychotherapy gives us a place to be witnessed as we tell our stories. These healing modalities feed our strength, allowing us to then open to deeper levels of truth in our meditation practice.

Having a teacher who is trained and skilled in working with trauma is enormously helpful. I had a teacher for many years that was essential in guiding me through the territory of deep practice and healing from trauma. When I met with her during times of intense retreat experience, I would sometimes say, "I feel like everything is pretty crazy. Am I okay?" (Sometimes I would say, referencing the old nursery rhyme, "I feel like Humpty Dumpty. Am I going to come back together again?") She would reply, "Yes, you're all right," giving me the courage to keep going. Knowing that she understood where I was in my practice and could assess what I needed created safety that supported the unfolding. It was an invaluable gift.

As we heal, a beautiful journey unfolds. What a strange thing to say about engaging with trauma, and yet this journey of sorrow is also a pilgrimage of joy. As the heart relaxes, as the protective cage of fear dissolves, alienation is healed and we know that we fully belong here. Life is a package deal: joy and sorrow unfold hand in hand. Embracing our sorrow and learning how to take care of it, we also discover increasing joy and wonder at the beauty and love in this world. The journey is not easy, requiring all our skill and love, but it's worth it. It's everything we could ask for.

THE HEAVENLY HOMES

Beautiful Heart-Mind States

Several months into my first long retreat, I'm standing at the sink washing pots. Early winter is upon us and snow has fallen the night before. Now the sun is shining brightly on the sparkling snow, and I am struck with the deepest joy. Tears running down my cheeks, I stand mesmerized in amazement at this world. I had not known that I could feel such joy, especially while washing pots!

Meditation opens us to many afflictive emotions, yet it also reveals the depth of beauty we can experience in our own heart-mind. We discover ever deeper and more expansive peace, calm, tranquility, joy, bliss, enthusiasm, lovingkindness, compassion, wonder, and equanimity. These, too, we meet with mindful intimacy. Mindfulness is an incredible quality that both disempowers afflictive emotions and strengthens wholesome emotions. Bringing mindfulness to beautiful emotions, we nourish them and they thrive, becoming ever more rooted in our being.

As we familiarize ourselves with these beneficial states with mindful awareness, our heart becomes our friend. We receive these beautiful heart-mind states and marinate in them all the way down to our cells until they become easy companions for us. When a woodland path isn't used very often, it grows over, but when we walk on it frequently, the trail becomes well marked, the brambles get cleared away, and we can traverse it with ease. As we travel the beautiful pathways of the heart, the trail gets well-trodden and simpler to follow. As we walk the path of calm, compassion, or joy, that trail becomes well established. Our feet find easy landing.

As with afflictive mind states, we explore wholesome mind states with curiosity and mindfulness. How does this beautiful mind state feel in the body? How does it manifest in the mind? How does it change? And most importantly for our freedom, how are we relating to this emotion? Are we grasping and trying to keep it? Does the heart cling and contract, hoping that the emotion won't go away? Well, it will! Can we accept that? Can we enjoy this pleasant experience with openhearted equanimity, surrendering our tendency to control and micromanage the beautiful experiences of this life?

For these states to arise, grow, and strengthen is wholesome and beneficial. But we can mistakenly believe that we facilitate this by grasping after them and hanging on to them. If we want something to last, we think we should hold on tight. On the contrary, these qualities strengthen through letting go of holding on. It takes a while to get our heads around this notion because it's so contradictory to our deep conditioning to grasp after what's pleasant. In meditation we discover that when we get attached to these blissful states, they decrease and even disappear. Their existence is inconsistent with and cannot arise with the reactive heart-mind. Beautiful heart-mind states arise precisely because we're *not* holding on. They emerge from the heart-mind unobstructed by grasping and aversion.

We learn the freedom of letting go through mindfully experiencing the process of holding on. We land in states of joy and calm, and, of course, we want more. We start to contract around the state, and it dissolves. Observing this in our own practice, we gradually understand in a visceral way that we can enjoy these mind states but we can't control them. All that arises is of the nature to pass away. Holding on can't reverse this fundamental truth. The deepest peace comes from living gracefully with this knowledge.

While we can't control these wholesome heart-mind states, we're not powerless. We develop and encourage them by nurturing the causes and conditions that support them to arise and continue. Mindfulness is the primary cause. During my five-month retreat, I experienced my first effortless and deeply calm meditation period. When I shared this with my teacher, he asked me, "What did you do before this meditation period?" I replied, "I was doing walking meditation, and I walked mindfully from my walking place to my cushion and I sat down mindfully." I practiced meditation as one whole, what we call *seamless practice*, and this facilitated the arising of calm.

My teacher was asking me to explore the causes and conditions that led to the arising of effortless ease. We can use the cognitive mind to investigate which behaviors feed and increase wholesome mind states. What develops calm in our lives? What conditions lead to the arising and strengthening of concentration? Investigating proximate and contributing causes and conditions, we can ask ourselves what changes in our lives and habits might facilitate the more frequent arising of beautiful states of heart-mind. In this way, we can steer our lives toward that which is wholesome and leads to the deepest happiness.

Please remember to enjoy the beautiful heart states that are the fruits of practice. Just don't hold on. Ha! (And if you do hold on, explore that mindfully.)

The Heavenly Homes

In natural resources management, an ecosystem restoration approach called *rewilding* lets nature heal by repairing damaged lands and permitting them to return to their natural state. Wild areas that have been altered, developed, and tamed are allowed to go back to their unmanaged condition. Dams are deconstructed, walls taken down, and native species of plants encouraged to grow. Even native animals are reintroduced. The altered areas are encouraged to return to the beauty, biodiversity, and majesty of their original state.

The practice of the Brahmaviharas or Heavenly Homes rewilds our hearts. Our hearts have been unhelpfully developed: walls have been built; the soil has been depleted; and our inner beauty and majesty may have been lost. With Brahmavihara practice, we deconstruct the dams and take down the walls, feed and nourish the soil, encourage the growth of natural love and compassion, and allow the vibrancy and beauty of our hearts to shine forth. We return them to their natural state before they became obstructed.

Buddhism is described as having two wings: wisdom and compassion. A bird can't fly with just one wing; a bird needs both. The same is true for our meditation practice. We need both wisdom and compassion. Compassion in this sense includes all the heart qualities known as the Brahmaviharas: lovingkindness, compassion, appreciative joy, and equanimity (*metta, karuna, mudita, upekkha*).[1] *Brahmavihara* means "heavenly home" because abiding in these qualities is lovely and sublime. These four flavors of love form a package that, developed together, cultivates a friendly, engaged, robust, and balanced heart. The first three are heartwarming, and the last one teaches us to let go.

The Buddhist monk and scholar Analayo describes the four Brahmaviharas as the phases of the sun and moon. Lovingkindness, or metta, is the midday sun that shines in all directions on everything and everyone equally. Compassion, or karuna, is the tender, poignant flavor of the sun at twilight. Darkness is close, yet the sun still sends out earthy rays of color. Appreciative joy, or mudita, is the morning sun offering the freshness and brightness of the new day. And equanimity, or upekkha, is the full moon, shining cool and gentle in the vast sky. Together these four qualities teach us to engage the complete range of human experience with tenderness and spaciousness.

We start this meditative journey hoping that we can progress through the force of our will and the strength of our mind. This emphasis can lead to a dry practice and bleak heart—symptoms of imbalance between heart and mind. Willpower can take us only so far. We need to develop love to nurture a sustainable practice. Love allows us to relax and develop the trust needed to go deeper into the inconvenient truths of reality. The four Brahmaviharas of lovingkindness, compassion, appreciative joy, and equanimity strengthen us to fully meet this crazy wild world.

We can't say enough about the beautiful benefits of Brahmavihara practice. The Brahmaviharas strengthen our relationship to ourselves, other people, and all beings. They dissolve the grasping and aversion that separate us from others, counteracting judgment, ill will, cruelty, envy, and self-centered attachment. This love with four flavors encourages us to connect through our shared humanity, melting the delusion that we are separate and different from others. We learn to share our hearts impartially, without preference. We see people more clearly as they are, not as objects interpreted through the lens of our self-centered needs and wants. The Brahmaviharas meet the complexity of others in a wide and tender embrace, moving past any tendency to distance or condemn. We free our own hearts, and we also free our relationships. Our hearts emerge from their small cage of self-interest, willing and delighted to encounter the rest of the beings in the world.

The Brahmaviharas are often developed through meditation practices designed to cultivate them directly. These meditations use visualizations and phrases to prime the heart to bring forth the Brahmavihara quality. For example, in metta practice we may visualize our dear grandmother and silently wish, *May you be happy and peaceful. May you be safe and protected.* The intention with these Brahmavihara phrases is not to make things better for our grandmother (although this would be very nice), but rather to beautify our own hearts. They are not affirmations meant to make things be a certain way, but rather openhearted wishes inviting expansiveness. Sometimes called a purification practice, they expose where our ability to love is stuck and blocked and slowly retrain and rewild the heart.

We start Brahmavihara practice with easy people to help familiarize ourselves more deeply with these qualities. We then move on to more neutral people, those we find difficult, and finally outward to all beings. In this way, we uncover our impartial and boundless heart that cares not just about those dear to us but also those we don't know, those we may not even like, and all beings without exception. We explore the breadth and depth, the love and the complications, of our own human heart, and in the process we discover that our heart is vaster and more capable of love than we had imagined.

The heart qualities of the Brahmaviharas can also be nurtured informally in our insight practice by consciously infusing their flavor into the quality of mindfulness. We can meet all experiences with awareness flavored with the friendliness of metta. When suffering arises, we can embrace it with mindfulness imbued with the tenderness of compassion. When pleasant mind states and experiences arise, we can appreciate them with mudita. Lastly, we hold all experiences in the spaciousness of equanimity, letting go of hanging on or pushing away the pleasures and pains of human life.

In our journey together, I would like to reclaim the word *love*. Kathleen Dean Moore in her book *Earth's Wild Music* says, "Hallmark has kidnapped the word *love* and beaten it senseless."[2] Let's revive the term in its spiritual fullness. A park ranger, afraid that people would be turned off, had asked Moore not to use the word, so she asked him what word they should use instead. After thinking for a long time, he answered, "Maybe, instead, we should say 'listen to.'" Okay, let's *listen*. Love listens deeply to our own heart, to each other, to the wild earth, and to life itself. Let's listen with our whole heart to the voices of all beings and let them teach us about our freest expression.

The Heart of Lovingkindness

I have a confession. In my early practice, I did not like metta practice or anything related to the Brahmaviharas, even to the point of skipping the meditation periods when these practices were taught. Contemplating them made me nauseous. They felt fake to me, so far from the reality of my own heart. After eight years of practicing meditation, I felt stuck. I was quite aware that I was suffering, but nothing was shifting. I explained my stuckness to my teacher and asked for advice. To my horror, he said, "Do a metta retreat." Desperate enough to follow his instructions, I signed up for two months of Brahmavihara practice focusing mostly on metta. This period of cultivating love did shift my practice, gentling and strengthening my heart. Hour after hour, day after day, I brought to mind images of myself and others and silently repeated phrases of blessings: *May you be happy and peaceful. May you be safe and protected. May you be strong and healthy. May you take care of yourself with ease and joy.* At first the practice stuttered. My heart was not so sure about this plan. *Is it really a good idea to open the heart to love? Giving love to others might mean there won't be enough for me.* With time, metta strengthened, and I felt love and kindness not just for myself and those whom I liked and cared about but also for people I didn't know and even those I found difficult. Eventually I radiated metta in all directions to all beings, and yes, it's like living in heaven. A heart filled with metta is a blissful place to abide.

Metta can present in myriad flavors. Sometimes metta is just a quiet intention to wish somebody well. Metta can also manifest as a warm feeling of friendliness. At times metta flows in a powerful stream of kind-hearted energy. The discourses often describe metta as the absence of ill will, the heart that is not obstructed with ill will. One time I asked a very happy Burmese monk, "Why are you so happy?" and he replied laughing, "Because I have no ill will toward anyone, I have no ill will toward you, I have no ill will toward the snakes!" We don't have to aspire to a lofty ideal of metta, but rather can discover its flavors in our own heart.

We want to integrate metta on all levels of our being. As we marinade in metta, we feel lovingkindness throughout the mind, heart, and body. Even our cells can know the feeling of friendliness. My teacher Michele once asked that happy monk to tell her more about metta. He just patted down his body, saying, "Metta, metta, metta." She didn't need a translator to understand; rather than relate to metta as a concept, we are meant to embody metta. While we use images and phrases to support the practice, we transform our hearts by feeling metta throughout our being.

Metta is inspired by seeing the good in oneself and others. We practice focusing on innate worthiness and beautiful qualities, such as acts of kindness and generosity. Counteracting the tendency of the heart-mind to fixate on problems and suffering, we repeatedly orient ourselves toward what is good. When the mind migrates toward difficulties, we simply come back to this innate goodness. Using metta phrases like I did on my retreat can help orient us toward loveliness. While not denying that there are big problems in the world, the default setting of our hearts migrates toward goodness.

The active part of metta practice is the conscious cultivation of the intention to be kind and to bless ourselves and others. Receptivity includes the willingness to let the heart navigate its own journey. Too much goal-oriented demand that our heart be friendly will cause the heart to not want to cooperate—the heart, after all, does not like to be bossed around. Metta practice is an exploration of the joys and concerns of the heart, and the heart is a complicated creature. We let the heart tell its story through embodiment, feeling, and intuition. Establishing the intention to cultivate unconditional love, we meet the heart's response— both its hesitations and enthusiasm. Eventually, our heart concludes, as stated by Dr. Martin Luther King Jr., "I've decided to stick with love. Hatred is too great a burden to bear."[3]

Through metta practice we extend the boundaries of our love. As stated above, we start with ourselves and the easiest person possible in order to familiarize ourselves with the nature of metta. Then we proceed through increasingly complicated categories of family and friends, strangers, and difficult people. Most of us can easily care about those who are close to us, but face more challenges with people we don't know. We turn our hearts toward a stranger, someone we don't feel strongly about one way or the other, and wish them happiness, safety, and ease. On my metta retreat, I cultivated lovingkindness for a staff member I didn't know very well. While I wasn't familiar with her personal story, I connected to her through our shared humanity, and she became a very good friend. After the retreat, when I ran into her, I had to hold back impulses to be overly friendly, because she didn't know that she was my good friend! We can have many friends when we feel metta for those whom we don't know. The bank teller, the supermarket checkout person, the people in traffic around us, the FedEx driver, all can become our friends. Up to eight billion people!

We expand the limits of our heart even further with the person called the difficult person, although this label is misleading because it insinuates they are inherently difficult. Someone else might think they're just great.

More honestly, we should call them "a person whom we find difficult," but for shorthand we call them the difficult person.* How do we include this person in our hearts? We can contemplate their good qualities and remember that they have people in their life that love them. They suffer just as we do and want to be happy just like we do. We feel our way toward including them too in our friendly heart. Feeling an absence of ill will or even some warmth for those whom we find difficult is a relief for our heart and offers a possibility for change in the relationship.

The hardest category of difficult person may be those who cause suffering to others, especially those who harm the powerless and vulnerable. In this case we can start by setting the bar at the absence of ill will. We understand that those who cause suffering are themselves suffering, and our hearts might soften a bit and include this challenging person in the circle of metta. Alternatively, we can ask the Buddha or Kwan Yin to take care of them. Though we ourselves can't extend warmth in the moment, we can wish that they are held in love. Sometimes we need to take the time to contemplate the causes and conditions that have led to this person manifesting as they are. Henry Wadsworth Longfellow said, "If we could read the secret history of our enemies, we should find in each man's [sic] life sorrow and suffering enough to disarm all hostility."[4] Reflecting on our own ability to cause suffering can serve as a pathway to heal the sense of separation. We, too, have caused harm. We, too, have not always acted in alignment with our highest values. Connecting to our shared humanity, we experience viscerally that we are them. We also remember that practicing metta for somebody causing harm does not mean condoning their actions. We may not want to have lunch with them. We may actively confront them or organize and oppose their policies. With a heart of metta, however, we are released of the burden and weight of ill will and hatred and can come forward with more clarity and flexibility. Anyone whom we feel inclined to exclude provides an opportunity to further ease open our hearts. Who is our teacher?

* It's also helpful to remember that we are someone else's "difficult person."

As metta strengthens and becomes increasingly the default of our heart, we sense our kinship with all beings. The heart softens, and we connect with the truth that all of us just wish to be happy. We feel that all beings—even ourselves and even those who cause harm—possess fundamental goodness. From the littlest insect to the biggest creature, we incline toward the wish that all are happy, safe, and peaceful. Metta increasingly becomes the default of our hearts, a natural response to this world.

Nani Bala Barua, better known as Dipa Ma, a Bangladeshi woman, mother, and lay meditation teacher, exemplified this boundless love. In her thirties, she lost two children and then her husband died. Overcome by grief, she almost died herself. She began to study meditation to heal herself and quickly surpassed even the realizations of her teachers. Once somebody asked her what was in her mind. She answered, "Concentration, lovingkindness, and peace." "That's all?" the questioner persisted. "That's all," she replied. Dipa Ma loved to bless everything, both people and objects, with metta. During one visit to the Boston aquarium, she spent her time blessing the fish through the big glass windows. Her love was without limits.

As metta dissolves the shielding obstructions in our heart, all things become more alive—not just people and animals, but also trees, plants, and even rocks. We become more sensitive to their life force, perhaps stronger in a tree than a rock, but in a rock nonetheless. To the rational and logical scientific mind, plants and minerals are inanimate objects. To the metta-inspired heart, they are alive, vibrant, responsive beings. We may pass by a familiar rock on the trail and want to give it a pat of appreciation and metta. Which version of reality is true: the scientific or intuitive? Perhaps there is no objective answer. We don't need to box up the mystery of the world. But I know which world I want to put my feet down in.

For many years I co-taught a metta retreat at IMS in the springtime, when sugar ants tended to show up in the kitchen. I was usually careful to clean without killing them, but one morning I was impatient and carelessly killed several ants. The next morning when I came to the kitchen, there were no ants. My first thought was, *Where are my friends?* I felt kinship with those little ants even though I didn't want them to take over my kitchen.

With metta, we aspire to approach life itself with less aggression and more gentleness. We put down a book softly as an expression of metta. We walk on the earth expressing this gentleness. Thich Nhat Hanh suggests, "We have to walk in a way that we only print peace and serenity on the earth,"[5] and "Walk as if you are kissing the earth with your feet."[6] We spread metta while stuck in traffic and talk to our spouse with kindness. When we want to measure our spiritual progress, a good question to ask is, *Am I kinder?* The answer to this question can tell us if we're headed in the right direction.

Creating a Kinder World

The great scientist Albert Einstein is said to have stated, "The most fundamental question facing humanity is, 'Is the universe a friendly place?'" Perhaps there is no objective answer to Einstein's question, and yet the world becomes a friendlier place for us when we practice metta. We are not naive. We know that there is racial violence, sectarian violence, violence against women, that there are militaristic white supremacists and other people who want to do harm. And yet we have some choice about the flavor of our heart, and this flavor influences how we experience the world. I like to do metta in airports, as I pass people, silently wishing, *Happy, happy, may you be happy.* While this alone doesn't solve these larger problems, people treat me with greater kindness. My experience is of a friendlier world, a safer and more benevolent place to reside.

The classic Black church song "This Joy" by gospel music legend Shirley Caesar, recently popularized by the Resistance Revival Chorus, reminds us of this strength in our hearts from knowing how to touch the metta that resides there: "This love in my heart, the world didn't give it to me. . . . The world didn't give it and the world can't take it away."[7] We have the power to create a world of love right in our own hearts, independent of the state of the world around us.

One recent winter day I stood outside attempting to feed the chickadees. They will often eat out of my hand when the conditions are ideal. This day, due to the snow-covered ground and empty feeders, was perfect for feeding them, but they were not landing on my hand. After ten minutes I was ready to give up, but then noticed that I had been thinking about a problem in my life and my energy hadn't been settled. I changed the flavor of my heart to softly radiate metta, and within seconds the chickadees began to eat out of my hand. I had become kind and trustworthy, and they responded.

In creating a kinder world, we uncover our biases, investigate where we create separation from others, and open to truths deeper than conditioned beliefs. In November 2020, I did a monthlong meditation retreat on the ocean in a neighborhood with closely spaced houses. As I moved into my retreat home during this time of a politically contentious presidential election, I noticed paraphernalia in neighboring yards strongly suggesting that my neighbors had different political leanings than I did. I watched my heart-mind lean toward "othering" the people around me, focusing negatively on our perceived differences. This was not the world I wanted to inhabit, so I sat down with myself and said, "This won't do. I'm going to like these neighbors." Over the coming days the decision to like them morphed into reality. Talking with the elderly man next door, we discovered that both he and my husband love to putter. Most days he doodled around his yard and the sounds grew comforting to me, even his leaf blower! And other neighbors helped me with the complicated schedule and regulations regarding trash and recycling. When we start with goodwill and add in familiarity, we can connect with our commonality with even those from whom we would tend to separate ourselves.

Metta gives us the courage to relax and trust this world. We are not pretending that nothing bad ever happens, but our basic orientation inclines toward friendliness rather than threat. As metta becomes the flavor of our heart, we still take care of ourselves, but without the ongoing background hum of fear.[8] This trust and relaxation facilitate the deepest meditation, which develops in an atmosphere of internal safety. When the world looks unfriendly, we feel restless and jumpy. Feeling held in love gives us the faith and courage needed to keep exploring.

Metta is powerful medicine. The Buddha tamed a wild elephant set upon him by his envious cousin by radiating metta, causing the elephant to stop charging and kneel in front of him. I thought this story must be hyperbole until I read about a woman who tamed snakes with metta. In the 1940s, Grace Wiley had a facility for wayward snakes called the Zoo for Happiness. She took in snakes that were going to be destroyed and gentled them with the energy of metta. People could watch her at work in her taming room, showering the snakes with positive regard, appreciating their beautiful qualities, telling them they were worthy of all love. Eventually the snakes would warm up to her and even let her pet them. I'm not recommending that any of us try this. One meditation teacher tried to shower aggressive dogs with metta and got bitten. While metta is indeed powerful, as we move through the world, we combine metta with discerning wisdom that assesses the safety and appropriateness of our actions. We can see, however, that when we approach people and other beings with metta, it is possible to create a kinder and gentler world.

Metta's Near and Far Neighbors

Each of the Brahmaviharas has what is traditionally called a *near enemy* and a *far enemy*, qualities that can arise as we develop that Brahmavihara. A set of friendlier and more contemporary terms are *near neighbor* and *far neighbor*. I prefer *near miss* and *far miss*. The near miss is a quality that can be mistaken for the Brahmavihara, one that is similar in certain ways but is self-centered rather than expansive. The far miss is a quality opposite of the Brahmavihara and easy to distinguish from it.

Cultivating metta brings to light what blocks metta. We don't so much create these radiant heart qualities as uncover what obstructs them. Metta is a natural quality that we all possess; it's part of our human birthright. We don't have to build it up, but rather work with what blocks its natural light. Because of the many ways we've been hurt, we have learned to shield the heart with attachment and aversion. Lovingkindness is a solvent that slowly dissolves this defensive shield, letting our natural friendly heart shine forth.

The near miss of metta is selfish or attached love. We need the other person to be a certain way, or we are attached to our metta practice having a certain outcome. We wish for them to be happy, but the intention is not openhearted; it's a wish with a clenched fist. If they're not happy, we're not going to be happy. The metta is no longer about our wish for them but rather about our own needs and preferences. One student described doing metta for her baby, finding herself saying, "May you be happy and peaceful, may you sleep through the night without a bottle, may you not peepee in Mommy and Daddy's bed," and she laughed as her agenda infiltrated her unconditional love.

Metta practice teaches us the difference between self-centered love and unconditional love. Self-absorbed love operates from our personal agenda. We want something out of this situation: either something from this other person or some result that makes us feel better. When our self-centered agenda enters the space between us and others, our vision is distorted, and we no longer see them as they are. We see them through the filter of how we want them to be. When we relax our agendas, people become delightfully themselves, often surprising us. The world regains vibrancy when we experience other beings through the eyes of unconditional love.

Unconditional love—love with the fist released, the open hand, the open heart—is not attached to outcome. There's no grasping, no aversion, just the simplicity of friendliness and kindness supported by a deep equanimity that can hold it all as it is. We feel the purity of the wish, the lack of turbulence, the unobstructed nature, and we know our hearts want to live here. Increasingly, this purer love becomes our default setting. While we may not feel metta all the time, we know the metta pathway in our hearts. We have cleared out the brambles and obstructions, and having walked the path often enough, we now follow it more easily.

The far miss of metta is aversion or ill will. We don't like this person, we don't particularly want anything good to happen to them, and we may even wish them harm. We may feel anger, fear, or even hatred. At the very least, we exclude them from our heart and the field of our kindness. Since metta practice is designed to bring up the obstructions in our heart, when these mind states arise, we're not doing the practice wrong. Rather, it's a sign that the practice is working as we're seeing clearly where we hold back, where our love is still limited and conditional. We need this emotional honesty in order to grow. Metta is not a quality that we slap on top of what is really happening. And yet we continue to explore. Is there any way to open our hearts, even a little bit, in this situation? What contemplations might ease the ill will and encourage understanding that leads to kindness? Through the practice, we receive all the complexity of our heart and help it find its way to its deepest unobstructed nature.

The Caring Heart of Compassion

Several years ago, the owner of the wooded land next to our house decided to clear-cut his lot. The logging continued for over a year and was loud, disruptive, and poorly executed. Many days when I would hear the trees fall, I felt my heart break.[9] I promised both myself and the land spirits that when it was all over, I would sit and offer metta and compassion to the earth and the remaining trees to support their recovery. Finally, on a beautiful spring day, I hiked up to the ridge, sat near the edge of the clear-cut, and prepared to send caring wishes. Yet something didn't feel right. I sensed the trees wanted me to sit with their pain rather than try to fix it. Instead of sending metta, I sat feeling into the trauma that had happened to the land and sharing in the grief, exposure, and vulnerability. We sat together, the tree spirits, the earth, and I. After some time, grief dissolved and equanimity dawned as I fully accepted that this was the way things were now. Now felt right to rest with the trees in caring and wishing for their healing. Around us, green buds were sprouting from the earth, new life springing forth. The trees reminded me that compassion isn't about fixing but rather about feeling with and caring.

The Brahmavihara of compassion turns the friendly heart of metta toward the reality of suffering within ourselves and others. The unobstructed heart, when it encounters suffering, feels tenderness, warmth, and the wish to alleviate pain. It is wide and large enough that it can include suffering without needing to get rid of it. (Hating suffering is not compassion.) Compassion is not heavy. When balanced, it includes spaciousness, accepting suffering as the reality of this moment—which is different, of course, than being passive or condoning it. In Brahmavihara practice, we encourage the development of compassion by bringing forth images of ourselves and others and contemplating our suffering with an intention to respond with tender warmth. We may use phrases that support this intention, such as "May you be free from suffering," or "I care about your pain." Informally in our insight practice, we hone our ability to bring compassion to our own suffering and set it as the default of our heart when we encounter pain.

Like a beautiful jewel, compassion has several facets. First, it manifests as warmth, a softening. Compassion melts the ice in our hearts that protects and shields us from suffering, and we find tenderness waiting right here. When physical or emotional pain arises, we soften into it rather than brace against it. We apply mindfulness like dabbing with cotton balls, tenderly touching that which is in pain. Compassion is soothing, like spreading warm oil on our skin on a cold evening. This warmth might have a poignant flavor or even a bittersweet quality, the sweetness arising from the connection and the bitterness from the pain of suffering.

Second, compassion is an empowered state of heart. We may misconceive compassion as a wimpy state, too soft to stand up strong. Yet compassion's strength comes from its capacity to not crumble or shrink in the face of suffering. Rooted in the earth, it can radiate power. X González (who previously used the name Emma González) manifested this compassion power when, after the shootings at Stoneman Douglas High School in Florida, they stood tall on the Washington Mall, silently weeping for six minutes in front of thousands, bearing witness for the length of time the gunman was shooting in their school. Compassion can powerfully hold what is difficult to bear.

Compassion responds. Thich Nhat Hanh said, "Compassion is a verb." Kwan Yin, the bodhisattva of compassion revered in Chinese and

Japanese Zen Buddhism, is often depicted with one leg up, knee bent, ready to spring into action to respond to the cries of the world. Our compassionate heart, large enough to hold suffering, at the same time is moved to alleviate it. Students often describe feeling overwhelmed by the enormous amount of suffering they hear about on the news and ask what to do. I tell them to respond in some way, however small. The littlest act can empower us, countering the feeling of powerlessness that can arise in the face of enormous suffering. A well-known quote jokes, "If you think you're too small to have an impact, try going to bed with a mosquito in the room." Responding to suffering serves as an antidote to collapse and despair. We have agency. We can focus on the integrity of our actions, even knowing the results are out of our control. If we can't change the suffering of another person, we can at least be by their side listening and caring, acting as a healing balm.

Lastly, compassion is spacious. Rather than being limited by aversion to suffering, our heart is boundless, able to hold pain, misfortune, and trauma. The Zen hermit poet Ryokan describes this combination of warmth and spaciousness like this: "O that my priest robes were wide enough to gather up all the suffering people in this floating world."[10] We understand that the world operates according to wider principles not immediately apparent to us. Compassion sees that things are always changing, unfolding in a vast web of cause and effect that we cannot always understand nor control. We act to alleviate suffering, and we know how to let go of demanding that these actions manifest as we wish. This wider perspective saves us from getting bogged down and burnt out by the enormous amount of suffering in the world.

If mindfulness doesn't cut it, try compassion. At times, the suffering we are experiencing feels very intense, immovable, almost unbearable. No amount of mindfulness is loosening its grip. Can we touch the edges of what is painful with tenderness, softening just a little, caring just a bit? The pain won't necessarily go away, but the warmth of compassion makes it bearable. Sometimes this change in orientation will initiate some transformation. As we soften, space is created for flexibility and movement. We can always try compassion.

Compassion's Neighbors

The Brahmavihara of compassion can be confusing for us as it's not uncommon to carry distorted beliefs, conditioned by family and society, about this heart quality. Sometimes these beliefs are closer to the near neighbors of pity and despair than the true quality of compassion. With practice we learn the flavor of authentic compassion and distinguish it from these near misses. Compassion may be misunderstood as pity, for example, an orientation that shares the quality of caring. Pity, however, separates us by feeling sorry for the other at a distance, lacking the warm connection of the Brahmaviharas. Paternalism and helping with a savior mentality are also near misses because of the distance created by the attitude of superiority. True compassion manifests as a relationship between equals. Without the distancing of pity or paternalism, I could be you, and what is happening to you could happen to me.

We may also mistake despair as compassion, believing that to be compassionate we need to be all in with the other person, sharing their agony. If we aren't in distress ourselves, that means we don't really care. This is not compassion, but rather empathetic distress. When caught in empathetic distress, we feel others' pain so deeply that we fall into it, losing ourselves as a separate person. This codependency is a recipe for burnout. With so much suffering in the world, the heart becomes exhausted.

The Dalai Lama was once asked if compassion hurts. He replied that a little spark of pain occurs with the initial connection with the person's suffering, but then the sweetness of compassion becomes the predominant experience. As we practice, this transition to sweetness happens more quickly. We do connect fully, but then put the emphasis on the care, rather than continuing to focus on the suffering. This wise compassion is not a betrayal of caring, but rather compassion balanced with equanimity. This orientation can be more helpful for the suffering individual, too. We stay clear and able to respond in a more selfless and skillful manner, rather than reacting to their suffering because we cannot bear it. True compassion is underscored by equanimity: the capacity to bear witness to suffering without falling into grief and despair.

The far miss of compassion is cruelty, responding to suffering with meanness. We more easily distinguish cruelty from compassion, but sometimes cruelty is sneaky. Notice how we talk to ourselves when we are in pain. We may blame ourselves and scold ourselves to get it together. Our inner critic might give "helpful" advice that in reality reflects callousness toward our very self. This harshness in the face of suffering is a form of cruelty.

We can also see this callousness manifest in political discourse, where qualities such as compassion, care, and community can seem hard to find. Our economic model institutionalizes cruelty by condoning lack of accountability and placing profitability over environmental and community impact. Power and privilege can insulate one from the experiences of those with fewer resources. This isolation can obstruct clear seeing of the causes and conditions creating poverty and oppression, making it difficult to feel the reality of those who are suffering and easier to respond coldly and with blame rather than care and compassion. Whether at the individual, community, or global level, cruelty turns away from genuinely caring and responding to suffering. Compassion calls for us to be watchful for our own callousness, especially when holding a position of power. Compassion encourages us to listen more deeply and respond with warmth, concern, and action directed toward alleviating the suffering in our communities.

When doing compassion practice toward loved ones, we notice when we slip into the near misses of pity or despair. When practicing with more difficult beings or situations, we root out any tendency to slip into callousness and cruelty. We aim toward unconditional care, with everybody included in our hearts. This aspiration is a tall order, and yet any separation rends the fabric of our heart. Undertaking the exploration of our heart's response to our own and others' suffering, we feel our way toward compassion. We familiarize ourselves with true, genuine caring and cultivate our natural compassionate heart, just waiting to respond with warmth and assistance.

Forgiving Ourselves with Mercy

This world is a challenging place for our tender human hearts, and the stress of modern life may leave them sorely in need of nourishment. Due to the tendency toward deep imbalance in the Western psyche, exacerbated by the emphasis on individualism over community and independence over interconnectedness, many of us suffer from deep ambivalence about human relationships, about whether the world is a loving place and whether we ourselves are worthy of love. We may suffer less from this desert of the heart if we are raised in a loving community or extended family, but even this doesn't erase the wear and tear of modern life. While not serving as a substitute for the life work of establishing and maintaining loving relationships, practicing metta and compassion can contribute to healing our hearts.

When the heart suffers from these relational wounds, we may need a lot of practice receiving and absorbing metta and compassion. We can practice metta in ways that remind us of our innate worthiness, letting it permeate all levels of our being. We might receive metta from someone that we know holds us in high regard, such as a favorite aunt, uncle, or grandparent; a niece, nephew, or grandchild; or our dog or cat—anybody who presently or in the past has delighted in our presence. For example, my tenth-grade school counselor, who believed in my worth and competency during a troubled time in my life, served to remind me of my own goodness. If a person seems hard to find, an archetypal being like the Buddha or Kwan Yin can serve well. We imagine this person or being gazing at us with kindness-filled eyes and delighting in our presence. They are so happy that we are who we are. Some people imagine sitting in the middle of a circle of friends showering them with metta. We can also practice metta like the happy monk, gently patting our body, encouraging our being to absorb metta's warm energy.

Receiving metta reassures our heart of our own worthiness and primes us to share metta with others. We counter any tendency to use our practice to further entrench ourselves in separation by joining self-compassion with sharing love and compassion with others. Offering metta to others dissolves any conditioning that love is scarce and we don't have enough of it to give away. We notice when our heart is full and wants to flow over, sharing our feelings of lovingkindness. Giving metta to others then teaches us the power and strength of our own heart. Our practice moves beyond our individual sphere of suffering and connects us to the greater world where suffering is part of every human life. We transcend the sense of our own scarcity and limitation and increasingly feel our hearts as boundless and connected.

Forgiveness is integral to this process of learning to love ourselves. As we gain intimacy with our own heart and mind, our imperfections become very clear. We see the "size of the beast": the forces of craving, aversion, and delusion in our very lives. We recognize where we have caused suffering through actions we regret. This down-to-earth practice is sobering, yet important. Opening to our unethical behavior and difficult personality traits is a natural part of the process of deepening in meditation. Being human is messy business. In my early practice, participating in group check-ins was a relief because I could see that all our minds basically worked the same. Maybe I wasn't such a terrible person; maybe this is just the challenging condition of being human.

To normalize this process, as a teacher I share stories about the trials of my own heart-mind. I don't take them as personal shortcomings, but rather as examples of the entanglements of being human. Anger, fear, and craving are not unique to any of us and are not a personal failure. One time—along with the cataloguing of fears as previously mentioned—I made a list of twenty-four kinds of anger I had worked with in my meditation practice, including killer rage, powerless fury, bulldozer anger, frustration, and mild annoyance. One student told me that he came up with forty-six, and I congratulated him.

Receiving kindness and compassion can feel like being showered with mercy. Not a word we hear much in Buddhism, *mercy* implies unconditional forgiveness and compassion. It's not something we need to earn; therefore, we don't have to prove ourselves worthy. We are forgiven for our mistakes, as we are only human. As the Zen teacher Lin Jensen says, human lives are "ten thousand beautiful mistakes."[11] We don't need to be perfect. We can rest our striving to be better, to excel, and to prove ourselves. In boundless mercy, we can fail and fail again. We can rest.

Suzuki Roshi had a balanced viewpoint: "Each of you is perfect the way you are . . . and you can use a little improvement."[12] We accept ourselves as we are, and we recognize that we want to transform unskillful tendencies that cause harm. They're both true.

Forgiving ourselves is letting ourselves be imperfect. In practicing mindfulness, we develop a willingness to feel and hold all our human experience. We bring the pieces of ourselves home, both the good and the bad, the beautiful and the not-so-beautiful, developing a feeling of unity and wholeness. This embracing is the practice of worthiness, giving up our quest for perfection. We rest in being an ordinary human being who makes mistakes and stumbles on the road.

In the process of forgiving ourselves and allowing ourselves to be imperfect, we often come up against a pattern of conditioning that we can call our *inner bully*. This bully manifests as a harsh inner critic, berating us for everything we do wrong and watching every move to make sure we don't make mistakes. This voice tells us that we are only worthy when we do everything right and we are unforgivable when we make a mistake. Because this inner bully can be so unforgiving, we need to learn to manage its energy.

When our inner bully is acting particularly cruel, we may wisely set limits. We can say, *Thanks for sharing*, and move our attention away. We can call forth determination: *No, I'm not going to engage in this pattern of thinking*. Trying to argue with the inner bully is contraindicated, because it's quite smart and almost always wins. Not engaging may be difficult to do because we are convinced that this inner bully is going to save us, but we can practice just stepping aside. We can invite the critic to sit in the corner in an easy chair, enjoying a cup of tea. It's not a bad life.

When we feel some confidence in setting limits with this inner bully energy, we can become interested in its manifestation, recognizing it as anger, fear, or self-doubt. What does this emotion feel like? What stories does it tell? (The bully really only has a couple storylines.) How does it express itself in the body? Through intimacy, we learn to identify less with these harsh inner voices, get less caught in the narrative, and are more able to see this conditioned story as habit just repeating itself. As we know this inner bully more completely, it loses its power.

Bullies aren't what they appear to be. Think of the schoolyard bully: they're usually one of the more wounded kids on the playground. Our inner bully may just be our inner woundedness. This strong energy often arises when we feel vulnerable. As a form of care, the bully wants to keep us in line, safe and protected. Its protection gives us the illusion of control. We beat ourselves up before anybody else can and try to prevent more mistakes. At the very core of the inner bully lies our yearning for connectedness, wanting to be part of the group, and our fear of being kicked out. The deepest wish of the inner critic is loving care. Realizing this true function of the inner critic, we can soften into compassion. When the harsh inner critic shares its opinions, we think, *I don't want to do that to myself,* and we're able to step back. We increase our vulnerability tolerance, finding within ourselves space to allow and hold our tender humanity. The inner critic gets to relax in an easy chair practicing useless gazing.

Forgiving Others with Understanding

The Brahmavihara practices nurture the beautiful qualities of metta and compassion, yet also bring forth where we are stuck, including old regrets and resentments. Forgiveness is the practice of letting go of bitterness and anger, freeing our hearts of their burden. Learning how to forgive elicits the deepest peace of mind and heart. Please read that sentence again. I'm not saying that we should forgive because that's what spiritual people do or because other people deserve it. Forgiveness doesn't mean condoning others' harmful behavior, letting them off the hook, or forgetting what happened. Rather, forgiveness releases our own heart-mind of the corrosive power of seething, scheming, churning resentment, and rage. This turbulence destroys our heart, so ultimately forgiveness is about tending to our own health and happiness. A common quote describes forgiveness as giving up hope for a better past. We clean up the places of the heart-mind where we are still stuck, the issues we've been holding on to that bind up our energy. This process allows us to relax and receive all the love that this universe is always sending our way. Benefit for others is extra credit.

We live in an imperfect world. We ourselves are imperfect; other people are imperfect; life itself is imperfect. Practicing forgiveness, we acknowledge imperfection and quit demanding perfection. While we hold people responsible for their actions, we stop blaming others or circumstances for our current unhappiness and take responsibility for our own well-being. Through forgiveness, we empower ourselves and transform anger into compassion and letting go. No longer at the mercy of those who have harmed us, our heart is free to choose its response.

The deepest wish of our heart is to forgive, because in forgiveness, our weary hearts can rest. We let go of the restless strategizing for revenge, the twisted bitterness, and the hard resentful heart. Hanging on causes suffering, and freedom arises when we let go. A heart-mind of forgiveness is at peace. Deepest forgiveness is unconditional, freely given, openhearted, expecting nothing.

Let's dispel a couple of myths about forgiveness. We may start with the idea that forgiveness is a "should." It's spiritually correct: we forgive others because it's the spiritual thing to do. From this perspective, when we hold a grudge, we are making the other person pay, and forgiveness is a favor we do for them. The Buddha said, however, that thinking somebody else will pay when we're angry is like throwing excrement into a headwind. We ourselves are the ones who get soiled. (As you can see, he tended not to mince words.) Forgiving is not about benefiting the other—although it can have that result—but rather about unburdening our own heart-mind of anger and resentment. When we are angry with someone and carry a grudge, we are bound to them. Forgiveness cuts us loose. We don't squander our energy anymore on this issue. Archbishop Desmond Tutu, head of South Africa's Truth and Reconciliation Commission, said, "To forgive is not just to be altruistic. It is the best form of self-interest."[13] If we can forgive, we are no longer chained to the perpetrator and can move on.

Another myth suggests that forgiveness can be slapped on top of what our experience really is, like putting sweet frosting on a rotten cake. Forgiveness can't be forced. It involves an honest journey through our own emotional process. We start where we are. We get intimate with our hearts' evolving response to having been violated or treated harshly or unjustly. The other day a student said to me, "Anger is not very loving." He was worried that anger wasn't spiritually correct. Maybe this emotion is not in line with our spiritual aspirations, but as the truth right now, we explore it with the wish to understand. And that's wholesome. Letting go may take moments, decades, or our entire life. We are not in charge of the timeline. If the harm was small, perhaps the process evolves quickly. When the harm or injustice was great, the heart may need a lot more time.

We may start with not wanting to forgive. The pain inflicted may feel unforgivable. Anger and hatred are protections that harden the heart, giving the illusion of impenetrability. Hatred feels strong, powerful, and invulnerable. We like this feeling and may not yet be ready to give it up, so we get to know that. Perhaps anger gives us the strength to move forward in our lives. Sometimes we need to protect our hearts for a long time. Sometimes we may not get further than the intention to forgive. Even that is powerful, as it plants wholesome karmic seeds that can sprout in the future. We can check in occasionally and ask whether anger is still serving us. What do hatred, bitterness, and resentment feel like? Is this really where we want our heart to reside? Is our heart ready to start letting go, just a little bit?

Eventually we feel that anger and resentment don't answer our deepest yearning for peace. They ossify the heart, isolating and separating us. They're tiring and don't allow us to rest. The twisted quality of bitterness and corrosive energy of hatred erode our own heart, and we wonder about the price we pay for protection. At this point, the wish to forgive can become authentic, emerging from our desire for freedom.

We continue on the heart's journey. We meet whatever emotions come up—anger, fury, hurt, grief, sorrow—and feel them mindfully. Sometimes we grieve that things were not as we would've wished or feel fury that we had to endure this harm. We are careful not to inadvertently feed the anger and resentment through rehashing the stories, but rather anchor our exploration in the body. When these emotions are allowed space, they unpeel in layers as our heart feels its way to letting go. Eventually, understanding dawns on us and blame is released. The heart lets go, landing in compassion. We can't skip layers, however. We have to journey our way through the realms of sorrow to arrive at our deepest wish of kindness.

Forgiveness matures when we finally understand that there's nobody to forgive. We are all dependently coarisen; we don't develop in a vacuum but rather are the result of many causes and conditions. Where do we start blaming? With resentment and judgment, our vision gets narrowed. With forgiveness, a wider lens reveals complexity that leads to understanding. Byron Katie said that forgiveness is "understanding that what I thought happened, didn't."[14] The story we had told ourselves shifts. We may even see we were complicit in the unfolding. We can ask, *How did I contribute to this?* When I've been angry at my partner, I go for a bike ride, and usually see that what I thought happened, didn't. I may have said or done something that caused suffering to my partner. Our view widens, and anger and resentment shift toward humility and compassion.

Forgiveness is facilitated by remembering how capable we are of causing pain. With healthy humility, we see that we are all just human, stumbling along. Just as we cause suffering out of our own reactivity and ignorance, so do others. When other people act unskillfully, we know that we have the same potential to cause harm, through our own obstructions of heart and mind. We all get caught in the mindless grip of unwholesome states and act unskillfully. Forgiveness of others comes out of this recognition of our shared humanity, and the heart is released through understanding. The Russian dissident Aleksandr Solzhenitsyn wrote, "If only it were so simple! If only there were evil people somewhere insidiously committing evil deeds, and it were necessary only to separate them from the rest of us and destroy them. But the line dividing good and evil cuts through the heart of every human being. And who is willing to destroy his [*sic*] own heart?"[15]

The last myth: forgiveness is passive and condones harmful behavior. Of course not. We may still choose to protect ourselves or right a situation of injustice. When someone is doing something wrong, if it's within our power, we should stop the deed. Anger can morph into a beautiful fierce compassion that wants to protect and heal this world. We can see situations with greater clarity and respond more wisely. Firmness or limits may be called for. We may choose not to be around the person yet make this decision free of resentment. We respond to the needs of the situation, anchored in a heart of spaciousness and love.

Finally, we forgive life itself. Have you ever felt angry at life? This world is always changing. We had hoped for permanence, solidity, and some final satisfaction, but we don't live in that kind of universe. Our bodies disappoint us by manifesting sickness, limitation, and aging. Our hearts need to be closed at times. What is pleasant ends, and what is unpleasant comes whether we want it or not. Life disappoints us, and we learn to forgive over and over, day after day. We forgive this wild unmanageable world that isn't perfect, that is instead a mix of happiness and sorrow, pleasure and pain. We let go of any tendency to resent this flow and open our hearts freely to how things are.

Gladdening the Heart with Mudita

Feeling delight in the success and good fortune of others increases our chances for joy eight billion to one. The third Brahmavihara, mudita, is an unselfish joy that delights in the happiness and good fortune of others, wishing for it to grow and flourish. Known in English as sympathethic joy or appreciative joy, the Buddha called this Brahmavihara "the heart's release of gladness." One Tibetan Buddhist teacher called it rejoicement therapy. Sounds good, doesn't it? No problem! Yet the Buddha said that this is the most difficult Brahmavihara to develop. We'll see why.

With our formal mudita practice, we start with someone who is currently experiencing happiness and success and then move through the categories of beings from easiest to most difficult. We may use phrases such as *I appreciate your happiness and success* or *May your happiness and success grow and flourish.* Traditionally, we wouldn't include ourselves in the development of appreciative joy. However, many Western teachers do incorporate practicing mudita for ourselves. This practice can serve as an avenue to moisten our dry hearts, enlivening and refreshing them. Because of our human negativity bias to notice problems more readily, we might overlook all the happiness in our lives, so we practice appreciating our joy, success, and good fortune: *I appreciate the happiness and success in my life.* Life isn't just problems and suffering; we also experience beauty and delight. This Brahmavihara turns our attention to what is going well in our lives, such as our good fortune in a new job, a successful relationship, a marriage, the birth of a child, or a new home. We can also appreciate all the daily delights that are available. How fortunate are we to have wildflowers growing by the road? To experience the sun warming us? Birds sing and trees whir in the wind. Warm tea to drink, beautiful music to listen to, people to love—the list is endless. The world is always offering beauty, nourishment, and wonder. Feeling delight only requires that we slow down enough to notice.

Mudita is energizing and refreshing. We can marinate in this joy through the heart and body, all the way down to the cellular level. Delighting in our good fortune and in the beauty around us balances out compassion, saving us from drowning in the breadth and depth of suffering also surrounding us. It helps us, in the words of the Buddhist scholar and ecopsychologist Joanna Macy, "to sustain our enthusiasm." She was referring to social activism, but we can also apply this principle to our meditation practice. Sustainable farming ensures that inputs are mixed into the soil, keeping it fertile year after year. Appreciative joy is sustainable farming for our heart: nourishing the soil with energizing inputs so that we can be present for life enthusiastically, day after day, year after year.

Even in the most difficult situations, some joy or delight can be celebrated. The author Peter Gay said, "Life is a shipwreck, but we must not forget to sing in the lifeboats."[16] Mudita is our song in the lifeboats. When my father was dying, I was able to notice that he was comfortable, had access to pain medication, and was surrounded by love and care. The dharma teacher Christopher Titmuss tells the story of a woman confined to an iron lung who was asked how she could bear it. She replied, "Every so often somebody opens the window and a breeze comes in."[17] Incarcerated people often describe the small joys that give them needed nourishment, like the bird that lands in the yard to eat the treat left there. Noticing what is beautiful can fortify us for the suffering we must endure.

Appreciating joy and success can also free us from defining others primarily by their suffering. Years ago, my first job as a psychotherapist involved working in an environment where I encountered enormous amounts of suffering, including trauma, racism, poverty, and violence. As a naive white thirtysomething, I felt overwhelmed and distressed with the suffering I encountered day after day. Over time, however, I understood that I was limiting the lives of those I worked with by focusing solely on their suffering. I began to appreciate the joy also present—the birth of a grandchild, close family ties, a good meal, music, and laughter. Not only did I feel more refreshed, but everyone benefited when the whole of their lives was seen and included.

When appreciative joy is strong, we develop contentment, which the Buddha described as the greatest wealth we can possess. Assuming that our basic needs are met,* we have enough. We don't need to run here and there, accumulating more and more in order to satisfy our hearts. What we need is right here. Rather than scrambling in greed and fear, we can relax in appreciation. Mudita teaches us how.

Our hearts nourished by appreciation, we turn toward the success and happiness in the lives of others. We start with those closest to us or with someone we know who is experiencing happiness. We contemplate what is going well for them, and we wish for it to continue and flourish. We strengthen mudita by encouraging ourselves to delight in the success even of those whom we find difficult. We explore the heart's response to this intention. How is it for us when others are happy and successful? Do we feel wholehearted delight and gladness? All over the world right now people are experiencing happiness and success. What's it like to rest in feeling

---

* Admittedly, this is a big assumption for some.

that? Concerns and reservations may manifest; envy or competition may block our hearts. In the following pages we will explore the near miss of overexuberance and far neighbors of envy and judgment that can obstruct the natural empathetic response of the heart to delight.

Mudita's Neighbors

Many years ago when visiting IMS, I experienced a lot of envy of a fellow practitioner who appeared to have everything that I wanted: people liked them, they had close connections with the teachers, and they were starting to teach. Previously, I hadn't been aware of feeling envy. (I thought I just didn't like them very much.) No one wants to admit to being envious. It's embarrassing. And yet . . . Eventually I became interested in envy and allowed space to explore it. I let myself feel the insecurity viscerally and learned the story of scarcity and insufficiency underlying it all. Then one day I entered a staff area and there they were. I saw my finger reaching for the play button on an old cassette tape player, ready to repeat the story I had rehearsed so many times before. This time, I said to myself, *I know this road. I know every twist and turn of it. I don't think we need to go there.* And I didn't. Through honest mindful inquiry, I developed the ability to have a choice in whether I went down that road. Later, when I was training to teach, we participated in a retreat together. They gave a beautiful dharma talk, and I appreciated their ability to share the dharma. What a relief! Mudita is a much lovelier home for the heart than envy.

As with all Brahmaviharas, mudita has near and far neighbors. The near miss of appreciative joy, the quality we might mistake for genuine mudita, is overexuberance. Overexuberance and appreciative joy share delight in good fortune, but overexuberance gets a bit too carried away. It says, "I've got it made! This is it!" But we never really have it made because everything is impermanent. This excitement, cut with self-centered wishes, can hide our attachment to the good fortune continuing. Overexuberance is like falling in love: everything looks beautiful, but we're not exactly grounded. Fully mature mudita incorporates equanimity, which lands us in reality. Robust love can hold the truth of impermanence. We celebrate and delight in what is beautiful even while understanding that all is ephemeral and subject to change. This joy might be a bit less ecstatic, yet it's more deeply anchored and restful.

As we practice joy for others' good fortune, we also explore the heart's hesitation around delighting in the success and happiness of others. The Buddha recognized mudita as the most difficult Brahmavihara because envy, the far miss of mudita, is deeply rooted in human patterning. We find ourselves thinking, *But what about me?* We want what this other person has. With difficult people, we may not wish for their happiness to continue at all; we may actually wish for them to suffer. This practice uncovers where our hearts perceive scarcity, thinking that there is only a limited amount of happiness parceled out in this world and, when others receive good fortune, we won't get our share. These far neighbors of appreciative joy, not easily mistaken for mudita, are brought more clearly into consciousness by our intention to share in the happiness of others. Envy, covetousness, and stinginess are felt and known. With mindfulness, we loosen the underlying stories and beliefs and the twisted energy of the heart. Released from covetousness, we enjoy the capacity to truly appreciate other people's success.

Appreciative joy also releases judgment about how others enjoy themselves. If they are not causing harm, we can feel happy for them. As a teenager, my godson enjoyed heavy metal music, a genre of which I'm not very fond. So I spent time while driving around town tuning the radio to heavy metal stations to see if I could appreciate it. And I found I could! Heavy metal is very energetic and willing to meet raw emotion. My judgment had gotten in the way of being able to enjoy aspects of this music. Developing this appreciation, I could delight in my godson's interest. With mudita, we move from judgment to appreciation, a much lovelier place to live. Cultivating this ability to choose what kind of world we create, the reality of our heart, empowers us. We shift from inhabiting a world of separation, ill will, judgment, and envy and choose instead the heavenly home of mudita.

Expanding Our Heart with Gratitude

A quality close in heart to mudita is gratitude. We don't talk nearly enough about gratitude. I get it. I used to think it was a second-class quality, one that we could add to our practice if we needed extra fluff. I have come to understand, however, that gratitude is a deeply spiritual and supportive quality for opening the heart-mind. Gratitude falls within the feminine archetype, as it acknowledges interdependence and appreciates all that we receive. This quality is seldom celebrated in the American myth of individualism, which assumes that people are "self-made." But of course, nobody is self-made; we are all made from others. We are here because of the infinite gifts that we have received from our ancestors, other humans, the nonhuman world, and the earth itself. When we understand that we are not independently made, we know our efforts succeed because of the support of many beings, and we are indebted to the world in every moment. As we emerge from prevailing cultural beliefs of individualism, competition, and a self-centered view of the world, with gratitude we land happily in the community of all beings.

When we explore gratitude with mindfulness, our heart expands and relaxes. We feel uplifted, connected, energized, and joyful. Celtic culture has a special word, *buiochas*, which translates as "tender gratitude." Diana Beresford-Kroeger in her book *To Speak for the Trees* says, "The feeling of buiochas is like a medicine of the mind that holds your life together."[18] We recognize that with every breath of air, the earth supports our journey. Every bite of food nourishes this body. In this wild world, we are tenderly cared for.

In a *Lion's Roar* magazine article, Macy described visiting an Onondaga Nation school. A teacher/clan mother named Frieda told her that the schoolchildren were engaged in their morning thanksgiving ritual. She explained, "We begin, of course, with the thanksgiving. Not the real, traditional form of it, because that takes days. We do it very short, just twenty minutes or so."[19] Imagine how our world could change if all schoolchildren started their days with twenty minutes of gratitude. I vote for this.

Gratitude shifts our perspective from one of lack to one of abundance.* When we are accustomed to seeing the world through the eyes of scarcity, we cultivate fear, stinginess, and aggression. Gratitude softens the aggressive tendencies of our hearts by deepening our understanding all the way down to the cellular level that this world is generous. Moment by moment we are receiving countless blessings, including air to power our cells, food to energize our bodies, sunlight to brighten our hearts, and beauty to nourish our nervous systems. It is extraordinary to be a live human being on this vibrant earth.

With gratitude, we let ourselves be touched by the generosity of life. Taking the time to slow down, we receive with delight the uplifted blossom of the black-eyed Susan, the smell of the spring rain, the chirping of the chickadees, the taste of fresh bread, and the smile of our child. We understand that the beauty of this world is limitless, always here for us. Thich Nhat Hanh said, "Happiness is available. Please help yourself to it."[20]

Gratitude introduces a healthy sense of indebtedness. We are humbled when we acknowledge that we are who we are through interconnectedness. As we receive, it only makes sense to give back. It's like a garden hose filling with water: if you put water in but the outflow is stopped up, everything gets stagnant, and no more water can come in. The water enters and needs to flow out. The Buddha talked about two rare beings in the world: *kataññu,* someone who knows what has been done for them and feels grateful, and *katavedi,* someone who pays back the debt. A compound word formed with them—*kataññu-katavedi*—means feeling gratitude and paying it forward.[21] Many Indigenous societies honor this understanding. Dr. Robin Wall Kimmerer of the Potawatomi Nation shares that, following the customs of her culture, when she harvests a plant, she not only first asks if it's okay and abides by the answer, she also leaves behind an offering to complete the circle.[22]

---

* It is important to pause and acknowledge that not everybody has everything that they need. When talking about abundance, we do not want to erase the reality of people who lack healthy food, clean water, a safe and secure home, basic health care, and community. Contentment and gratitude come easier when our basic needs are taken care of. This is an important truth.

The unbalanced energy of dominant Western culture encourages us to take whatever we can get and discourages us from thinking of the consequences of our taking, developing entitlement rather than gratitude. We view receiving as a line rather than as a circle. With gratitude, we can understand the circular nature of respectful relating to the world. When we take, we also give back. Living in a world of interconnected embeddedness, we look after each other, engaging in a revolution of gratitude and offering back. Kataññu-katavedi releases us from the self-absorption of a worldview based on acquisition and independence and merges us into the feminine paradigm of interdependence. We land on this earth ready to share what we have received.

The Spacious Heart of Equanimity

The well-known Serenity Prayer captures understanding of the Brahmavihara quality of equanimity.

> Grant me the serenity to accept the things I cannot change
> The courage to change the things that I can
> And the wisdom to know the difference.

We like to control other people. We appreciate it when they do what we want and don't do what we don't want. We like to think we have the power to decide how their lives will be. The fourth Brahmavihara, equanimity (or, in Pali, *upekkha*), addresses our human tendency to want to manage the lives of others to suit our needs. It teaches us to rest in the understanding that we can't control other people and the unfolding of their lives. We can't decide their destiny; they have to work that out themselves. We can wish them well, care for them, and delight in their success and happiness, but ultimately, they have their own journey. To abide in peaceful, mature, unconditional love, we let go of self-centered attachment to people manifesting according to our agendas.

The equanimity Brahmavihara teaches us the limits of what we can do, putting realistic boundaries around our caring. We learn to let go of taking too much responsibility or getting too entangled. We are not responsible for fixing other people or making them be the way that we want. As a form of respect, we recognize others' sovereignty and capability. People are an unknown, a mystery, and we open to this freshness in our relationships, unburdened by our attachments, fears, and projections. In this way, equanimity encourages a grounded, realistic love. We recognize that this world is an unknown, vaster and more mysterious than we can pin down.

And giving up control—or, more correctly put, giving up the *illusion* of control—requires living with the shaky tenderness of life. Things change, people will do what they want, and we never know for sure what that will be. They'll even die on us. We build the strength of equanimity as we are increasingly able to meet others and life as they are. Equanimity is grounded in reality, solid and steady. We give up bargaining with life . . . and it turns out to be the best bargain yet.

While the other Brahmaviharas warm the heart, the equanimity Brahmavihara cools and calms it. We practice letting go, again and again, of our agendas, expectations, and desires. It is described as parents letting go when the child leaves home, realizing that their child has their own individual destiny. This equanimity manifests as relief from tension and contraction, both conscious and unconscious, and allows us to relax into spaciousness. Love deepens as our heart is freed from the restriction of our desires and fears.

With the equanimity Brahmavihara, we bring to mind an image of a person and say, *You are the owner of your karma. Your happiness and your sorrow depend upon your actions and not my wishes for you.* This traditional phrasing can be confusing to Westerners not thoroughly schooled in an understanding of karma. Coming from a misunderstanding of karma as punishment for what we've done, this phrase feels like turning a cold shoulder to the ones we love. However, when we approach karma from a correct understanding as the law of cause and effect, we know that whatever actions we take of thought, speech, and deed will have effects congruent with the energy of the action taken. This phrase expresses the empowering truth that our actions matter; our actions go a long way toward creating a happy or sorrowful life.[23] Understanding that this natural law will have greater influence over others' lives than our wishes for them, we release attachment to the results of our well wishes. We respect others' agency to create their life.

When the traditional equanimity wording triggers an unhelpful response, we can use other phrases that communicate this same flavor of letting go. We can try them on and feel when a particular one facilitates the relief of relaxing control. Here are some options:

- *Although I care for you, I understand that I cannot control your destiny.*
- *I respect your sovereignty and your own unique journey.*
- *I let go of my expectations and demands for how your life is.*
- *Things are as they are.*
- *Things will unfold for you according to life's natural laws.*
- *I release you from my demands and attachments.*

Do you feel the flavor? Letting go, letting go, letting go. *I'm giving up trying to control how things are for you and respect that you have your own life.* Practicing this Brahmavihara with those whom we want to manage—perhaps our spouse, children, parents, or a work partner—can be particularly freeing. We acknowledge that they are a separate person with their own life. In this way, we give them a gift; people like to be respected and treated with dignity. This Brahmavihara offers others release from the burden of our demands. It's freedom for both of us.

If the Buddha were alive today, he might express this last Brahmavihara as setting appropriate emotional boundaries. After developing the first three Brahmaviharas to melt the boundaries between ourselves and others, we need to clarify those boundaries, too. We open our hearts to others through metta, compassion, and appreciative joy, and then we ask ourselves: *What are the limits to what we can do? What can we control, and what can't we control? How much space do we give other people? How do we let go of our wish to meddle and fix other people's lives? Where do we end and they begin?* The equanimity Brahmavihara reinforces that in this relative reality, I am one person and you are another. You have your own life.

This Brahmavihara isn't passive and doesn't mean that we never negotiate our interactions with other people. True equanimity is flexible and adaptable. When our partner or coworker is treating us with disrespect or abuse, we address it and protect ourselves. We may establish a strong boundary about what we're willing to tolerate. When our children leave their dirty dishes lying around, we may have a conversation about household responsibilities. We work out differences and figure out how to live together more harmoniously. We distinguish demand or control—that is, telling others what to do or how to be—from negotiation of authentic relational dynamics. With equanimity we work things out from a stance of engaged respect.

Equanimity's Neighbors

When dharma teachers like myself talk about equanimity, students start to get concerned. *You mean that we just accept suffering? We just become passive in this world? We don't care anymore?* These common misunderstandings about equanimity are in truth the near misses of equanimity. Equanimity without heart can morph into indifference or detachment, near neighbors of the true quality. Detachment masquerades as equanimity because it shares the spaciousness of nonattachment, yet it is missing the connection that is the lifeblood of all the Brahmaviharas. We pull back, safe in our own world, disconnected from the messiness of the relational world. Equanimity is not detached and indifferent, but rather maintains the caring and appreciative connection of the first three Brahmaviharas even while letting go of attachment to outcome. We then respond. We engage because we care. We take our place as loving citizens in our family, our work, and our society.

Detachment and indifference are easier than equanimity, as we are just not involved. They are a form of spiritual bypass that avoids the real challenges of living with family, friends, and communities. Heartfelt equanimity removes any propensity toward indifference. Genuine equanimity, this combination of connection and nonattachment, requires feeling our way to skillful balance. When we sense the stress of attachment, we practice letting go of our demands. When letting go leads to detachment, we warm the heart through connection. We learn a fully mature unconditional love that remains openhearted, nonattached, and fully present in this world, ready to respond.

The far neighbor of equanimity is reactivity: needing things to be different than they are. The heart says, *No! I cannot open to this. It must not be this way.* This Brahmavihara exposes grasping and aversion, the tendency to manage the world (and others) to suit our desires. We feel the self-centeredness of our loving wishes and our reactivity to the truth of things as they are. We wish for others to be happy because we can't tolerate their unhappiness. We want them to be free of suffering because their suffering makes us suffer. We can't bear the thought of their happiness ending. With equanimity, we loosen and release the tight fist of demand.

The equanimity Brahmavihara unfolds as the practice of rooting out self-centered forms of love, encouraging the widening and deepening of the heart into the peace of unobstructed connection. Rather than bypass our reactive attachments, we make them conscious so we can face them, feel them, and understand viscerally that they are not where our heart wants to abide. Then the heart knows what to do, knows that letting go leads to peace. The nondemanding heart of equanimity remains, graceful and peaceful in the midst of caring.

Equanimity as the Foundation of Love

Equanimity is a strong undergirding for the Brahmaviharas of lovingkindness, compassion, and appreciative joy. Practicing the warmhearted wishes of these three flavors of love, our own agendas can inadvertently taint the openheartedness of genuine unconditional love and shift our well-wishes from blessing to demanding. The other three Brahmaviharas reach their fullest depth and maturity only when imbued with the spaciousness of equanimity. As long as our self-centered desires and fears are present, they distort the expression of metta, compassion, and appreciative joy. When we are connecting through these other Brahmaviharas, equanimity protects us from stress due to attachment to things being a certain way. Equanimity dissolves grasping and aversion, the reactive shielding of the heart, and we feel the other Brahmaviharas in their fullness. By teaching us to let go, equanimity strengthens the other three Brahmaviharas, making them robust and durable.

In our metta practice, for example, we wish for others to be healthy, safe, happy, and peaceful. However, in this world of joy and sorrow, pleasure and pain, we know that they aren't always going to be so. They will also experience ill health, danger, and sorrow. How do we extend these metta wishes while also holding the truth of the way this world is? With equanimity, we expand the size of the heart, its willingness to hold it all. We realize it isn't our job to determine the outcome of our wishes. Brahmavihara practices focus on cultivating the loving spaciousness of our own heart rather than determining how things are for others. We wish others well, and then the unfolding is not ours to decide. This letting go deepens the unconditional nature of our love—no demands limiting our boundless heart.

In compassion practice, we wish for others to be free from suffering, while also holding the truth of their suffering with spaciousness. Equanimity encourages us to respond to suffering not with aversion, but rather with softening. Equanimity rests in "this is the way things are right now" while simultaneously allowing our heart to be touched by the poignancy of pain. Compassion deepens when openhearted allowing, rather than reactivity, is our response to suffering. No longer limited by self-centered concerns, the heart expands; the unconditional nature of compassion grows. When equanimity flavors compassion, it becomes broad, deep, and quiet. Equanimity teaches us to rest our hearts in the wider truth that all is well.

Equanimity keeps compassion from becoming weighty. We avoid confusion about who we are, establishing appropriate boundaries. When I worked as a psychotherapist, at the end of each day I imagined each of my clients, connected with them warmly through metta and compassion, and then let them go, consciously acknowledging that they had their own lives to live. These kinds of warmhearted unburdening rituals can free us from carrying suffering in ways that deplete our energy.

Equanimity also deepens appreciative joy. In the practice of mudita, we wish for the happiness and success of others to grow and flourish. However, in this world happiness and joy do not necessarily abound, and sorrow and tribulations also visit all of us. Happiness is impermanent; it won't last. We have a koan: How do we wish for happiness to continue while knowing that it's going to end? Again, equanimity encourages us to let go of attachment to the outcome of our wishes. We celebrate happiness and success even while accepting that it is impermanent. Equanimity supports a grounded love, erasing any frivolousness from our mudita wishes. Equanimity keeps us real.

With brilliant understanding of the human heart, the Buddha provided us with a framework that outlines these four great qualities as the foundation for boundless love. Using these guidelines, we explore for ourselves our experience of these qualities. We engage in a down-to-earth embodied investigation of love and the obstructions to love. We clear the heart of our conditioned hesitations, making room for our natural love to shine. We develop fully the Brahmaviharas, these heavenly homes, encouraging them to become the default of our hearts and the flavor of our consciousness.

PART THREE

WISDOM

IMPERMANENCE

Anicca Is Our Foundation

Meditation practice develops wisdom by moving us closer to the ways things really are, thereby allowing us to discern the underlying truths of this world. This investigation messes with our deeply cherished illusions about life. We like to think life has stability and permanence. We assume that we can find happiness through accumulating things and experiences. We view ourselves as separate independent selves that can control what happens within and around us. In meditation, we discover truths that disavow these illusions: *anicca* or impermanence, *dukkha* or stress/suffering, and *anatta* or not-self. These three principles are the foundation of all life, and the closer we are to the earth, the clearer they become to us.

Experiencing these three truths intimately, rather than as an intellectual idea, transforms how we perceive the world and our relationship to it. Our own embodied reality is our teacher. Each of us is said to incline toward one of the three and that one is our doorway into freedom, our access point. However, they are intricately entwined, and exploring one in depth means that all three become alive for us. With these three characteristics, the Buddha hands us the key and says, "Walk through that doorway," showing us a pathway to unbind the heart.

Anicca is the underlying truth of all life. Better said, anicca is life. There is no life without change and impermanence. Think about it: if things didn't change, we would inhabit a dead universe, and that's not where we live. Bubbling, boiling, swishing, growing, waning, roaring, whispering, coming, going—it doesn't stop. We see impermanence minutely from the restless energy of a cell all the way to macro levels like a changing climate. The suddenness of the COVID-19 pandemic was deeply shocking. People are losing it a lot lately. We feel the shakiness of surrendering the certainties we had thought we could count on, like the predictability of the weather, a functioning democracy, and dependable supply chains. All is shifting; we're walking on the deck of a ship at sea.

Meditation is a personal exploration of change. Each breath changes. Each moment changes. Breathing, thinking, itching, craving, hearing... life is flow, and we are always in transition. The more aware we are, the more change we see. Sometimes when concentration is very strong, the moment-by-moment change is so rapid that mindfulness can't even keep up with it. Everything arises and slips away so quickly. When we stop and pay close attention, we notice just how constant change is.

And, of course, we experience the bigger display of change in our lives as circumstances evolve. We face birth and death. We experience illness and aging. We get married and divorce. Our children grow up. We lose our job and get a new one. Business runs as usual and along comes a pandemic. The climate seems stable and then becomes wild and unpredictable. Our centuries-old democracy begins to wobble and crumble. In our own lives and in our communities, conditions and circumstances cannot be pegged down.

Many years ago, I led a meditation group at Mount Holyoke College. One day we were talking about anicca, and I asked the students, "It's obvious that everything changes, but why does this matter so much? Why do we talk about it?" One young woman answered, "Because this is the way it is, and if you have issues with this, you need to deal with them." We all have issues with change, and in meditation we're dealing with them. The unbinding of the heart-mind evolves from our intimate encounter with our emotional reaction to incessant and largely uncontrollable change.

We let change affect us, teach us, and steer us into a graceful relationship with life based not on illusion, but rather on truth.

Intellectually we all know that everything changes. If you ask people, "Do things change?" most people will say yes. Many years ago when I was a new teacher, I surveyed a number of people with this question. Everybody said things change. Then I upped the ante by asking them, "Does everything change?" This question produced more confusion. One person said that 95 percent of things change. However, knowing cognitively that everything changes doesn't transform us. Moment-by-moment intimate contact with this truth and our response to it deconstructs our conditioning and lets us choose fresh and freer ways to be in this world.

Our usual conditioning in the face of change is reactivity. When an experience is pleasant, we want it to stay, so we hold on. When one is unpleasant, we don't like it, so we push it away. (When it's neutral, we don't pay much attention.) This holding on and pushing away—our basic restlessness—is happening moment by moment. Because things are changing so constantly, this conditioning doesn't give us a chance to rest. We're so tired from this business of micromanaging the universe. In one meditation inquiry, a woman raised her hand and asked simply, "Where can we rest?" This poignant question lies deep in our hearts. We obviously can't rest in the changing conditions of our lives. We can't rest in scrambling to make things be the way we want. Because that's our usual life strategy, we're left restless and confused.

We can rest when we are able to flow with change without resistance. Pleasant, unpleasant, and neutral experiences arise and pass away, and we don't have to push one away or hang on to another. When we experience this freedom, we know the rest possible in the middle of flow. Ajahn Chah called this "still moving water." The water is moving, yet the awareness is still, resting without agitation. Life is moving, yet the quiet heart-mind abides in peace.

Each time we engage in formal meditation practice we are learning how to live harmoniously in this world of change. When we sit down to meditate, we don't know what's going to happen. Maybe we'll hang out in bliss, or perhaps we'll meet pain deep in our heart. We study our conditioning to hang on to the pleasant and exile the unpleasant. We learn how to flow with the whole shebang with an uncontracted heart-mind, unbound by clinging and reactive conditioning. Meditation gives us seaworthy legs by increasing our tolerance for the shakiness of change. We meet anicca with emotional honesty, feeling our way toward peace and acceptance. The moment-to-moment awareness of change offers us the opportunity to explore close up and personal our relationship to the shifting tides of life and teaches us to flow with uncertainty rather than resist it. We choose an evolutionary leap: to hold all of life in a large compassionate embrace.

The timeline of our journey to acceptance is not in our control and often depends on the intensity of the change. Rather than tell ourselves that as evolved meditators we should be equanimous when things change, we allow ourselves to feel our heart's journey in the face of anicca. We may start with denial or numbness (*it's not happening*) and then move on to reactivity, the hope that we can control this reality. We may feel grief, sadness, anxiety, anger, disappointment, yearning, or just plain shaky. We allow these emotions to unfold, with mindfulness, not needing to suppress or change them, yet also not feeding them. By respecting our emotional journey, we finally relax into the truth. This is how life is right now. Meeting the heart where it is, we develop authentic equanimity—rather than detached coolness fabricated as a spiritual response. As we become familiar with navigating this terrain of loss with kindhearted awareness, we journey more gracefully, trusting the heart to find equilibrium at its own pace.

As our practice matures, our capacity to flow with change grows. Before we were mad about the broken computer all day long, then maybe for only a couple of hours, then maybe only a few minutes. The journey to equanimity shortens. We get hung up less, spending less of our life fighting the changes that inevitably come our way—whether it's little things like the unexpected traffic jam or the bigger losses that our hearts must face. It's a lot of work fighting the way things are, and we no longer want to waste our time in opposition. We gracefully surrender to the ups and downs of this human experience. We learn unconditional cooperation with the unfolding show.

Learning to live gracefully with anicca, we take increasing delight in the magical display of this unfathomable world into which we have taken birth. Anicca manifests as this very vibrant and dynamic world. We experience impermanence in the wild dance and spirited vitality of this very life. William Maxwell said, "So strange, life is. Why people do not go round in the continual state of surprise is beyond me."[1] Right now, I'm looking at the autumn leaves changing: the green, gold, red, and yellow; the mauve, purple, and orange. Then they let go, flutter off, and the bare branches share their unadorned beauty. What a world! We can't comprehend it, but we can feel and enjoy this vibrant and dynamic wild ride.

When I was young, I played the violin for a few years. I learned two styles of playing: *staccato*, marked by abrupt and choppy strokes, and *legato*, which is flowing and smooth. When we resist the truth of change, we live our lives in staccato mode, feeling jumpy and out of balance much of the time. Meditation practice teaches us to relate gracefully to change and play life in a smooth and flowing style, legato all the way.

Uncertainty Is the Only Certainty

Anicca is poignant. Dynamic tension exists between the truth that everything is always changing and our deep human wish for certainty and security. Ajahn Chah, going right to the heart of the matter, translated *anicca* as "uncertainty." He said, "People say, 'Ajahn Chah only talks about *not certain*.' They get fed up with hearing this, and they run away from me. 'We went to listen to Ajahn Chah, but all he talked about was *not certain*.' . . . I guess they're going to look for some place where things will be certain. But they'll come back."[2] Yep, he's right: we're not too happy to contemplate this basic truth of life. We like our universe more certain, thank you. The tension between the shakiness of life and our wish for certainty is the source of suffering. The desire for security causes us to try to nail down life, which simply can't be nailed down. It causes us to resist the flow of life, which doesn't stop changing no matter what our wishes are.

Many years ago, I experienced neurological symptoms a few days after getting a flu shot. The neurologist informed me that there were two possible causes for my symptoms. One prospect suggested that I had had an autoimmune reaction to the flu shot and the nerves would heal. Alternatively, I was showing early signs of a progressive neurological disease such as multiple sclerosis. The neurologist told me it would be some time before we could determine which was true because if it was indeed only an autoimmune reaction, the nerves would take months to heal. I sat with this uncertainty in my life and in meditation for these months. At first, the mind scrambled for certainty, jumping back and forth between landing on an autoimmune reaction or a neurological disease. I wanted certainty, even if the outcome turned out to be horrible. (We prefer any kind of certainty to uncertainty; we just want to know what kind of world we are inhabiting.) Resisting the uncertainty caused fear and suffering, and I felt restless and exhausted from the relentless struggling of my mind.

Slowly I came to accept that the outcome was undecided. I did not know what was going to happen. This uncertainty was the only thing that was certain right then. Resting with a softer heart in the truth of uncertainty, my world opened wide and spacious with possibility. The mind and heart had no edges, no place of resistance to things exactly as they were. I felt tenderness for all of us living in the truth of uncertainty. Eventually, after three or four months, the nerves began to heal, though it took almost two years for the symptoms to disappear. This medical crisis helped me learn to relax into uncertainty. It is the truth of our lives every moment of every day, so we better get used to it.

Anicca means that we are always in a state of not knowing. We can never tell what's coming our way. In this relative reality, of course we make our best guess and plan our lives. Given uncertainty, however, our best allies will be responsiveness, flexibility, and trust in our capacity to deal with life. With climate change we talk about adaptability—another way of saying the same thing. Our intimate connection with reality gives us the information we need to be responsive, and our flexible heart-mind not caught in reactive conditioning provides the freedom to respond in fresh and appropriate ways. Because of its spacious and nonreactive nature, the trained heart-mind is highly adaptable, which is a quality we need now and are certainly going to need in the future.

We hold uncertainty as best we can with an open heart. We connect with the groundless nature of this life, which also means freshness and possibility. When we can tolerate the dynamic and uncertain nature of things, we can move closer to life and participate more fully. We hold life's perpetual ethereal nature in a great tender compassion, knowing that it's not only our personal reality, but also the truth for all living things. We've taken birth in a challenging universe. Because of impermanence, we're always navigating loss. Our practice teaches us to traverse this terrain with gracefulness. The ongoing losses inherent in a world of change tenderize the heart, training us to truly love and to love while letting go, the deepest and fullest kind of love.

Heartbreak and Joy

Heartbreak is the natural consequence of living a life of relationship, whether with your spouse, your children, your friend, your dog, or a tree. When we engage in close connection with the things of this world, we experience their leave-taking as well. Every September, the hummingbirds that spend the summer with us depart. They fly south, and I miss them. I'm heartbroken because I don't know if they'll be back. In a world of anicca, loss is built into the fabric of life. One of the five daily recollections recommended for serious practitioners reminds us that we will be separated from all we hold dear. Life is an apprenticeship in loss.

Heartbreak is the price we pay for connectedness. We sign up to live in the heart of the human predicament: to love in an unfixable world. As we connect with ongoing leave-taking, the heart navigates its way to peace and acceptance by traversing the terrain of sorrow and grief. Yet heartbreak also translates into poignant tenderness toward oneself, others, and this world itself. I hope we're getting more tender through practice, because if not, what good is it? Are we building more sophisticated walls to shield ourselves from basic heartbreak, cocooning within our illusion of a separate protected self? Or will we be touched by this heartbreaking beautiful world?

Approaching loss from the transcendent masculine paradigm, we rise above grief. There is no problem; knowing that all that arises passes away, we accept things just as they are. Transcendence does provide spacious balance, yet when it is our unexamined default, we run the risk of disconnecting from our humanity. From the heart, loss does matter. Part of our biology involves feeling grief and compassion. The sorrow of heartbreak deepens our ability to be in this world with all of ourselves on board. The down-to-earth, embodied heart connects us to our own humanity and to everyone else's. We're all in this together, pioneers in the land of loss.

Grief, the journey of the heart coming to terms with loss, is the companion of heartbreak. Denying or blocking grief dulls vibrancy and love, so it's important to let the heart navigate through the terrain of loss, not telling it what it can and can't feel. We allow, we feel, we ground in the body, and we let the heart grieve. Grief is a wilderness landscape. Starting off ragged and violent, it can propel us into anger and fear. Bleakness, despair, and an apparently endless loneliness can travel with us. Grief shifts and morphs, like a river on the way to the sea—sometimes a roaring waterfall, other times rippling over rapids. Over time grief becomes warmer and quieter. Slowly it spreads out in the delta lands of compassion, a tenderness that can hold the goodbyes. Like sunset, soft and poignant, we come to rest in the truth of loss.

Heartbreak is an initiation into the unfathomable mystery of this wild life. Our familiarity with grief accompanies us on our journey into the truth of this uncontrollable world. Heartbreak meanders its way into tenderness toward this predicament we all share. We cohabitate this vulnerable existence in a wild world of loss with all other human beings, animals, plants, and trees. Even rocks are vulnerable as they slowly wear down from heat and cold, water and ice. We've all taken birth in this universe of such change and unpredictability.

Grief is the emotion of our times as we live in a period of accelerated loss. Our collective sorrow is vast and mostly unacknowledged, particularly in dominant cultural spaces. We're holding immense anguish at the state of our communities, societies, and planet. Our sorrow may express itself as anxiety or just plain irritability, both of which can act as cover stories for the deep well of grief. We try to avoid feeling the grief, distracting ourselves with the endless entertainment options offered to us. Yet we sense the heartbeat of grief thrumming underneath the glossy patina of the slick advertisements and scripted news bites. Not hearing it named, we're confused, stuck between the sense of impending doom and our fear of letting the truth in. Individually and collectively, opening to grief might help us move forward into the world as it is now. In this heartbreaking world, we feel so we can be in touch enough to care and act.

Surprisingly, the flip side of heartbreak is joy. The sun rises in the morning, with energy, beauty, and splendor. We made it to another day! From a rational point of view, we want to protect ourselves from heartbreak. From the receptive paradigm, heartbreak is part of life, and when we try to avoid it, we also miss the beauty. Life is a package deal; we don't get to pick and choose. Joy and sorrow are married and travel together. A protected heart doesn't feel; an open heart feels both joy and sorrow. We wear out our insistence on experiencing joy over sorrow and open fully to both, knowing they are partners in this vibrant world. We learn to cohabitate with heartbreak, holding it close as a reminder that we feel and love. This broken-open heart springs into connection with joy and delight.

Sometimes we rest. Life is intense, and the heart needs a break. We pull back, protect, take thought vacations, or just numb out. No problem. Our heart works hard and deserves some time off. We don't demand more of the heart than it is able to give. When it rests, eventually it hears the beckoning call of the world—the hum of a school bus passing on the road, the whispering trees, and soft giggle of our child—and once again it relaxes into intimacy with life. We can come back at any moment, and the world is here waiting for us, fresh and new. Isn't that a miracle?

9

STRESS AND SUFFERING

Happiness and Suffering

We come to practice hoping we can think our way to freedom. If we just understand things deeply enough, then our problems will be solved. We think and we think and we think, and yet we don't feel closer to resolving our suffering. In a goal-oriented way, thinking is even satisfying. We're very busy and feel like we're getting something done. Yet we don't feel free. We are just as tangled up as we ever were. The Buddha said, "This generation is entangled in a tangle"—a statement that's still true! How do we untangle the tangle?

To free the heart and mind, we have to feel. Resting in this animal body, we touch the wild nature of our heart. We make space for yearning and sorrow, joy and deep pain. Practice doesn't at some point become miraculously pain-free. Quite the contrary: as we become stronger, awareness opens to deeper levels of pain and suffering. So, also, peace and joy deepen. Allowing suffering space in the heart-mind-body frees us. I wish there were an easier way, but if one exists, I don't know it.

Thich Nhat Hanh explains that happiness and suffering inter-are. We can't open to only one half of life, choosing happiness and ignoring suffering. When we attempt a life just of joy and avoid the suffering present within ourselves and others, this very act of denial creates a wall. Building walls takes work, and a wall is not freedom. In practice we take the walls down brick by brick so that the whole heart-mind inter-is. Joy and pain inter-are. We liberate ourselves from the walls within that separate what is allowable from what is not: *This I will experience and this I will not. This is acceptable and this is not. This is who I am and this is who I am not.* A free heart-mind includes the whole catastrophe. We are all of it.

Why would we sign up for this encounter with messiness? How many of you want to sign up for suffering? I don't see a lot of hands. However, when I first heard the Buddhist teachings on dukkha, I felt such relief. Finally, somebody was talking about the world as it is. I once read that the true religions of the United States are denial and optimism.[1] We work hard to disavow the tragic nature of life, creating the cognitive dissonance of denial as we also know that life includes a large amount of suffering. We undertake a meditation practice when we have worn out the alternative of feeling entangled, ensnared, and imprisoned by our own heart-mind. We become willing to pause long enough to know this entanglement and develop motivation to cure it. Meditation involves stopping, looking, listening, and getting on with the business of working out our freedom.

Dukkha Is Our Challenge

The Buddha said, "I teach one thing and one thing only, dukkha [stress/suffering] and the end of dukkha." Never mind that that's two things, we get the idea. The breadth and depth of this word are hard to translate. We often use *suffering*, but dukkha is subtler than that. It is suffering plus unreliability plus unsatisfactoriness plus stress. The Buddha's statement suggests that when we sign up for meditation practice, we must be willing to suffer. The spiritual path is not for the fainthearted. We need an arduous wish for freedom and a gnawing dissatisfaction with the current situation in order to be motivated for this journey that involves facing dukkha. We engage with serious meditation practice when the alternative of living unconsciously, repeating our habits over and over again, proves unworkable. We're willing to consciously face suffering in the hopes of transformation. The Buddha said that not only does he teach suffering, he teaches the end of suffering: dukkha and the end of dukkha. Facing suffering leads to the end of suffering. We take a leap of faith to verify this for ourselves.

The Buddha was a brilliant scientist of suffering, putting forth a clear and thorough description of its nature. He outlined three ways that we suffer, each one increasingly subtler. More specifically, these are three ways that we potentially suffer. Without mindfulness and understanding we get caught and entangled in these challenging aspects of life; with wisdom and letting go, we can settle into life just as it is with grace, poise, strength, and love.

The first way we suffer, called *dukkha dukkha*, encompasses the aches and pains of the body and afflictive emotions in the heart-mind. This double dukkha always makes me smile. Let there be no doubt! This dukkha includes all the unpleasantness that we must bear in this heart, mind, and body, including aging, sickness, death, sorrow, lamentation, and despair. Nobody is likely to argue with this description as it concurs with conventional ideas about suffering.

When suffering in the body or heart arises, what's our first inclination? To get rid of it, naturally. We start our exploration with the wish to transcend. "Get me out of here" is reportedly the most common human thought. Most of our early practice involves getting familiar with our strategies to avoid painful experiences of body and heart. We try ignoring them, concentrating on something else, commanding them, controlling them, and being with them so they'll go away. We attempt these strategies repeatedly, and we watch ourselves fail over and over again. We think we're doing the practice wrong, but we're right on track: learning for ourselves that avoiding suffering does not transform it.

Ajahn Chah said, "There are two kinds of suffering. There is the suffering you run away from, which follows you everywhere. And there is the suffering that you face directly and so become free."[2] We are working on the latter one. From the intimacy of the receptive paradigm, we move closer to dukkha so that it can be known and included. We muster up some courage and determination and turn toward these painful experiences to see what we might learn. What can knee pain teach us? What can anger teach us? These become our instructors, coaching us in dukkha and the end of dukkha. We turn toward them in a sustainable manner, touching into the pain and skillfully moving away when it's too much to hold. Slowly, our capacity grows; we can stay with what is painful and let it teach us.

Studying dukkha, we see for ourselves that facing suffering leads to its transformation. Turning toward and surrendering to pain changes the experience. Minus the tension and struggle of trying to avoid the difficulty, we feel some relief. Maybe for a second or two we rest in this pain just as it is and it's no problem. Those few moments of resting teach us that the unpleasant experience is not the problem. The suffering comes from resistance to being with things as they are. This valuable understanding encourages us, and we more willingly dare to face suffering directly. This shoulder pain—I can let it be. This trembling fear in the heart—it is what it is. Of course, the conditioning to avoid is deeply ingrained, and we retreat to wanting to get rid of the pain once again. Yet willingness grows. We become less afraid of these unpleasant experiences. Not needing to avoid them, we reduce the endless restlessness of trying to control unpleasant experiences in life. We stop running and find peace in letting be.

For those willing to risk further, we explore the second kind of suffering: *viparinama dukkha*, a subtler type of suffering due to change. Not only are unpleasant experiences suffering, but even pleasant experiences contain the seeds of suffering because they end. This dukkha points to the unreliable and the unsatisfactory nature of things in this world. Everything is going to disappoint us because it's not going to last and give us the enduring happiness we seek. Life just keeps moving. Trying to hold on, we experience dukkha.

Our exploration into viparinama dukkha requires us to look more deeply when feeling pleasant experiences. We're generally not as motivated to look for suffering when things are going well. *I'm doing okay, thank you!* But are we really? What happens when our pleasant experience ends? If we haven't developed wisdom, we are bereft. We pull out all our strategies to avoid this kind of suffering, too. We try to hold on, denying impermanence and thinking if we grasp hard, the pleasure won't slip away. We get excited and exuberant about what we like and want, accumulating as many pleasant moments as we can. And of course, these strategies fail, too. Thomas Edison is reported to have said, "I have not failed, I've just found 10,000 ways that don't work." In meditation we find 10,000 ways that don't work until finally a light comes on.

Our basic happiness strategy as "untrained worldlings" involves accumulating as many pleasant moments and avoiding as many unpleasant ones as we can. Viparinama dukkha messes with our blueprint, and we don't like that. Exploring this dukkha requires us to get comfortable with impermanence. Yes, we can enjoy what is pleasant, but it's not going to solve our search for happiness because everything that arises also passes away. Letting go of holding on is the key to transforming this kind of suffering. Once again, we don't give up easily. Repeatedly we hope that pleasant experiences will satisfy us. Repeatedly we are disappointed. We had wished for so much more out of pleasant experience, and yet we find we can't take our refuge there. This disappointment is our teacher, instilling in us the lesson to let go. Letting life flow, there's no problem: just pleasant experience and its ending. This is the way things are. We can stop our restless scrambling to accumulate enough pleasant moments to make life okay and rest in our ability to hold life's inevitable changes.

The third kind of suffering, called *sankhara dukkha*, is even subtler and more existential. Having taken birth in this world of contingency, we are constantly impacted by the environment in ways largely out of our control. Any experience—whether pleasant, unpleasant, or neutral—is suffering because of the uncontrollable nature of this sense impingement and our continual adjustment to ever-new circumstances. We are always responding, moment by moment, to the ever-changing impact of our environment on our senses. We grow weary trying to manage our world. We experience an underlying edginess, a not-quite-rightness, never knowing what is coming next. We're so damn vulnerable. This low-grade hum runs through our lives, but mostly we don't notice. For those of us who experience trauma, forced dislocation, assault, ongoing poverty, or oppression, this thrum may be louder. We've learned that it's a worrisome universe and we'd better stay on guard. Even checking the news too often or ongoing windy weather can activate this vulnerability. It's not our fault: it's an edgy universe. Being repeatedly impacted by our environment is wearying, yet it's hard to rest. This subtler kind of dukkha can go unnoticed because we keep pretty darn busy with the first two kinds.

Exploring the third kind of suffering is for the bravehearted because it requires that we inhabit our vulnerability in this world. Turning toward the nature of uncontrollable sense impingement means recognizing that we can't make ourselves into a separate, independent, safe being. We certainly try. We deeply wish for security. We like things ordered and predictable, thank you. We employ many strategies to protect ourselves from this vulnerability, including every variety of grasping, pushing away, and dulling out and distracting. This game plan may give us the illusion of protection, so we try to take refuge here.

Yet we are intimately embedded in this world and can't stop the impingement, so we have to make peace with our vulnerability. Suffering comes from identifying with and holding on to the sense experiences of the heart, body, and mind in order to manage them. As soon as we grasp the changing experiences as who we are, we suffer sankhara dukkha. The deepest peace comes from releasing this hold, or not taking it up in the first place. Experiences are allowed to arise and pass away in the vast spaciousness of the heart-mind. There is no problem.

Turning toward these three kinds of dukkha, we become familiar with our deeply conditioned human strategies for dealing with a world of change. Resisting these basic truths of life—that unpleasant things happen, pleasant things end, and we human beings are embedded in vulnerable interconnectedness—there is dukkha. Without heart-mind training, we try to manage this dukkha by relying on control strategies to try to get rid of what we don't want, get and keep what we do want, and protect ourselves from our intimate vulnerability in this world. Maintaining these approaches keeps us restless, our life energy consumed in the exhausting task of micromanaging our experience. On the other hand, letting go of struggling with dukkha, we experience the peace and freedom we yearn for. We open up space in our usual conditioning and cultivate the alternative of letting be and letting go. We experience for ourselves the truth of dukkha and the end of dukkha. Our own life just as it is becomes our teacher.

Illness as Our Teacher

In my early thirties, I suffered a period of several years of poor health. Due to environmental and emotional stressors, my body succumbed to a viral syndrome that caused fatigue and unpleasant experiences of body and mind. During this time of not knowing how the illness was going to unfold and whether I was going to regain my prior health or continue to sicken, I experienced a lot of fear. I had taken pride and refuge in having a lot of energy, willpower, and initiative, and now, without access to these same mental and physical resources, I was at sea.

This health challenge was one of my greatest teachers. Accustomed as I was to relying on the active paradigm to navigate the world, illness and limitation forced me to develop more receptive qualities. No longer able to depend on managing the world with energetic willpower, I had to develop my underdeveloped softness, gentleness, love, and surrender. Illness is a great gift, as we generally won't move toward this more receptive paradigm until we see no other option. Illness gives us no choice.

Of course, illness is also a real drag, and I resisted the process. At first, in denial of my condition, I tried to keep operating as normal. I wasn't going to go down easy. Eventually, it became clear that I couldn't go on, and I took a leave of absence from work. After some initial healing, the illness manifested as "relatively normal" days and "symptomatic" days. At first, on the normal days, I was elated. Now I was decidedly going to get better and not suffer anymore. On the days when I was symptomatic, I despaired, fearing that I was never going to be healthy again. In fact, it was likely that I was going to become completely disabled. I rode this roller coaster up and down, up and down, depending on how my symptoms manifested on a particular day. I suffered attachment and disappointment, hope and despair. Finally, it dawned on me that I needed to bring careful mindfulness to this unfolding process to see how I could find freedom right then amid the changing conditions of my life.

As the symptomatic days left me drained and stuck in afflictive mind states, I focused first where I had some space—on the days when I felt good. I explored the attachment that manifested in getting lost in elation, just a bit too much exuberance that unconsciously denied the impermanence of this pleasant phase. While continuing to enjoy the sensations of feeling relatively healthy, at the same time I reminded myself, *This is not going to last; this is impermanent.* When this period of relatively good health passed, as it inevitably would, and I entered a symptomatic phase, I suffered less than before. I didn't feel dejected as I had not convinced myself that I was cured forever. I expected change.

During the symptomatic days, I then focused on increasing my tolerance for the unpleasantness of what I was going through. I committed myself to arresting any catastrophic stories about the future, asking myself instead, *Is this moment okay?* Often the answer was, *Yes, I can deal with this moment.* If the answer was no, then could I be okay with lack of equanimity in this moment? It became very simple: *Can I accept this moment?* Increasingly surrendering to what was present in the moment, infusing mindfulness with kindness and compassion, I learned to approach the unpleasant sensations with less identification and more care.

Rather than rejecting my experience with aversion, I encouraged softness of heart and mind in relationship to what was happening. I surrendered to each day, to each moment when I remembered, recognizing that what was happening was impersonal and uncontrollable. When I got caught in reactivity, I surrendered to that, too. When we land fully in the wholeness of the moment, however it is manifesting, this is the deepest healing. Any moment of life can teach us this, including moments of illness and being caught in reactivity to illness.

Illness is an uninvited, unwelcome, and yet excellent teacher of the truth of life, providing perfect conditions for freeing the heart and mind. When the body is ill, we can't argue with it. We can't will away sickness; we can't control it away; we can't just demand that it leave. It is the way it is—like a fierce Zen master hitting us with a stick. *Pay attention here! How are we going to deal with this? How can we find peace amid illness?*

Illness can teach us to convert willpower into gentleness, doing into being, hardness into softness, and control into willingness. Rather than relying on predominantly masculine archetype qualities, we learn to embrace more feminine archetype energies. Navigating illness can deepen our understanding of equanimity, the heart-mind that doesn't react to the ups and downs of life but rather can stay poised and balanced. We learn about letting go.

It's so strange how we can feel some kind of injustice when we get sick or experience age-related limitations. *This isn't supposed to happen to ME!* The truth of illness also applies to aging and death. We're all going to get sick and we're all going to die. None of us are exempt. When my brother received a diagnosis of an inoperable glioblastoma, he so poignantly said to me, "I always thought I'd have more time." A friend who had AIDS back when this syndrome was considered a death sentence would say, "I'm not in any different position than you. We're both gonna die. I just know it." Whomp! Fierce Zen master! Health and sickness, life and death are all part of the whole. Did we think we were going to get one without the other? Did we hope we were the exception? How we respond to the inevitable dukkha of life determines our freedom. Unfortunately (or fortunately?), we do not lack opportunities to learn. This is our human condition.

NOT-SELF

Not-Self from the Feminine Paradigm

What is our visceral embodied experience of self? How do we feel not-self? These questions are central to exploring not-self from a feminine paradigm. Rather than using conceptual analysis, we feel our way into a direct relationship with self and not-self. Metaphorically speaking, self feels claustrophobic, like a dark dungeon or a caged bird. Our experience of not-self is like taking off a tight shoe, a breath of fresh air, the *shrrrr* of the wind in the pine trees, the wide-open ocean. We know these experiences for ourselves, in heart, body, and mind.

The teaching of *anatta,* or not-self, is considered the most liberating tenet of the Buddhist teachings. Describing how we are bound, fettered, and limited by the sense of ourselves as separate and self-existing, this teaching offers the possibility of unbinding and freeing the heart and mind. While many practitioners find anatta difficult to comprehend, it's even harder to conceive how we believe ourselves to be separate independent beings when we are so intimately connected with our environment. With every breath, every sound, every bite of food, every step, we're here, immersed, embedded, inextricably linked. The belief that we can separate ourselves from life and be truly independent is illusion. Yet as humans, this is what we do: we create separation as a survival strategy. It may help us survive, but it doesn't make us happy.

To be clear, not-self teachings are not suggesting we wipe out some essential part of our programming that helps us get through the day. We're not declaring that I don't exist, you don't exist, and everything is an illusion. We don't get rid of our functioning everyday self. We do, however, note that the usual way of experiencing self is limited for freeing the heart-mind. With anatta teachings, we expand our options, discovering the freedom of not-self, the dissolving of the contraction of the heart-mind caught in separation. We could call anatta "a different understanding of self."

The Buddha offered several conceptual paradigms related to the constructed nature of our self, giving us useful frameworks for our experiential exploration. Not-self teachings in the sutras are often conceptually based, emphasizing analysis and deconstruction. For example, the Buddha explained not-self by describing the composite nature of the self through the six senses. Is there anything else, he asks? Is there anything beyond seeing, hearing, tasting, smelling, feeling the body, and the experience of mind? He further breaks down the six sense experiences into eighteen components: six sense bases, six sense objects, and six sense consciousnesses. The same set of experiences, arranged in a different format, are included in the teachings of the five aggregates of clinging: the body, and four experiences of mind, including feeling tone, perception, karmic formations, and consciousness. The Buddha asks, "Are these experiences permanent? Are they controllable?" (Spoiler alert: They're not.) "Is it proper to take what is impermanent and uncontrollable as my self?" (Spoiler alert: It's not.) These questions loosen our conviction that we exist solely in the way that we thought, as permanent and self-contained.

Another teaching on not-self—dependent co-origination—describes twelve steps that lead to the creation of self and, consequently, suffering. The CliffsNotes version of this teaching starts with basic ignorance about the way the world is. Influenced by our accumulated conditioning, experiences of the body and mind and consciousness arise along with an affective quality. Out of ignorance and habitual conditioning we react to this affective tone in increasingly contracted and confining ways, leading to the birth of ourselves as separate. Therefore, we suffer. Our human life (and lives) is this endless round of the creation of self and suffering, until we find a way to break the chain with mindfulness and wisdom.

These conceptual frameworks are useful, yet understanding them intellectually only carries us so far. Conceptual understanding doesn't unbind the heart-mind. We use these frameworks as pointers toward our direct feeling experience—experience that teaches us in an unmediated way. From the feminine paradigm, we feel our way into not-self. Not a theoretical and abstract exploration—it's visceral and embodied. We experience the creation of self up close and sense into its release. When self feels strong, we experience contraction, clinging, binding, tension, stress, self-preoccupation, limitation, tightness, and inflexibility. What happens when awareness directly contacts this experience of self in the mind, heart, and body? As we get intimate with clenching, the willingness to open and relax the tight fist grows. How, then, do we experience not-self? We also familiarize ourselves with this openness of the unbound heart-mind, manifesting as ease, spaciousness, flexibility, softening, allowing, relief, freedom, and the healing of estrangement.

In our meditation practice, we feel the protective nature of contraction and clinging and grow willing to risk the vulnerability of letting go. We see that the self is composed of control strategies. These strategies limit us, confining our hearts in a narrow cage in order to feel safe. What do we do with this dilemma? Our evolutionary and biological imperative calls for us to create safety and security for ourselves, and yet these very strategies cause suffering. The heart yearns for more space, for more freedom.

From the background of conceptual frameworks, we delve from the perspective of the heart into our felt experience of self and of not-self, of suffering and freedom. Kindhearted awareness allows us to soften our way into melting or dissolving the barriers created by these contractions of self. This melting uncovers the radiant heart, the unbound heart, the heart that is not contracted around me and mine, but rather is open to touch life and be touched by life. This unbound unmuddled heart responds to life with more clarity and compassion.

In his teachings on the Four Noble Truths, the Buddha explained in the first noble truth that life involves suffering in the form of mental and physical pain and the stress due to the unreliability of phenomena. The second noble truth stipulates that this suffering is caused by our grasping and contracting around experiences in order to control them. The third noble truth frees the heart-mind through the relaxing of the grip, the opening of the clenched fist. The heart and mind unbind from the patterning of hanging on, holding on, and contracting. In the meditative process, awareness meets contraction, whether on gross levels such as fear or anger or subtle levels such as the slightest tightening in the heart-mind. Recognizing the stressful nature of holding on, awareness considers letting go on all levels: the physical body, energy body, mind, heart, subtle body, even the cells. With continued application of soft kindhearted awareness these hard and rigid protections dissolve, allowing contraction to unbind itself. We feel our way to freedom through intimacy with both the binding and the release.

Not-self, then, is referring to letting go, to not hanging on to experience. It's not something that we do, but rather something that we don't do. We don't hang on. We don't contract around experience. We don't imprison our hearts and minds in a cage of separation. We have a functioning relative self that can respond to arising experiences in skillful ways, but not a rigid inflexible self that shuts down, contracts, owns, and tries to micromanage what arises.

As we let go of contraction and grasping, the heart disentangles, opens, and widens. This openness of not-self is natural, nothing special. It's a relief, like coming out of a dark tunnel into bright daylight. This unbound heart, strong in understanding, equanimity, and love can engage with this wild crazy world with wisdom and compassion. Trust and confidence are the path and the fruit of this exploration. Our heart is flexible enough to accommodate what comes our way and respond skillfully and heartfully. We settle into our spacious heart-mind, down-to-earth, unfettered, and engaged.

Not-Self as Relationship

As clinging dissolves, our natural condition of nonseparation from the world around us blossoms. Intimacy with all things becomes possible because we aren't barricading ourselves behind walls in our heart-mind. We're free to be part of all this. Absent the contracted heart-mind of self, everything just is. We just are with it. The philosopher Thomas Aquinas said that we are universe capable.[1] We are capable of a heart and mind as wide as the universe, deeply intimate with all things.

The Zen master Dōgen said, "To know the self is to forget the self, to forget the self is to be made real by myriad things."[2] Through the intimacy of knowing this self in all its manifestations, we learn to forget the self, to let go of clinging, of holding on to anything as who we are. Dōgen reminds us that the flip side of nonclinging is to be made real by all things, to be in relationship with all of life. Our journey melts the barriers that separate, and we are left with . . . just life. Just this wild, wild life unfolding moment by moment.

The heart paradigm relates to not-self through relationship. When self-feeling is strong, we try to establish our independence, pulling out of relationship and separating ourselves for safety and control. From this stance, we aren't fully alive. Self is estrangement, confined to the narrow parameters of what feels acceptable to us. Because the nature of all things is relationship, we're only wholly alive in relationship with this world within and around us. With practice, we develop the courage to land fully on earth and dissolve the obstructions that shield, protect, and separate us. We feel our intimate unfolding relationship to sense experience, to other human beings, to all things. In the process, we heal the estrangement of self.

As our relationship with life grows, we increasingly feel that we are made real through love. A more porous connection with life gives birth to tenderness. Not separating ourselves, touched and being touched, we fall in love with this world. We love the red squirrel hunting for acorns, the light shining on the Kwan Yin statue, and the drivers on the distant highway. We care for suffering, the pain in the knee, and the dying maple tree.

We delight in joy, the song of the hermit thrush, and the purple blossoms of the wood aster. We are universe capable, able to hold it all in the great expanse of the heart-mind.

Both masculine and feminine paradigms of expressing not-self are important. The masculine paradigm points toward the transcendence of the spacious mind, not stuck anywhere or to anything. The more feminine archetype expressed from the heart feels our embeddedness in this world, our tender connection with other living beings. Our embodied self knows that we are in relationship with all things, including bears, daisies, and rocks. With an unobstructed heart, we belong fully to this earth and to all upon her. We are actualized by myriad things.

Becoming Ordinary

When we first start practicing meditation, we hope it will make us special. People will notice, of course. Maybe it's better to aspire to be ordinary. Ha! Seriously, being special is too much work; we have to continually maintain it. Being an influencer must be a horrible job. Imagine having to be special day after day. So much stress.

Many of us begin meditation practice hoping to improve ourselves. We'd like dramatic things to happen that give us a place to hang a sense of self—a good self, we hope. We would like to be superhuman or transcend being human entirely. However, when we meditate properly, there is no way to avoid seeing how very human we are. Down-to-earth dharma involves learning nonresistance to our humanness.

Resting in our humanity does not come easy, however. We resist our human nature in many ways, both subtle and overt. Pablo d'Ors reports that his Zen teacher "makes it clear that I'm not yet who I truly am, but rather still someone too cunning and unnecessarily complex."[3] If we are practicing right, rather than becoming special, we regularly become disillusioned. Sawaki Roshi said, "No matter how many years you sit doing zazen [meditation], you will never become anything special."[4] Fantastic! Meditation is just connecting to life passing through, nothing extraordinary. We just become more ordinary.

Our life is made of run-of-the-mill moments. What parts of life are worth our attention? Where do we draw the line? Attention helps us cross the divide of disconnect and connect to our ordinary lives. Relaxing into our everyday reality, we may have to risk producing absolutely nothing. We worry about this. Yet connecting with being ordinary, the heart-mind cools off. It's refreshing, like a dip in a cool lake on a hot day. We can settle into the present moment, all the insignificant moments that make up most of our lives. We don't need our next hit of entertainment or self-aggrandizement.

Meditation practice helps us to drop more deeply into the truth of our own unique lives. As we come back to our own experience repeatedly, we learn to trust it. *What is the truth right now, in this moment?* It is as it is, not better than, equal to, or less than anybody else's experience. Life manifests from causes and conditions. All that arises passes away. None of it can truly be owned. There's no point in getting too dramatic. We still have passion for life and love, but the afflictive drama wears itself out. We are our own crazy, idiosyncratic, eccentric self. Beautiful! We settle into authenticity.

The Buddhist teachings on *mana* point to the deepest binding of the heart. Translated as "conceit" or "comparing," mana describes any inclination to see ourselves as better than, equal to, or worse than others. Essentially, these three views emerge from conceiving of ourselves as separate. We pull out of embeddedness and assess from a distance. Trusting ourselves to be ordinary is an antidote to this binding of self. Of course, there are times and places to shine—for example, in our careers. Yet in meditation, trying to excel just gets in the way by strengthening the sense of a separate self. Maybe we will have to settle with not looking so spiritual after all. Maybe we will just become more alive.

Less concern about ourselves and our placement compared to others leads to the growth of humility. My teacher, Michele, once said to me, "If our meditation practice isn't making us more humble, what are we *doing*?" Humility is a quality of great depth and freedom. We may mistakenly believe that humility is about feeling less than. No, its great freedom is stepping out of the whole paradigm of comparing. We are less interested in shoring up the ego and more interested in playing our role in life as best we can, learning as we go. Humility embraces "don't know" mind, beginner's mind, receptive to whatever feedback we get about where we still have work to do. We trust ourselves enough to not need to posture. In fact, we welcome feedback, whether from others or the phenomenal world. The Catholic priest Richard Rohr said, "I have prayed for years for one humiliation every day and then, I must watch my reaction to it."[5] Our reactions help us spot our shadow and self-aggrandizing strategies. As we release ourselves from perfectionism and the pressure to be extraordinary and acknowledge where we need to grow. we can express our own unique personality and talents.

As we connect more with the truth of our experience, we develop humble authenticity. With humility strong, we let go of defensiveness, strategizing, arrogance, and worthlessness. We release ourselves from posturing and comparing. Humility rests on a sense of total adequacy, freeing the energy we have put into trying to shore up our sense of self. The Japanese hermit poet Ryokan expresses the lightness of humility in a short poem recounting playing with the children in the village. He ends, "Last year a foolish monk; this year no change!"[6] Humility recognizes that this spiritual path is a long road and constantly measuring our progress is fruitless, bound to lead to suffering. The task is to keep walking, putting one foot in front of the other. Then, being ordinary, this unique life shines out with authenticity as a gift to this world.

Emptiness and Love

On retreat, I walk at the seashore accompanied by the late afternoon sunset. The sound of the ocean waves is the sound of emptiness, including both the crash and the silence between them. The arising crescendo and the dissipation of the waves exist in vast silent stillness. While we hear the silence under it all, there's so much wild action! The infinite and the startling vibrant beauty. Each wave is unique and yet part of the whole. The waves can't manifest without the ocean; the ocean has the nature to manifest as waves. This image of the ocean and waves is commonly used to describe the union of form and emptiness.

Early Buddhism emphasizes *sunyata*, or "emptiness," as emptiness of an independent self. We subtract and subtract and subtract everything that we think is truly independent, including our very selves, and arrive at nothing. *Nada, nada, nada.* Everything can be broken down into parts made of parts made of parts until eventually we arrive at wide-open space. In the resulting spaciousness we find the lack of solidity of anything that can be nailed down. What is there to hold on to? Our understanding of emptiness comes from feeling the all-pervasive truth of impermanence; everything is in flux. The rapid and fluid nature of change creates a world in which nothing is fixed or dense.

For some, however, the word *emptiness* can be problematic. We may associate it with a frightening void where nothing is happening. Why would we want to go someplace that's so, well, empty? The word *sunyata* could just as well be translated as "fullness" or "boundlessness." Everything is in relationship. Because nothing has an independent existence, everything is intimately connected to everything else, linked in a vast net of relationships. At no time are we separate from this fabric of reality. This dynamic field includes you and me and the sun and the earth and the flowers and the sewage and every emotion and every cause and condition, and it's all shifting, vibrant, and alive! From this perspective, the ground of being is seen as a great potentiality from which life springs forth and to which it returns. Always springing forth, a boundless fullness continually manifests.

Chan Master Hua from the City of 10,000 Buddhas said, "The actual Dharma is just this Dharma of true emptiness and wonderful existence. True emptiness is not empty. Why? Because it contains wonderful existence. Wonderful existence does not exist. Why? Because it encompasses true emptiness.... It is said, 'True emptiness does not obstruct wonderful existence; wonderful existence does not hinder true emptiness.'"[7] Did you get that? Perhaps not, but we feel the coming together of the wide-open space of heart and mind infused with this amazing world of form. Yes, this existence is ephemeral, arising and passing away like bubbles in a stream. And it's also true that life exists and it's wondrous. Emptiness and existence do not cancel each other out, but rather coexist. The freest heart-mind has no preference for emptiness and no preference for form, but rather abides in the intermingling of the two in this amazing universe.

These two perspectives of emptiness and fullness support each other. The wisdom aspect of emptiness cautions us not to subscribe to independent existence anywhere in this fullness, to not own anything in this wild manifestation of life. The profound wisdom of emptiness reminds us that everything arises and passes away. The perspective of emptiness saves us from drowning in the suffering and drama of the world. Less identified with passing phenomena, we don't get so trapped in aversion and craving. The heart-mind can be flexible, wise, and loving in its responses, of true service in this world of full emptiness.

The heart orientation of fullness reminds us not to consider emptiness as a cold void where nothing is happening. Fullness reminds us that we are in relationship with the world around us and drifting off into the ether is not mature spirituality. The perspective of fullness invokes love and compassion. Life is met through the heart imbued with spaciousness.

We can consider these two paradigms of sunyata as the meeting of wisdom and love. Seen from the angle of wisdom, we are nothing. Approached from the perspective of love, we are everything. "Wisdom tells me I am nothing, love tells me I am everything, and between these two my life flows," as summed up in the well-known words of Sri Nisargadatta. We embrace both aspects of existence because between them our life streams and carries on.

When we drop awareness into the heart and experience emptiness from this space, it becomes obvious that emptiness and love co-arise. The heart not bound in the conceptual or energetic realm of separation is naturally touched by the world of form. The spontaneous response to unobstructed connection is love and compassion. We genuinely allow ourselves to be touched by the world, and the heart responds.

Emptiness without love and compassion is void. It's too cool, like outer space, and can result in detachment. Nothing really matters, and the heart is whisked away from engagement and care. We want a juicy and alive emptiness, not a void and stark one. Compassion brings in the tenderness that moistens emptiness into fullness. Unconditional love blooms from deep in the heart and shines upon everything equally, recognizing relationship everywhere it turns. Love's juiciness makes the ordinary world sacred. We don't need to get out of here to find sacredness because we're drowning in it.

It's getting later in the fall, and the leaves are falling off the trees. There's so much light and uncluttered space. That space, that openness and lightness, remind me of emptiness. When the leaves fall down, space and light remain. The trees are still there, life still goes on, but with a luminous background. In the same way, when we clear out the clutter of our own hearts and minds, our lives go on, sweetly connected with all this against a backdrop of luminous spaciousness.

FREEDOM

Letting Go

I get off the plane in Chicago and walk to the board to check my connection to Hartford, the last flight of the evening. CANCELED. I think, *No, it's not true.* I check again. CANCELED. *Really, is it possible?* I check again. CANCELED. Now I'm stuck in Chicago for the night. *Ugh. I hate this. I really wanted to get home. Why do they cancel the last flight of the day? I so wish this weren't true. Damn airlines!* Sitting with my aversion for a few moments, it starts to shift and I finally let go. *Okay, this is the way it is right now. What do I need to do next?*

Letting go is coming to peace with the way things are. What are we letting go of? Our attachment. We aren't letting go of the desired thing, as that has moved on quite well on its own, but rather releasing our grip on the desired thing. *Letting be* might be a more appropriate term. Moment by moment we have the opportunity to settle into life as it is manifesting right now, releasing any resistance. We let things be, minus any struggle with the flow of change.

The process of accommodating unwanted change unfolds in several phases. Our first line of defense typically involves denial that things have changed. The computer won't work. *No, it's not true!* The flight is canceled. *No, it can't be! It's not happening!* The water heater broke. *No, it must just be taking a break!* My earring is lost. *No, it must be around here somewhere!* With this form of holding on, we aren't ready yet to even acknowledge that things have changed.

Once we connect with the truth that the computer is not working, the flight is canceled, the water heater is definitely broken, and our earring is nowhere to be found, then reactivity sets in. *No, this is not the way I wanted it to be! I want the computer to work. I want the flight to take off. I want hot water. And I want my earring!* The fantasy of grasping and aversion maintains the illusion that wishing things to be different can make them so. Depending on our skill in letting go and the intensity of the situation, this phase can last anywhere from a couple of seconds to many years. David Foster Wallace described our human predicament when he said, "Everything I've ever let go of has claw marks all over it."[1]

Another flight scenario (flying is an excellent opportunity to learn about letting go) unfolded after I spent three weeks on retreat in Upper Myanmar, when mindfulness and equanimity were strong. I arrived at the airport in Yangon for my flight to Bangkok where I was scheduled to give a talk to an English-speaking sangha that evening. After I approached the airline counter and handed the attendant my passport, she looked through her list with growing puzzlement and asked for my itinerary. I gave it to her, she examined it and said, "That flight was yesterday." I watched my mind process this information. *Not true. Not true. Don't like. Don't like. What do I do next?* The whole sequence lasted about two seconds. Then I was able to pay for a new ticket and get on the flight. With mindfulness and letting go, we can process change more quickly, sparing ourselves the turmoil and stress of reactivity.

From an active paradigm we hope that we can command letting go, that if we tell ourselves to let go, we will. *Just let go!* We all try it. It doesn't work. We cannot make letting go happen because letting go is a not-doing rather than a doing. It's not hanging on. From the receptive paradigm we allow our heart to have its experience. With mindfulness, we feel our way to letting go by anchoring viscerally in the body. We notice when we keep thinking the same story, attachment continues or even grows. Stories fuel holding on. When we proliferate about how the airlines messed up, we feed anger. When we feel the emotion within the body, a shift is possible. Sometimes we have to feel through several layers before we are ready to let go of our grip. Mindful awareness assists the heart to move toward resolution.

Letting go ends our argument with reality. We fight reality when we insist that what's unpleasant should go away and what's pleasant should come and stay. We argue with reality when we turn away from and deny the way things are right now. The three roots of suffering—grasping, aversion, and delusion—are really three ways of resisting reality. Reality always wins because this moment is just the way it is. Ending our argument with reality is fully accepting that things are as they are. We cultivate wholehearted unconstrained cooperation with life.

Letting go leads to the peaceful mind state of equanimity, what the Buddha called the highest happiness that we can experience in this mundane realm. The equanimous heart-mind remains balanced and graceful in the face of the ups and downs, the pains and pleasures, and the joys and sorrows of life. Equanimity gives up magical thinking of an improved reality and lands here fully. We engage in life with poise and dignity, letting go of attachment and aversion and resting in the truth of how things are right now. We grow up and become a mature adult.

We can practice surrendering to reality with the small challenges of our daily lives, like having a headache. We don't want to have a headache, but that's our reality right now. We may hate the headache, wish that we didn't have a headache, resist the headache, but the truth is that right now we have a headache. We end our argument with reality when we settle into the pain and open our hearts to our experience in the moment. And yes, please take a pain reliever. Letting go does not mean that we don't respond. We still act skillfully, with wisdom, from a place of greater clarity.

Because letting go is a process, we learn to make peace with the process itself. Radical equanimity is the capacity to be okay with not being okay. In another flight scenario, I arrive at the airport in Portland, Oregon, after seventeen days of travel, ready to fly home to the East Coast and sleep in my own bed that night. I put my credit card in the machine and am informed that it's too late to board the flight. After being refused an exception, I sit down and observe my reaction. I'm upset. This is the last flight home. My ride has left, and I have to figure out where I'm going to stay for the night and fly the next day. A voice on my shoulder says, *Rebecca, you're a dharma teacher. You should be doing better than this!* Another voice replies, *Well, I'm not and that's okay.* I feel fine with the fact that I am upset. Every few minutes, I check in with myself, *Am I okay with this yet? Nope, I'm still angry.* After a while, the reactivity shifts, and I am ready to think about my plans for the evening. Radical equanimity is okay with not being equanimous. We trust the heart's capacity to find its way.

All the little annoyances of our life teach us about letting go. We experience a number of them every day. People don't do what we want them to do; situations don't turn out the way we want them to turn out; we lose something; we have to deal with something we don't want to deal with or don't get something we want. All these little annoyances can strengthen our capacity to let go and rest in equanimity. We don't like them, but we can appreciate them as our teachers. *Here's a chance to practice letting go.*

We also practice letting go when bigger changes happen. Climate change has given us a chance to see how we collectively argue with reality. Attachment to the way things have been manifests as denial of our current reality and our need to change. Accepting that we live in a different world now is a struggle. We still fight this emerging reality, not fully embracing that things have changed. The climate of our planet is not the same as it was before. We are clawing our way to accepting this truth. We can then be more creative and compassionate in our response to the world as it is now.

The bigger challenges in life—like climate change, losing a loved one, a serious health diagnosis, or a pandemic—require us to cultivate even greater capacity. It takes longer to let go, and that's okay. We humans take time to process big changes. Demanding that we be perfect spiritual practitioners who always know how to let go quickly is oppressive. It's not kind. Compassion assists us on this journey. We care about the pain as it's unraveling. We care about ourselves as we claw our way to letting go. Although we can't demand letting go, we get better at it. We learn the pathway, we come to trust it, and our heart is drawn toward the sweet freedom of release.

I teach at Common Ground Meditation Center in Minneapolis where a sign on the office wall reads, "This is the way things are right now." When I find myself lacking equanimity, this phrase helps me surrender to the truth. Short mantras like this can help us consider the possibility of letting go by inclining the heart-mind toward relaxing our grip. We drop in a suggestion and see if it takes. Here are some examples.

This is life manifesting.
Just this.
Just unpleasant.
Just pleasant.
Is this moment okay?
Do I have a problem right now?

These invitations can help turn the heart-mind in the direction of letting go of struggle and resting in current reality, down to earth.

Equanimity is not the end of the story but rather the beginning of the response. Obviously, we have agency and we should use it. With a more peaceful heart, we respond with more clarity, flexibility, and adaptability. Having calmed down the story of *what I want*, we can ask, *What does this situation call for?* From this stance of less reactivity, we are more likely to respond in helpful ways that avoid causing harm and contribute to the greater good. We fully acknowledge the wildness of the world and learn how to meet it—even to dance and thrive in it. No longer confined by our agendas, we can be truly responsive to life as it manifests.

When I was a child, my father would rent movies (yes, real movies on reels) from the local library, and we would watch them as a family. Almost every time my dad went to the library, I begged him to rent my favorite movie, *The Railrodder*, featuring Buster Keaton, a famous silent movie comedian. (Disclaimer: This movie might not be anything like what I remember.) The story follows the journey of an Englishman who, after reading a newspaper article about Canada, jumps off a bridge in London and walks out of the surf on the east coast of Canada. Buster discovers an old open-air railway car that he uses to journey across Canada. His little car has a box in the middle from which he pulls out everything he needs. Many wild things happen in this movie, and I loved his steadfast poise in the face of a series of obstacles. With a background *do-dee-do* soundtrack, light and easy, he sits tall and dignified, enjoying the scenery and responding skillfully to whatever comes his way. When it rains, he pulls an umbrella out of the box, and when it snows, he finds a down coat. When buffaloes cross the track, he stops to watch them. When he needs to sleep, he pulls out a blanket and pillow, and when it's teatime, he draws out tea service. As a child, I delighted many times over in seeing his ability to respond without being perturbed, the essence of equanimity.

There Is No Perfect Kuti

A recent online ad features a car set against a background of wide-open space and majestic mountains. A person gets in the car and turns it on, and the voice-over says, *This is what freedom sounds like.* Then a hand puts an air freshener in the car and the voice-over says, *This is what freedom smells like.* While I appreciate the sense-based intimacy, the message is problematic. This ad encapsulates our conventional idea that freedom is the ability to get away from it all to someplace better and more beautiful. Freedom is masking what is unpleasant, trying to make everything pleasant. In Buddhism, we propose a different idea. Freedom doesn't need to mask anything; it includes both the pleasant and the unpleasant. When we are free, we don't need to escape. We can land fully right here, right now. With mindfulness as our vehicle and the dharma as our air freshener, we explore a freedom not dependent on conditions.

During my first long retreat, when I was only twenty-four, I spent a month trying to figure out how I was going to be happy for the rest of my life. This pressing question kept arising: *How am I going to be happy?* My mind imagined many possible alternatives, but they all had downfalls. I would be a hermit living in a hut in the mountains, and then I would be happy. But I would get lonely. I could join a spiritual community and have companionship, but then again, some of the people would very likely drive me crazy. I should get married and have children and that would make me happy. But oh, so much responsibility! I experienced tremendous fear this month as no option seemed viable. When I woke up every morning, the first thing I noticed was fear.

Then one afternoon during my meeting with my teacher, Sharon, I found myself saying, "It looks like nothing in this world is going to make me permanently happy." "Yep," she agreed. I continued, "So it looks like the only place I might find happiness is in the moment and my job is to figure out how to be happy right now." "Yep," she nodded. That afternoon the fear disappeared. I stopped looking for happiness in a misguided way, causing despair and discouragement. Once I knew where to focus my gaze, I was no longer afraid. I found happiness by giving up looking for it anywhere but here and now.

One year on retreat in Myanmar, a friend and I found ourselves comparing our meditation huts, each secretly hoping that ours would turn out to be the better one. My kuti was smoky, noisy, and hot, but it had few bugs and a lovely view of the Irrawaddy River Valley. Her hut was quiet and cool and the air was cleaner, but it had more bugs, mosquitoes, and snakes and was stuck back in a narrow grotto with no view at all. We concluded that there is no perfect kuti. This phrase became my shorthand for giving up the expectation of finding some perfect circumstances that would make me happy and a reminder to land right where I am and find happiness here. *There is no perfect kuti.*

Our hunt for perfection may spill over into our meditation path. We try this teaching and then that teaching, looking for the perfect teaching that will save us. We believe accumulating more teachings must be better, but too many options may just leave us confused. We are not sure if we should practice this technique or that technique, and sometimes, they even seem contradictory. There is no perfect teaching. Perhaps we can learn from monastic life where, for the first five years of training, the monk or nun stays with their preceptor studying one set of teachings. After this time, their teacher may recommend that they study with a different teacher in order to augment or balance their practice. I stayed in the same lineage primarily with the same teachers for the first thirteen years of my practice, and this consistency provided clarity and depth. Yes, do some spiritual shopping, but when you find a place that feels like home, remain there for a while. The Buddha said you are more likely to find water if you dig one well one hundred feet deep rather than ten wells ten feet deep. Stay and dig deep.

Surrender and Trust

We come to meditation practice hoping to find strategies that will help us control this wild world and our untamed heart-mind. And yes, we do encounter techniques to manage the inner and outer turbulence and find some peace. We learn how to rest the attention with the breath or another home base in order to strengthen calm. We become more skilled in meeting emotions mindfully, gaining dexterity so that we don't have to repress or drown in them. We develop awareness of our impulses to act and learn to pause, reflecting on the skillfulness of what we're about to do. We increase our ability to call forth kindness for ourselves and others. These learnings build our confidence that we can face life as it is. We trust our increased capacity to deal with the world. We have faith in these techniques that protect us from being overwhelmed with the wildness of life, now better able to manage our responses to the changing conditions around and within us. This trust grows moment by moment, day by day, year by year, as we turn toward the reality in the here and now and deal with it. Our progress is not usually linear—we face peaks and valleys—yet over time we can notice the evolution of this strength and trust. Having this confidence is a huge blessing in our lives, as it facilitates our ability to relax into the present moment however it manifests.

At some point, however, these strategies begin to fail, and that's a good place to enter more deeply into practice. Yes, we have found techniques to manage our hearts and minds better, yet the world is still wildly uncontrollable. The mind is chaotic, wandering this way and that as it wishes. Emotions arise and plague us even though we wish they wouldn't. Our body experiences pain and sickness no matter how well we take care of it. It's all so very messy, wild, and ungovernable. Meeting and accepting this truth with an open heart is the ultimate strategy that brings us the deepest peace.

The feminine paradigm accepts that life is untamable. We enter this realization slowly, as we don't exactly experience it as good news. It incrementally dawns on us as we sit with these ever-changing bodies, hearts, and minds, that things are a bit wilder than we had assumed. Attempting to control what is happening within us, we experience increased frustration as this strategy doesn't pan out. We fail time and again to get this heart, body, and mind to obey our wishes. In our struggle, the peace we have been seeking seems further away than ever. Yet failing is necessary because it teaches us that we are looking in the wrong place.

After failing often enough, we give up and surrender to whatever is happening. We are surprised to find that this brings tastes of the peace we had been seeking. We think, *Now that I know what to do, I'll just surrender!* Yet we find surrendering cannot be commanded either. We surrender only once we truly accept our control strategies aren't working. We have to wear out our usual tactics with mindfulness and slowly come to accept that control is not going to bring the happiness that we're looking for. We learn to surrender, giving up hope for a better present.

Over time, we deepen our knowledge of the flavor of surrender, another word for letting go. We learn within ourselves, viscerally, what letting go feels like. While it cannot be commanded, we can discover how to feel our way toward it. Our heart remembers the sweet relief and more easily risks the vulnerability of letting go. Surrendering takes courage, moment by moment, to leap out of our known ways of managing this unmanageable universe and fly free, groundless. Although we may experience moments of profound surrender, for the most part this willingness doesn't happen all at once. We try out surrendering and see what happens. Then our old habits reassert themselves. This is not a mistake. This is just how we humans learn: opening and then retreating to the safety of the known to check it all out. So we open again. Gradually, our taste for this unburdened heart-mind strengthens, and we increasingly trust this wide-open space of the heart and mind. We decide, *I think it's okay to hang out here a bit more.*

Trust is essential to surrender. With deepening practice, we learn to trust in something deeper than the logic and words of the conceptual mind. This wider space is a huge compassionate awareness beyond our small self. We develop faith in something bigger than our small life. We could say we learn to trust life. We could call it the unconditioned or Kwan Yin. We trust what is behind the manifest: the formless, the unborn. In this paradigm, we are gambling on something that has nothing to do with ourselves, that's bigger than ourselves. We aren't trusting that terrible things won't happen to us because they will. Life is a shipwreck. Something is always coming at us that we must deal with. Even if we're a hermit, this is true. This body breaks down, challenging life situations arise, we have to feed and shelter ourselves and heal our wounds. Life is a lot to manage, and it rarely goes according to our exact wishes. In this wider space of trust, life is unfolding according to its own laws and isn't about what we want.

Because the fear of death blocks the portal to this wider space, ultimately we must trust that it's okay to die. You may be thinking, *Well, that came out of left field!* Yet it all comes down to this and, of course, this trust doesn't come so easy. Our fallback mammalian conditioning is geared entirely toward survival. We don't yet have faith in this larger space because it's not enough about us. Our human conditioning entails being consumed by the needs and wants of this smaller self, yet to be trapped in this smaller self is basic suffering. We learn flexibility in crossing the portal into larger space by surrendering the compulsion to protect ourselves at all costs. Then the two spaces can live together: the space where we do what we need to do to take care of ourselves to survive and the vaster space that is bigger than our individual survival. Our lives go on, less encumbered, and we feel free to play in this universe.

The Heart Is a Feral Cat

The ultimate goal of practice is the freedom of the unobstructed heart-mind: the unbinding in the heart-mind of the fetters of greed, hatred, and delusion that manifest as limitation, contraction, hardness, and dullness.

The ten-million-dollar question is then, *How does the heart-mind become free of these obstructions?*

We unbind the heart-mind by meeting its myriad experiences with warmhearted awareness. The obstructions of the heart-mind dissolve through the power of this awareness. They don't melt through what we do, but rather through the inexplicable power of awakening. Of course, we do do something: we create the conditions that support this mysterious process in unfolding. But ultimately, the opening is not in our control. *We* don't do the unbinding; awareness does it. We can't really take credit.

Unbinding takes place throughout our physical, mental, emotional, psychological, energetic, and cellular bodies. Unbinding expresses itself as openness in place of obstruction, ease instead of tension, space where contraction existed, liveliness where deadness was present. A long process of becoming intimate with obstructions, honest about our experience, willing to meet it all, leads to increasing transparency. Blockage and entanglement dissolve. What's left is the open heart in touch with life.

We can also describe this journey as learning to relax ever more deeply. We settle into ever deeper relaxation on every level of our being: heart, mind, body, nervous system, cells. We soften our habitual defensive patterning of hardening and activating to make sure we aren't harmed and can get ahead in the world and relax the conditioning always on alert for what comes next. We nourish the ability to settle back into right here, right now.

This opening process is rarely linear and involves honest engagement with our heart's response to dissolving habitual protections. The human heart is a complicated and wild creature. Like a feral cat showing up at your door, it exhibits both fierce protection and the desire to open and connect. My husband and I have adopted several feral cats from the woods behind the Insight Meditation Society. The first one we named la Feroza (or La-la for short) which means "the ferocious one" in Spanish. La-la was about six months old when we took her in, and she never did tame up. She taught me that it is necessary to have immense respect for a feral cat and they make the rules. When we approach a feral cat too quickly, they run away, so we must wait until they come to us. When we patiently hang out, as they finally feel safe enough, they come closer. I learned to love La-la's ferociousness, her absolute commitment to her own safety.*

Our own heart is similar to la Feroza: ferocious in its need for protection and safety. We want to have immense respect for these requirements. When we approach too quickly, our heart will run away. Whenever we push our own agenda about how our heart should feel or when and how it should open, the heart will not share its secrets with us. The heart does not like to be bossed around. Nothing closes the heart faster than to be told what kind of experience it is supposed to have. When we hang out patiently, however, with kindness and respect, the heart begins to show itself to us. We establish a relationship based on accepting our heart just as it is, quietly letting it reveal its complications, despair, joy, sorrow, care, turbulence, and peace.

After la Feroza relocated, we adopted two kittens born to a feral mother, naming them Pearl and Sparky. Pearl was more skittish and protective, wanting connection and yet fearful of it. She was tamer than La-la but still needed lots of space in order to come forward. We couldn't move in on Pearl; she was the one who set the agenda. I appreciated that Pearl learned her whole life. At her own pace, she kept growing. Even up to shortly before her death of old age, she was still taking risks to trust more and to come closer. Sometimes our heart is like Pearl: more complicated, willing to open and risk, but the pacing is slow. We can appreciate the tempo of our hearts and not push them to open faster than they're ready, trusting their nature is to continue to grow.

Sparky, on the other hand, is unconflicted about his love of connection. He can be approached anytime and responds with lots of purring and cuddling. He delights in being close and loves to play. Sparky is uncomplicated. Sometimes our heart is uncomplicated like Sparky: open and connected.

---

* One time when we were away, la Feroza disappeared. A couple months later our neighbors told us about the new cat who had taken up residence in their woodshed: la Feroza. She lived out the rest of her years in peace in her own outdoor hut.

When we give our heart respect, no matter how it's manifesting, it finds its way toward connection and love. We learn not to demand results, but rather to trust our hearts' process.

Vulnerability and Resistance

This morning while walking outside, I was caught in thinking about teaching in person during the pandemic. With my mind absorbed in my drama, I didn't feel my feet or the breeze or hear the sound of the wind in the pines. Being wrapped up in my cognitive world, my contact with the environment was dulled. This cocooning in self-absorption removed me from more direct connection with the world around me. I was also less alive. Later, when my mind quieted, I felt my foot touch the earth, saw the bare trees clearly outlined in the woods, and heard the distant traffic. This intimate connection felt more alive, and yet also more vulnerable. I was penetrable, able to be touched. The wind could brush my cheek with a soft caress or hit me with a cold stinging bite. Landing fully in the present moment, we move closer to life, or we could say, life moves closer to us. As we become more able to be touched by life, we feel the true condition of our intimate vulnerability with life both within and around us.

Vulnerability is the ability to be affected as described in my morning walk. Vulnerability, the foundation of any authentic relationship, means letting our guard down so that we can connect in an undefended manner. Vulnerability is the courageous stance of the heart willing to forgo the protective cocoon of dullness and reactivity in favor of genuine engagement with this wild world. Melting the barriers of the heart-mind, we let ourselves be touched. We become more sensitive; sights, sounds, smells, tastes, body sensations, and emotions all become more vibrant and alive. Before, the reactive barriers of our heart and mind muted the experience of life. Now, with more transparency, we begin to feel the true nature of the world as alive, moving, and energized.

This exquisite vulnerability is both deeply moving and deeply terrifying. We feel moved to be so intimate with this world in which we are embedded. It's like being in love. It's also terrifying to be so intimate with this world in which we are embedded, so wild and uncontrollable! With our profound wish for intimacy, we work out our fear of being overwhelmed with the wildness of life. Our usual antidote to the wildness of life is control, the opposite of vulnerability. We busily demand that the experiences of life be the way we want. Using our protective strategies of grasping, aversion, and delusion, we micromanage life, conceptualizing, projecting, twisting, and manipulating the apparent outside world to do what we want. We are hoping for invulnerability, but we get the suffering of alienation.

With exquisite vulnerability we surrender our job as manager of the universe.. The seventeenth-century Japanese haiku master Issa wrote, "Simply trust. Do not also the petals flutter down just like that?"[2] Minus our defenses of control, life is less dense and more spacious. Rather than commanding the world, we receive it with trust, and we may be both startled and delighted by how different it looks from the one we have been making up. This universe is so much more alive, unpredictable, and refreshing than we had supposed. We can rest here, in this world of incredible possibility.

Meditation is a process of melting our resistance to life as it is. Life flows as ever-changing sense experiences, whether pleasant, unpleasant, or neutral, and mostly out of our control. Resistance is our attempt to control the uncontrollable, to manage life to suit our demands. Resistance is the heart-mind's way of buying time while growing strong enough to land in reality as it is. We can rest right there in our wish to stay protected, in this hardness that shields us from this direct connection with life. Eventually, we get tired of it. A willingness arises on its own to risk dropping the shielding. Over time the willingness becomes allowing, and gradually allowing becomes embracing. This process doesn't happen all at once; we go through these phases over and over again.

Resistance manifests as contraction, inflexibility, and hardness within the heart, body, and mind. Our job is to feel where we have hardened and meet these places with softness. When in doubt, soften, soften, soften. We can start with the physical body, noticing where there is contraction. We allow the hardness to soften just a bit, and in doing so, we let in what we've been trying to keep out. We connect with hardness or contraction in the mind, the heart, and the energetic field. We touch this tension with the softness of cotton balls. Anywhere we sense tightness, we encourage relaxation, embarking on a journey with many ups and downs and unexpected twists of the road. We slowly allow the heart to soften and grow in its ability to be fully present and alive. It's generally not a short-term project.

Living life changing in each moment, not knowing what the next moment will bring, is a wild ride. Cultivating the strength to hold so much vulnerability takes time. We call upon patience, kindness, and compassion. Opening unfolds on a timetable that's perfect, even if we can't see that right now. Many times I have felt that my practice is unfolding *sooooo* slowly, only to understand later that it couldn't have been otherwise. We resist, resist, resist, until finally surrendering becomes an option. We're finally ready and strong enough to be with things as they are.

As we move toward a closer engagement with life, we strengthen the heart-mind to be able to hold this greater sensitivity. We learn equanimity, poise, amid the pleasantness and unpleasantness that touches us. We strengthen love, the ability to soften, to take care, and to be kind. These qualities become our guardians and our protections. As they grow stronger, the wildness of the world feels increasingly manageable. We can be vulnerable without being overwhelmed.

Sensitivity and vulnerability do not always grow at the same pace as equanimity and love. We are challenged when the sensitivity has increased but we don't yet have the equanimity to hold it all. During these difficult times of practice, we're getting a bit more than we bargained for and may experience anxiety or overwhelm. Eventually, equanimity catches up and we feel peaceful, regulated, and capable. The two phases of practice—the turbulent and the peaceful—inter-are. Each feeds the other in deepening spirals of peace. The times of turbulence give us a chance to stretch our capacity and lead into more profound periods of peace. Then we see again where we're stuck. The cycles continue, with both more profound yet subtler levels of stuckness and peace manifesting. These cycles can happen in a meditation period, in a day, and in years. We learn to trust them, rather than despairing during the times of turbulence and getting attached during the times of peace. Together they are the whole package. We foster invulnerability by going through this vulnerability, not the pathway we expected. We cultivate the unshakable liberation of the heart-mind, the ultimate invulnerable vulnerability.

The Deepest Peace

The deepest peace and freedom of heart and mind fall in the realm of the nonconceptual, thoroughly embedded in the receptive paradigm. We can't peg it down or describe it conceptually, so it's hard to talk about. Surrendering the conceptual messes with us. We had hoped that we could think our way to freedom, that our reliance on the conceptual mind would liberate us. Yet any constructs are already outside of the nonconceptual realm of deepest peace. The best the Buddha could do was describe what it is not: it's the unborn, undying, uncreated, unformed. The realm of the unconditioned, of nibbana, is an inchoate mystery, supremely feminine. We can point to it, we can allude to it, but the actual experience is beyond description. Sometimes we glimpse it, in our peripheral vision . . . *Oh yes, there it went.* We might catch it in the shimmer of the trees, the sudden ringing beep of the truck, or the soft sunlight on the worn carpet. We sense it in our own quiet heart and luminous mind, but we can't grasp it enough to explain it.

This freedom is also an aspect of the world of form—of you and me, of the earth, of the crow, of the rock. This is much easier to pin down; this is the world that we know. Because the unconditioned is not separate from life itself, it has a nontranscendent partner in the world of form. It's both transcendent and immanent. The feminine paradigm of awakening doesn't place freedom in the future as a goal that we are going to reach in this life, in the afterlife, or in transcendence of life, but rather lands it solidly in the now, in the wild aliveness of this world, in our own radiant hearts that are strong and flexible enough to meet unceasing change in the vast splendor of emptiness. The unconditioned is not someplace we can get to that isn't here; it's embedded here all the time. We let go of striving to achieve some way out and rest our weary hearts and minds in the cradle of now imbued with wakefulness and compassion. Home is right here.

Letting go is the price to rest in this freedom. To repeat the poet T. S. Eliot: "Quick now here now always. A condition of complete simplicity costing not less than everything."[3] It's so simple that we miss it, and the price of admission is giving up our usual ways of making it in this world: in other words, everything. The complex world of conceptual knowing must surrender to the simple realm of not knowing. We give up all demands that the world conform to our preferences, all insistence that we exist as a separate being that needs management, landing us in the groundless ground of the mind and the wide-open space of the heart. Freedom is all subtraction, and once we have eliminated what is obstructing, awakening is realized. It dawns on us.

Touching this freedom requires complete surrender. The cost is abandoning any quibbles we have with this world—the way it is, the way it manifests. We tend to be willing to pay this steep price only when we have exhausted all other options. Meditation is the practice of wearing out failing strategies. Meditation must grind down our stubborn insistence on willpower as the means to save us. We genuinely accept that we live in a world of wild incessant change. We acknowledge that it is a challenging world, that we suffer from painful bodies and mind states, attachment when things change, and an existential tremor due to never knowing what is coming our way. We know deep in our hearts that holding on to any of it as ours, as controllable, is incompatible with the free heart. The heart-mind no longer confined by its own agenda opens to the unfolding play of the entire world.

Teijitsu, the eighteenth-century abbess of Hakujuan, a Japanese Zen Buddhist nunnery, experienced this release as an opening into the entire world. In *Women of the Way*, we read, "She saw that all phenomena arose, abided, and fell away. She saw that knowing arose, abided, and fell away. Then she knew there was nothing more than this, no ground, nothing to lean on stronger than the cane she held, nothing to lean upon at all, and no one leaning, and she opened the clenched fist in her mind and let go, and fell, into the midst of everything."[4]

Sometimes this groundless ground is more wide-open than our ego would prefer. We want the spaciousness of the unobstructed heart-mind, but maybe we don't want too much of it. It gets pretty quiet. *Where am I?* The ego gets concerned that there isn't enough of *me* in the unobstructed heart. *Let's think a bit so I can be sure that I exist.* Our ego likes its job of ensuring our survival by micromanaging the world to suit our preferences. The ego doesn't like to rest, because resting looks like death, enlightenment looks like death. The ego will reassert its ability to do its job. This is okay, just how it unfolds. Our conditioning is strong, built up over eons. We can include the ego doing its job in the larger space of holding this human life. Over time, the ego gets acclimated to taking a break; sitting in the armchair relaxing with a cup of tea, looking out the window at the view, isn't such a bad life after all. Things keep running okay without hypermanagement.

We acclimate to the silence that emerges from the vast spaciousness of our own heart-mind. Stillness, silence. We listen to the world and receive it rather than own and demand it. Backing off from our mind-activated assertive stance with the world, we rest in receptivity. We are not separate but at the center, just like everything else is at the center, because there is no center. By decentering ourselves, we come back to center. We can hear this space below the hum of the traffic and the symphony of the creek. We can sense it but never own it. It belongs to no one and to nothing and to everyone and to everything. We withdraw from putting ourselves into everything and let things have their own life without our interference. We pull back our overinvolvement in the things of this world and let them be as they are. Everything is released into its natural state. Unencumbered connection with this world frees our heart and everything else from the burden of our interference.

This wide-open space is responsive, attuned to the world of form, the world in which we are embedded. Friendly and wanting to respond, we are ready to take care where we see suffering and rejoice where we meet beauty. Open awareness holds it all without being perturbed or disturbed. The world of form is not a problem; it is as it is, including vast suffering and vast beauty. How big can this compassionate space of our heart get?

We practice where we feel any limit or resistance, and the size of this compassionate space continues to expand and grow.

From the feminine paradigm, nibbana is the heart as wide and spacious as the entire universe. We experience freedom from entanglement and burden right in the middle of this very life. It's really quite simple. And it's really quite difficult. Freedom is never further away than here and now, never some other time or some other experience or some other place. That's the simplicity. The difficulty is the entanglement we habitually add to life. That's what we subtract when we relax. Our freedom evolves as a process of subtraction, dissolving everything in the way of natural openness. When we take away the entanglement, we're left with just life—awesome, mysterious, ordinary, simple, and just what we're looking for.

PART FOUR

ENGAGEMENT

12

————

THE PATH OF LOVE

Wisdom and Love

In traditional Theravada teachings, the heart and mind unbind through wisdom.[1] The truths of impermanence, suffering, and not-self (anicca, dukkha, and anatta) teach us to let go of clinging to any experience, thereby freeing the mind. Understanding deeply the nature of reality—suffering and the end of suffering—we attain nibbana, the ultimate liberation. The heart practices, particularly in the form of the four Brahmaviharas, are considered supplemental teachings, an adjunct that supports this process but not a liberation path in themselves.

We Westerners can easily get on board with this perspective and become fascinated with the wisdom teachings associated with the mind, passing over the importance of compassion and the heart. Once an experienced practitioner was talking with a Tibetan master about her PhD investigating very detailed Buddhist wisdom teachings on the nature of self and suffering. After she explained the intricacies of her studies, this Buddhist master surprised her by asking, "And does this help you to become more compassionate?" Our enthrallment with the world of the mind can absorb us, and we may neglect the realm of the heart.

Let's reconsider this preference for wisdom over love. Perhaps this model emerges from millennia of patriarchal conditioning. These traditional

229

meditation teachings have a decidedly mind-based flavor, relegating the heart to second place. Let's consider unbinding the heart through love as a path to free the heart-mind. The practice of love, carried to its deepest potential, liberates the heart-mind.* Love calls at every stage of cultivation for us to let go of attachment and self-centered concern. To fully develop the Brahmaviharas, we need to overcome greed, hatred, and delusion—the three fetters that shield the heart and ensnare us in separation. We must purify the heart of wanting anything, letting go wherever we encounter clinging. As love develops ever more deeply, it becomes increasingly unconditional. Less dependent on any object, this unbounded love rests in this open heart, the self dissolved. The indestructible heart remains. Both pathways—wisdom *and* love—free the heart and mind.

Perhaps it's time to own the path of love within Buddhism. Let's place it as a valid route right alongside the three characteristics and the Four Noble Truths in the journey to freedom. The teachings on love deepen the wisdom teachings, and the wisdom teachings further develop our capacity for love. Wisdom frees the mind through understanding that nothing can be clung to. Love liberates the heart through letting go of any contraction whatsoever checking its limitless potential. Wisdom infuses love with spaciousness. Love infuses wisdom with warmth. In the end they unify as one: warm spaciousness.

This equal emphasis on love may be part of the West's offering to the evolution of meditation practice in the Insight Meditation lineage of Buddhism. The Hispanic expression of the dharma may lead the way. In teaching Spanish-language retreats in California and Massachusetts with coteachers Andrea Castillo and bruni dávila, we have noticed that the participants tend to tune in above all to the teachings on love. The resulting warm engagement suggests that the flavor of the dharma in Spanish just might be love.

This co-emphasis on love is particularly relevant for these and the coming times as our society falls apart on so many levels. We're going to

---

* In the Metta Sutra, the heart freed through love is said to lead to third-stage enlightenment (nonreturner). The fourth stage—full enlightenment—is taught to arrive through wisdom.

need love, so much love. We will need wisdom, too, but without love, how do we care about and respond to all the suffering? Love opens the heart to engage with the real problems unfolding in our world. Love makes us strong enough to stay connected as things fall apart. Love might be what saves us all.

Transcendence and Immanence

What is the final goal of our meditation practice? Are we trying to get out of here or to be here with more aliveness? Do we want to transcend or land fully in this human life? Most patriarchal religions emphasize the transcendence of getting above or beyond our human condition, and Buddhism is no exception. In Early Buddhism, our goal is to become an arahant, a fully realized person, utterly free of clinging, who escapes suffering and will not be reborn in any form. Early Buddhist emphasis on saving ourselves has an individual and independent orientation that reflects the masculine paradigm. This way of approaching Buddhism aligns with our individualistic culture, and many in convert communities undertake a meditation practice for our own benefit and with the wish to transcend.

We could say the arahant ideal reflects the androcentric conditioning of Early Buddhism. What would our goal look like from the perspective of acknowledging our embeddedness, both caring for and celebrating existence? From the feminine paradigm, we emphasize immanence or "dwelling within": arriving fully into our humanity. Buddhism from this perspective points toward being alive and present here and now. Later Buddhism (Mahayana) reflects a shift into this more feminine perspective. The bodhisattva vow from Mahayana Buddhism envisions a more collective freedom, where we renounce our own full liberation until all beings are liberated. We can adopt this Mahayana shift right in the heart of our Theravada insight practice.

We need both paradigms: transcendence and embeddedness. The ability to transcend involves knowing how to go beyond our usual reactive conditioning of heart and mind and abide in spaciousness and freedom.

Without this capacity, we become lost in this world. Too much emphasis on transcendence, however, encourages disengagement from this very life with the promise of rewards in heaven (the unconditioned or release from the wheel of suffering). Why should we worry about this world when the real prize is someplace else? Individualist aspiration can discourage us from paying attention to and caring for the suffering of the planet and those around us. We're just trying to get out of here.

We balance transcendence with a spirituality that values this very world and encourages engagement. We want to be here and connect with each other. We wish to acknowledge the state of the world around us, care about it, and respond to it. The Buddha taught that laypeople should emphasize three parts of the path: heart-mind development, ethics, and generosity. Cultivating ethical integrity and giving brings in this balance and points toward our interconnectedness. In the rush to transcend, let's not forget about the heart expressions of the ethics of nonharming and the generosity of giving. These bring us right down to earth where we learn to act as decent and caring human beings.

Awakening while being embedded in this world means releasing our hearts from greed, hatred, and delusion without trying to escape. We engage life with a heart free of turbulence and obstructions, a heart that is unshakable in strength, and yet responsive to the world around us. Our heart-mind reflects the transcendence of the mountain high in the sky and the rootedness of the bamboo that sways and responds to the world around it. Steady and strong, flexible and responsive. Together.

Equanimity from the Heart

When our neighbor clear-cut his land just feet from our house, my heart broke each time I heard a tree crash to the forest floor. I felt deeply the stress of the beings of the land as their home was destroyed. I repeatedly asked myself, *Where is equanimity in this? How does my heart find peace in the midst of this violence?* This koan reverberated within for the year and a half the logging continued, as I made room for my heart's responses and slowly felt my way toward peace. Finally, one day it clicked:

my heart-mind landed with no resistance—*This is the way things are right now*—and I felt peace. Under circumstances of violence and destruction, equanimity arises from the willingness to fully inhabit the truth of now. We give up fighting the way things are and land in full presence, eyes open, feet on the ground, heart engaged. In this circumstance equanimity meant fully accepting that these trees were being cut and the land was being desecrated and being willing for my heart to break. Staying with heartbreak long enough, we open to a tender spacious peace that hums and reverberates, without turbulence, with the suffering of this world. Heartfelt equanimity.

A lot of heartbreaking things are going on these days. After the murder of George Floyd, I asked myself the same question: *What does equanimity mean in this situation?* Of course, I landed in the same place. Equanimity arises when we open to the suffering in this world fully without resistance. On the road to peace, we may need to grieve the loss of our illusions that the world is a better place than it actually is. For some of us, equanimity might mean being willing to be heartbroken about the pain of racial violence. For others, it may mean making space within the heart to hold rage and sorrow. Rather than moving quickly into spacious equanimity without allowing ourselves to feel, we accompany our heart as it feels its way to tender peace. Heartfelt equanimity, in the process of accepting the truth of our world, allows our hearts to be touched and to break open. Being willing to feel awakens our wish to engage in alleviating the suffering that is in our world.

The climate catastrophe also challenges us to explore our heart's response to violence and destruction. We let in the heartbreaking changes in our immediate environment and our larger world and give space for our heart to respond. We may feel grief at the decline in bird populations. Some of us feel anger at politicians who can't get it together to pass needed policies. Guilt can arise at our complicity in polluting the world. Despair may emerge as it's unclear if we humans will be able to resolve the crisis we have caused. Engaging with mindful awareness, not feeding the stories but rather making space within the body for the emotions to have their life, our process is direct and simple. We ground in the body, hold the unfolding within the space of our heart-mind, and let awareness feel its way to equanimity. A surprising turn of events takes place. We learn that we won't be crushed. Tenderhearted peace evolves. The heart works its way to openness to the way things are now. Possibilities emerge; we can respond and engage because we are here. A great tenderness arises, knowing that we share this together. Making space for these responses of the heart, we have increasing access to rest in a larger expanse that acknowledges without resistance, *This is the way things are right now.* This expansive compassionate space is able to hold it all; this heart just loves.

One day while sitting on my favorite rock in the middle of the woods, I noticed that the woods were quieter than they used to be with less birdsong, and the trees seemed unhealthy, struggling. I felt such sorrow and grief for this world and all the innocent beings suffering because of my species' greed and ignorance. In the middle of my despair, the trees and land let me know: "We are still here. Love us as we are now." In that moment I saw that grief and despair, in the wish for things to be different than they are now, were hindering my capacity to love more deeply. The land and the trees wanted me to love them as they are now—not as they used to be, not as they might be in the future, but rather right in the midst of their struggles. My heart relaxed, no longer in denial of the truth and once more in attunement with the spirits of the trees and the land.

Heartfelt equanimity balances spaciousness with sacred love. We connect with our indestructible heart, this unconditional love that is able and willing to include it all. This love is not logical, not boundaried nor thought out. It's an undomesticated love that meets the whole world as sacred. The sacred is not only what is beautiful or transcendent; the sacred is all of it: animal and human, the rose and the dandelion, the hawk and its prey, you and me. We engage this feeling heart and ground it in soulful commitment to our dynamic suffering world.

ENGAGING WITH OUR WORLD

Intimacy with the Environment

The Buddhist commentaries relay an encounter between monks and tree spirits that led to the establishment of the metta practice. In this narrative, the Buddha sent young monks to practice in the wild forest. They set up camp but were disturbed by tree spirits unhappy with their presence. These spirits emitted horrible smells and made jarring sounds, frightening the monks who were then not able to practice their meditation. They went back to the Buddha, told him they couldn't meditate there, and asked to be assigned a different location. The Buddha, interested in freedom rather than avoidance, assured them that they could meditate there and gave them the lovingkindness meditation practice as protection. They returned and practiced metta for the tree spirits, establishing a friendly relationship. The tree spirits subsequently mellowed out and happily shared their space.

This story is usually recounted from the perspective of the monks. Let's reframe the narrative from the viewpoint of the tree spirits. These beings inhabited a lovely woodland environment and then a group of young men showed up. Reading between the lines, we can guess they weren't very respectful. Perhaps they didn't gather wood considerately, destroying trees to make fires. Maybe they themselves produced a lot of smells, especially if they didn't make proper latrines! Although they were monks, they were also young men, likely full of boisterous energy. The tree spirits may have felt disrespected and responded with frightful smells and sounds to scare the men away. When the monks returned and practiced metta, we can assume they also changed their behavior and approached this woodland home with more friendliness and respect. The tree spirits, sensing the change, became agreeable to sharing their space.

These teachings give us an effective paradigm for approaching environmental issues. As modern people, we often behave like those young monks. We can be boisterous, loud, and disrespectful to the environment around us. Collectively, we have established a dominating relationship with the trees, the plants, and the minerals, taking what we want from the land and the beings on it without respect for their right to exist in peace. And the spirits are responding. The fire spirits blaze in incontrollable burns. The water spirits respond with floods and drought. The earth spirits grumble in earthquakes. The air spirits whip up tornados and hurricanes. We, like those young monks, feel frightened and unsettled as the world around us responds in increasingly dramatic ways.

Like the monks, we can endeavor to establish a relationship with the earth and the beings who live here based on love, kindness, and respect. With metta, we become intimate enough with our environment to see that it's alive, rather than insensate matter to which we can do whatever we wish. We know the goodness of the magnificent forests, the great waters, and the beautiful mountains. We appreciate the flowers and the plants that feed us and offer medicine, savoring the incredible abundance of this planet that we live on. Connecting deeply, intimately, with all beings, the heart is touched and responds with kindness and respect.

Our attitude of human supremacy can then yield to an ethics of respect toward all beings. Odell states in *How to Do Nothing*, "To behold is to be beholden."[1] As we behold this beautiful world with intimacy, we also know that we have an obligation to protect it. We may not be able to ask the tree and mineral spirits in words how we can get along, but we can listen and learn through intimate observation and intuition. The earth tells us what is working and what is not. Clearly our current approach is not working, so we need to listen more deeply. Receptive energy, willing to be touched by the life around us, enables us to hear. Susan Murphy writes, "And the dearest thing about having this very body is how it establishes indissoluble kinship with all beings and all kinds of beings, as well as trees, oceans, even puddles."[2] Remembering and honoring this kinship will point us in the right direction.

As our attention becomes increasingly receptive, our gaze widens. We stop seeing the world solely in terms of what we want from it, and it becomes possible to see it as it is, in all its wonder and sorrow. This is how we learn to love. A breakdown in the old worldview of separation, materialism, domination, human exceptionalism, and individualism makes way for a more heartfelt worldview that honors and respects our intimate embeddedness in the wider world around us, coparticipating with all other humans, animals, plants, minerals, and the earth itself.

We expand our Buddhist path beyond what we can get from it and ask what we can give. Our meditation practice reminds us of intimacy with all things and what that intimacy engenders: love, connection, and respectful engagement. Buddhist teachings offer the world a concrete way to descend from the domination of mind into the felt sense of the heart and body, including practical instructions that facilitate this coming down to earth. By teaching us to embrace this sweet world with the whole of our being, mind, heart, and body, Buddhism shows up as an excellent religion for now and the future.

Intimacy with Social Identity and Justice

Embedded in the world with down-to-earth dharma, we explore all the ways that we show up with each other. We see where we create separation around differences and learn how to emphasize connection that embraces the wide range of human experiences. Our challenge is the conceptual mind's tendency to place other human beings into categories, as this hinders real seeing. This lack of intimacy may then engender absence of care. Through our embodied heart-oriented practice, we feel into the reality of our social locations and the ways we have all been shaped by our identities, both dominant and subordinate. While on the one hand we understand that we all share fundamental humanity, we also know the intersection of our experiences of race, gender identity and expression, sexual orientation, socioeconomic class, age, national origin, and physical and mental ability deeply affects the ways we perceive the world and the granular experiences of our daily lives.

When I was a college student in 1982, I attended a talk by trans trailblazer Kate Bornstein that startled me out of my usual ways of seeing things. She said, "I wake up every morning neither completely a man nor a woman. Think of the assumptions we make about our life and the world every morning when we wake up and know our gender."[3] We relate to the world through the filter of our identities. On our spiritual journey, we develop a willingness to investigate how our social locations and intersectionality have shaped our experiences and perceptions. We explore how to hold identity by both acknowledging the very real impact of our social location while also investigating how to free ourselves of internalized identification and encumbrance. At the same time, we receive and feel into the social realities of others, including suffering caused by social inequities and oppression. This intimacy motivates compassion and respect, leading us to ask how suffering and injustice can be alleviated.

Supported by curiosity and mindfulness, we develop intimacy with both our subordinate and dominant group identities by exploring emotional impacts and deeply ingrained conditioning. This process makes conscious the unconscious assumptions that we were taught in our families, learned through the influence of the culture, and absorbed from the social world in which we grew up. We become more deeply who we are: this vibrant ever-evolving intersection of many life experiences and social interactions. In the process, we also begin to understand the stress of holding on to our identity too tightly, letting our investigation teach us to engage our identities with the lightness of wisdom and the tenderness of compassion. The subsequent flexibility of heart and mind allows us to relate to identity in skillful ways in our world.

Identifying with marginalized or subordinated group experience, we may make room for the emotions that can arise including feeling deprecated and discounted due to one's social identity. In my own case as a cisgendered woman, I join with many women who have explored the impacts of sexism in our lives. Cutting through the normalization of patriarchal conditioning, we may feel rage and resentment as we heal the harm we have experienced due to personal and systemic exclusion, disrespect, and oppression. We may become aware of how we make ourselves smaller because of internalized sexism, the adoption of the views of a culture still deeply influenced by sexism. We move through the messages the dominant culture has broadcast about our inferiority, connect with our own power, and learn to trust in our own intuition. We defrag our internal systems and update to a freer program.

In addition to personal healing, those with subordinated group experience may choose, when we have the necessary energetic resources and willingness to step into challenging situations, to address oppression on a more systemic level. Writing this book is my contribution, highlighting implicit sexism and the androcentric slant in traditional Buddhism and offering a balancing perspective. In these situations, we may wait to step in until we feel prepared to deal effectively with any pushback or unexpected repercussions. The support of community and allies can give us courage to express ourselves and trust our path.

When our social identity places us in a position of power and privilege, down-to-earth dharma brings us face-to-face with the need to educate ourselves about the ways we have been protected by our identity and open ourselves to the experience of those who have been marginalized. We embrace this excellent opportunity to understand the ignorance that can arise with dominant group experience. For example, we can feel sure that we understand the nature of this world, while being unaware of the realities of those who are marginalized and even unaware that we are unaware! When we land down to earth, our instinct to connect and care can fuel our inquiry into the nature of power and oppression. We strengthen the commitment to develop humility and the willingness to be uncomfortable, expecting that we will make mistakes as we stumble toward understanding. As our hearts open, we ask ourselves what we can do to right the harm caused by oppression, inequities, and systemic exclusion. This work is not drudgery. On the contrary, it is mind-expanding and heartwarming and deepens our ability to land on this earth.

As part of my journey in understanding my social identities, I have deepened my understanding that as white people, our ancestral inheritance includes both great beauty and terrible pain. A positive influence is my Celtic ancestry, from which I inherited a spirituality grounded in profound love of the earth. My Irish and English ancestors valued place, connection, the aliveness of the land, and simple human kindness. Their relationships were embedded in reciprocity and respect—elements of the feminine paradigm. These gifts, part of my legacy as someone of Northern European descent, give me strength and historical rooting.

The history of whiteness in the United States naturally includes a great deal of oppression, racism, and violence. Exploring the terrible narrative of our ancestors' involvement with slavery, Indigenous genocide, and the exploitation and oppression of ethnic minorities puts us more in touch with being a white person in a white dominant culture and can instill a sense of responsibility to come down to earth and respond. There are many ways for white people to understand our genetic and emotional inheritance from this legacy of domination and to reckon with this history. Some ways I've engaged include reading books and seeing movies sharing firsthand accounts from people of color and researching my ancestors' direct involvement in perpetrating slavery and Indigenous genocide. Exploring our social conditioning with other white people can further open our eyes. Learning to listen, rather than presume and unwittingly dominate the discussion, when people of color share their views, perspectives, and lived experience, we can emerge from the ignorance of our preconceived ideas into deeper understanding and connection to the realities of a wider world. In addition, we may actively engage to alleviate the suffering caused by racism by, for example, making financial contributions to African American and Indigenous nonprofits, supporting the reclaiming of Indigenous ancestral lands, and advocating for anti-racist changes in institutions in which we are involved. In this way, we situate ourselves within our broader community and begin to heal our ancestral karma. Wherever we find ourselves in a socially dominant group, we can investigate broadly and deeply our place in the system of oppression and uncover ways to use the power available to us to alleviate suffering and create a more just, safer, and kinder world around us.

The suffering we encounter on our journey into social identity often brings up strong emotions. How do we not get caught in bitterness, separation, anger, fear, and grief? Or guilt and shame? As dominant group members, for example, we can experience excruciating cringe moments when, even with our best intentions, we inadvertently cause harm to others out of ignorance. Leaving room for our emotional response and taking time to care for it allow us to realign with clarity and love. While claiming responsibility for skillfully managing the feelings that arise, we also hold them in a larger context as socially conditioned and not so personal. With wise tender care, we can bring skillful energy to our response to our own and others' suffering. We acknowledge and hold these powerful challenging emotions so they can transform, finding support as needed through meditation, ritual, and community.

Many of our Buddhist convert communities are grappling with issues of social identities: racism, sexism, classism, heterosexism, transphobia, and the relationship between convert and heritage Buddhist communities. Harmonizing our communities across differences stretches our hearts and minds. At times these changes are messy, confusing, and very down to earth with human failings. One way to undermine the unseen shadows of dominant group conditioning is for members to sign up to be willingly challenged and disturbed. The dedication to enlarging the space of our heart-mind to truly include all beings overrides our desire for comfort. Together we as a community explore what feels truly welcoming to all and how to cocreate the future with many voices at the table. This journey, although challenging, refreshes and delights us as we grow into more expansive and lively ways of being and relating. The "practice of total inclusion"[4] gets manifest.

Sustainable Engagement in the World

A number of years ago, a fossil fuel company planned to route a fracked gas pipeline through my small New England town. This pipeline would travel through northern Massachusetts and southern New Hampshire and end at an export terminal on the coast. The company had completed surveying and were moving ahead with their plans. My husband and I joined our town's affinity group, part of a larger group called the Sugar Shack Alliance, opposed to this pipeline. We believed that fossil fuels should stay in the ground, building a new pipeline would encourage the use of fossil fuels, including fracked gas, for decades to come, and we needed to transition to renewable sources of power. We strategized how we could stop the plans of this powerful fossil fuel company.

One action centered around building a replica of Henry David Thoreau's Walden Pond cabin on the land of one of our participants, directly in the pathway of the proposed pipeline. Our town building inspector said that because it was a small structure, we didn't need a building permit, but if we got a permit to build it, a permit would also be needed to take it down. We got the permit. And we had a lot of fun. Neighbors became acquainted with one another as we held poetry readings, potlucks, and rallies at the cabin. Other resisters began to plan for more cabins in the pipeline's proposed path. Eventually we succeeded in our mission, and the fossil fuel company withdrew its plans. Our affinity group continued to work to lessen fossil fuel dependence by protesting the construction of a storage pipeline in a state park in the southwestern corner of Massachusetts. We moved our Thoreau cabin as close as we could to the path of this pipeline and rallied our state representative. We didn't win this engagement—the pipeline was built—but we had a lot of fun trying. We felt power and satisfaction in having stood for our values.

These days I frequently get asked, "What do I do about all the suffering? How can I engage and not get overwhelmed?" In addition, this unasked question lurks underneath for many: "How do I deal with the 'colossal anguish' I feel about the state of our world?" In situations where we commit to alleviating suffering, we both engage and take care of our hearts. The framework of the four Brahmaviharas supports engagement in a sustainable and joyful way. We establish goodwill, care enough to act, nourish ourselves through joy, and let go of attachment to the results of our actions.

First, we cultivate metta for all involved, both those who agree with our opinions and actions and those who don't. We may not necessarily like everyone, yet we endeavor to keep our heart open, checking any ill will that arises and proceeding with an attitude of connection. One meditation teacher tells the story of practicing metta in Myanmar during a time of political unrest. He told his teacher how well he was doing sending metta to the demonstrators. His teacher asked, "And are you also sending metta to the police and military?" Julia Butterfly Hill, the young activist who spent two years living in a redwood tree named Luna in order to protect it from logging, said to Benjamin Tung on the DVD *The Taoist and the Activist*, "Activism is about a spiritual practice as a way of life. . . . I realized I didn't climb the tree because I was angry at the corporations and the government. I climbed the tree because I fell in love with the redwoods, I fell in love with the world. So it is my feeling of connection that drives me, instead of my anger and feelings of being disconnected."[5] A story from Zen teacher Blanche Hartman's book *Seeds for a Boundless Life* illustrates this move from opposition to connection. In her early days of activism in the late 1960s, she "fought for peace. There was some contradiction . . . I hated the people who disagreed with me." She describes a moment in 1968 when she attended a strike at San Francisco State University and found herself face-to-face with one of the riot squad policemen, someone she had seen as completely "other." Their eyes met and she had a deep experience of shared identity with this man, seeing that they both were trying to do what they thought was good and right. She has called it "the most transformative moment of my life." Stunned by this unexpected meeting, she initiated a spiritual search to find a teacher who could explain to her what had happened.[6]

Having established our intention for goodwill, compassion inspires us to act. At times despair can arise in the face of the massive amounts of dysfunction, violence, and suffering we encounter. We may feel that we ourselves must fix everything. We can ask ourselves instead: *What is my passion? Where do I feel called to serve?* To maintain sustainable care, we can understand that we are not doing this alone. We trust that our fellow world citizens will also answer their passion and together we will bring about change. We relieve ourselves of the burden of feeling we ourselves need to do it all and take refuge in community. In his book *Blessed Unrest: How the Largest Movement in the World Came into Being and Why No One Saw It Coming*, Paul Hawken describes how millions of people around the world are working in nonprofits and community organizations to address environmental and social injustice. Reading about the amazing things people are doing to help others and our planet reminds us that we're in good company.

Balancing compassion, appreciative joy answers our need for lightness and delight. How can we have fun in our engagement? The famous activist Emma Goldman said, "If I can't dance, it's not my revolution." How do we dance while doing our work? How do we play? How do we celebrate? Even during times of great sorrow and mourning, for example at a Black Lives Matter demonstration, we can connect with the underlying solace of being together and the beauty of ritual and song. Writing letters to members of Congress is more fun in a group than at home alone. We consciously support the aspects of our activism that nourish and sustain our enthusiasm.

In a *Lion's Roar* article online, Sharon Salzberg describes how she asked Myles Horton, the founder of the Highlander Folk School of Tennessee, a training ground for civil rights protesters and later for people engaged in environmental activism, what he did to develop resilience or get a break from the pressure and stress of his work. He said, "I look at the mountains. I just sit and look at the mountains." Nature and "useless gazing" can provide solace and calming joy for our weary hearts.[7]

Lastly, equanimity cultivates the ability to let go of attachment to the results of our efforts, sustaining us for the long haul. In all activism and noble endeavors there are times of success and times of failure. On some occasions we feel our impact, and other times our actions seem worthless. Most important is acting, knowing that we are in alignment with our deepest values. We focus on the goodness of responding, whether it's a huge project or a small step. We do what we can, and then it's out of our hands. The late senator and civil rights activist John Lewis in a June 2018 tweet encouraged endurance, an aspect of equanimity: "Do not get lost in a sea of despair. Be hopeful, be optimistic. Our struggle is not the struggle of a day, a week, a month, or a year, it is the struggle of a lifetime. Never, ever be afraid to make some noise and get in good trouble, necessary trouble."[8] We cultivate the big heart-mind that doesn't depend on instant results. We develop flexible responsiveness that trusts in our capacity to adapt and persevere.

Whether through our paid work or through activism and volunteer work, the four Brahmaviharas give us strength and support. Bringing them to mind and checking on all four facets can help us to love and act in a balanced and sustainable way. When one aspect is lacking, we contemplate how to nourish it. When our work or activism is fueled by anger and ill will, how can we bring in more love? If our heart is dried out and uncaring, how can we warm it up again? Feeling drab and uninspired in our work, what cultivates more joy? When we are burning out in despair about not making a difference, how do we develop more equanimity? Using the Buddha's brilliant framework for the heart, we joyfully give of ourselves because that's what hearts are called to do.

14

OUR ETHICAL INTEGRITY

The Beauty of Sila

A number of years ago, a couple of teachers and I visited a Buddhist monk at a Cambodian temple in Lowell, Massachusetts. He asked what we do when we teach, so we told him about our retreats where people learn to meditate. He listened attentively, and then slowly shook his head and said, "Better to start with *sila*." *Sila* is a Pali word most traditionally translated as "morality" or "virtue." Since those words can have heavy connotations for some, we can instead say "ethical conduct" or just use sila. This elderly monk was suggesting that before teaching people to meditate, we should emphasize living in an ethical manner. In many Asian temples, both in the United States and in their home territories, ethics and generosity are emphasized as main components of the path for laypeople. Many Westerners, however, don't approach meditation with these two components in mind. We want to figure out what to do with the suffering in our minds and hearts. Yet the monk's suggestion is thoughtful. Strong ethical integrity is an essential foundation for the full blossoming of our practice.

Ethics occupy three steps of the Noble Eightfold Path, the Buddha's prescription for a spiritual life: skillful action, speech, and livelihood. Three out of eight means that sila is not just an add-on practice but rather an integral part of a spiritual life. In Buddhism, ethical integrity entails living in a nonharming manner, acting from the values of the compassionate heart. Deeper commitment to sila is an expression of the awakened heart and a natural consequence of walking the path. As we develop a softer, kinder heart, it's a no-brainer that we don't want to cause harm and suffering through our actions. Joko Beck, in her usual straightforward manner, says, "Practice can be stated very simply: It is moving from a life of hurting myself and others to a life of not hurting myself and others."[1] Sila extends our mindfulness practice from our meditation cushion out into our relationships in the world, landing clearly in the paradigm of interconnectedness.

Sila practice fine-tunes our inner moral compass. We commit to cleaning up our act on an ongoing basis. Rather than viewing this as a heavy task—a not uncommon response—we can recognize that sila points us toward the beauty of expressing our compassionate heart. We ask, *How are my actions aligned with my values? Where can I be kinder, more compassionate? How can I reduce the harm that I cause in this world? How can I honor and respect both myself and other living beings? How can I support my own flourishing and the flourishing of others in an atmosphere of nonharm?* These are beautiful questions to explore. With sila practice, we investigate the answers not only in our mind, but also in our heart and through embodiment. Devoting ourselves to sila, we unite and align mind, heart, and body.

The Cambodian monk we visited was pointing to ethical conduct as a prerequisite for calming the heart and mind. When we act unethically, not aligned with our deepest values, we create inner turbulence. For example, when we tell a lie, it produces stressful energy, which is why lie detector tests work. Harmful acts weigh, cloud, and disturb the heart-mind. When we sit down to meditate filled with the turbulence and stress caused by unskillful actions, the mind has trouble settling down as it jumps this way and that thinking about the problems we have created for ourselves and others. We feel remorse, worry, and fear of consequences, agitating the heart-mind. Our mind may twist and contort facts seeking to deny and justify our actions. This turbulence makes it hard to see deeply, like when the water of a lake is disturbed by a wind that hides any view of the depths. With sila practice we protect ourselves from our own destructive tendencies and actions and the harmful impact of these on our own heart-mind.

Integrity, the alignment of heart, body, and mind with our values, gives us a solid base for our meditation practice. The Buddha mentions nonremorse as one of the main benefits of living an ethical life, calling it the bliss of blamelessness. The happiness of a clear conscience blesses us and relaxes our nervous system. We can also note that beyond just avoiding unskillful actions, when we engage in skillful, wholesome actions aligned with our values, the karmic imprint also stays with us. In this case, actions based in wisdom and love lighten our heart-mind, filling it with happiness and joy. A happy mind settles and progresses more quickly in meditation.

In addition to the personal benefits to practicing sila, out of compassion we take care not to cause suffering to others. As we become more sensitive and attuned, we increasingly feel our heart's wish to avoid spreading suffering. We want to move through this world in the kindest way possible with a gentle wake left behind our boat rather than one that is turbulent and destructive. In addition to our personal ethical integrity with other humans, we also practice ethics in all our relationships, with the greater community of all beings on this planet Earth: trees, plants, animals, birds, dirt, all things. Relating with nonharm and sustainability toward all beings, including nonhuman ones, our heart delights in becoming a kind and responsible coparticipant in this world.

Protecting Our Ethics

Two heart-mind factors support and protect us in our commitment to sila. Called *lokapala*, these "guardians of the world" are our inner conscience reviewing past and future actions with heart and understanding. *Hiri* is traditionally translated as "moral shame" and *ottappa* as "moral dread." If these translations feel too heavy, we can alternatively translate them as "wise regret" and "wise respect." Although these two mind states are unpleasant, they're good for us. The unpleasantness of their visceral sting reminds us of how we want to live, encouraging us to bring wisdom and skillfulness to our actions.

Wise regret, a form of moral intuition, highlights when we have acted in a way that is not in alignment with our values. We have violated our inner sense of integrity. Hiri says, *I know this wasn't a skillful thing to do, so I feel remorse.* Like bitter medicine that's good for us but doesn't taste so nice, the pain of regret motivates us to live more from our values in the future. Joko Beck says that we know we're really practicing well when we find ourselves able to be truly sorry that we've hurt somebody. When we are tangled up in our own story, we don't care as much how we affect others. As we soften and open, we more readily see the reverberations of our actions and regret the pain we cause. Feeling remorse is a price we are willing to pay to attune our moral compass, gaining self-respect in the process. We feel good about ourselves when we act with integrity.

We distinguish wise regret from guilt, an unproductive form of self-hatred. Guilt is self-centered, still wrapped up in the story of me. When we find ourselves rehearsing a drama about what kind of bad person we are, we have likely slipped into guilt. We are "overowning" our mistakes. Wise regret is simpler: *This action was not skillful, and having committed it, I don't feel good and don't want to repeat it.* Stop. Rather than manifesting as a harsh inner critic, hiri, a feminine noun in Pali, can whisper softly with compassion.

Ottappa, or wise respect, involves pausing before upcoming actions and reviewing whether they are in alignment with our values and respectful of ourselves and others. We feel an unpleasant sensation of dread when we contemplate doing something that lacks moral integrity. *I know if I do this it will have unpleasant consequences, so I will practice restraint.* This bitter medicine protects and empowers us by introducing choice. In the process we gain self-esteem and self-respect when we restrain ourselves from engaging in actions that cause harm.

Mindfulness is a further guardian of ethical conduct. Mindfulness gives us the capacity to pause and assess whether our actions are in alignment with our values and whether the results will be helpful or cause suffering. In a discourse directed toward his son Rahula, the Buddha encouraged him to be mindful of actions before, during, and after, at every step assessing the wisdom of the action. Will this lead to suffering? If so, refrain. If not, it is okay to proceed. Is this leading to suffering? If so, stop. If not, continue. Did this lead to suffering? If so, avoid doing it in the future.[2] Every step of the way learning is encouraged with mindful reflection as our support.

When we talk about sila, we should resist the pull to get bummed out thinking of all the bad things we have done. To not get crushed under the weight of self-condemnation, we must know how to forgive our mistakes. It is precisely in those mistakes, which remind us of our deepest values, where learning takes place. Human existential dukkha includes the painful recognition that as long as we carry seeds of greed, aversion, and ignorance within, we will sometimes fall short and cause pain and suffering to ourselves and others. Noticing this pain is an important part of our meditation path because it purifies our motivation, inspiring us to free others from our harmful actions. During one retreat where I found myself repeatedly remembering the many ways I had fallen short, I made the vow to stay on the path if only to spare others my unskillfulness.

For support in forgiving ourselves, we can refer to a Tibetan Buddhist framework to transform unwholesome karma called the *four powers*. The four steps in this plan can be called the four R's: recognize, remorse, remediate, and recommit. First, rather than glossing over or denying our mistakes, we recognize that what we have done is harmful and unskillful. Next, we allow ourselves to feel remorse and regret, these skillful heart-mind states that strengthen our acknowledgment of the harmful nature of our actions. Third, we remediate, which may include making amends for what we've done or contemplating the causes and conditions that supported our unskillfulness and changing these conditions to support more ethical behavior in the future. Last, we recommit to living from our deepest values and expressing them in our conduct. Having undertaken these four actions, we have done what we can to repair damage and support integrity in future conduct, so I have a fifth "R" to add: release. We can let go of self-recrimination, forgive ourselves, and move forward. In this way, we develop compassion for ourselves and cultivate the ability to hold our shortcomings with gentleness, forgiveness, and care.

As we continue to explore sila, the motivation driving our action is considered of primary importance in our practice. What is propelling us to act? Is it greed, hatred, or delusion? If so, the outcome is likely to be harmful. Is it love, compassion, wisdom, or kindness? The outcome is more likely to be beneficial. This is the basis of the Buddhist teaching on karma: actions of thought, word, and deed tend toward consequences congruent with the energy behind the action. This is not some esoteric teaching; we can see in our own minds that the karmic imprint of our actions is determined by the motivation. What's the result in our mind and heart when we act out of hatred? How does the heart-mind feel when we act out of greed? On the other hand, what's the flavor in our heart and mind when we act out of generosity or compassion? When we feel the karmic impact of the motivation behind our actions, the teachings on sila come down to earth.

Understanding motivation is an imperfect science. As we check out our motivation for acting, we see that it is often mixed rather than a single clear-cut impulse. With mindfulness we get increasingly attuned to our motives—both hidden and less beautiful motivations and wholesome ones. Mindfulness gives us space to pause when the intention is unskillful and bring forth discerning wisdom about the best course of action. When motivation is wholesome, we know then we can move forward with confidence and wisdom.

The Power of the Precepts

It has been said that if one were just to engage with the five precepts deeply and wholeheartedly, that is the whole path. When I first heard this, I was surprised. *Just refraining from killing, stealing, sexual misconduct, lying, and misusing intoxicants—that's the whole path?* Now I understand that the precepts are a very deep practice. To keep them we must transform greed, hatred, and delusion. To refrain from causing harm, these root unwholesome tendencies of the heart must be tamed. So yes, precept practice can do it all. As a purification practice, it brings us down to earth into the ultrafine details of our conditioning.

We are fortunate that our Buddhist practice gives us concrete guidelines for sila. The five precepts offer a framework to express compassion and avoid causing suffering. These mindfulness training vows, taken by laypeople the world over, remind us of how we intend to live. Like a white flag that waves in my face when I'm about to do something unethical, they say, *Rebecca, remember the precepts! Take care in this situation.* I'm about to tell a lie to get out of an uncomfortable situation, and this little voice says, *Ah-ah, fourth precept! Do you really want to do this?* Thich Nhat Hanh calls the precepts navigational tools, like the North Star. They help us to steer through the tricky moral dilemmas of everyday life. Precept practice becomes ingrained as a way of living infused with curiosity and a joyous commitment to living with compassion. As we cultivate them, we develop moral fitness: the ability to respond in deeply ethical ways.

In traditional Buddhism, the five precepts emphasize in simple language restraining oneself from unskillful actions. Here is a short version:

> I undertake the mindfulness training to refrain from taking life.
> I undertake the mindfulness training to refrain from taking that which is not given.
> I undertake the mindfulness training to refrain from sexual misconduct.
> I undertake the mindfulness training to refrain from false and harmful speech.
> I undertake the mindfulness training to refrain from taking intoxicants that cloud the mind and cause heedlessness.

As a form of sila practice, we can read these precepts each morning, planting seeds of mindfulness that help us become aware when we are about to commit an action that violates them. The precepts can highlight where we are stuck, providing an opportunity for honest inquiry into the conditioning and the circumstances that propel us to cause harm. We may want to choose one precept, perhaps one that's tricky for us, and focus on it for months or years at a time.

The Theravada lineage traditionally follows a conservative literal reading of the precepts; these are strict rules that should be followed in all circumstances. There's wisdom in this point of view. When we start applying personal interpretations, our human tendencies toward delusion can make things very slippery indeed. With clear-cut rules, there is no ambiguity. Their specificity leaves little room to wriggle and justify unethical behavior. The first four precepts specify areas where it's easy to cause harm and suffering and best to take heed. The last precept helps us keep the first four by maintaining a clear heart and mind.

From the relational paradigm, on the other hand, we recognize life is complex, and making rules that always hold is difficult in an ambiguous world. The precepts are taken as guidelines to apply in context, orienting by the overriding compassionate wish to minimize suffering. At times we may create less harm by breaking a precept. For example, on a couple of occasions since I started practicing, I have consciously chosen to tell a lie as the appropriate response in a particular situation. I did not do it lightly, and I still feel a karmic imprint from having done so. On many other occasions lying would've been convenient, but since my convenience isn't a good reason to break a precept, I told the truth.* The precepts ask us to look deeply into our hearts and ascertain what the situation calls for, beyond our personal preferences and convenience.

From this relational paradigm, the five precepts can be expanded into great depth and richness. Extended versions of the precepts may include not only restraint, but also aspirations for positive action, broadening the training to include activities we encourage. Orienting from the heart, we explore just how far we can extend our commitment to living with kindness and integrity. Here is a brief expanded version. Each precept begins with "knowing how deeply our lives intertwine" in

* In addition, telling the truth can shock and delight people. One time my insurance agent suggested that if I told a little lie I could get damage to my car covered. When I refused to do so, she was so shocked that she proclaimed this news to the rest of the office.

recognition of interconnectedness and the truth that our actions affect each other.

1. Knowing how deeply our lives intertwine, I undertake the mindfulness training to abstain from taking life. I commit to respect the life of all beings, including humans, animals, plants, and minerals.
2. Knowing how deeply our lives intertwine, I undertake the mindfulness training to abstain from taking that which isn't given. I commit to simplicity, generosity, and conscious use of resources.
3. Knowing how deeply our lives intertwine, I undertake the mindfulness training to abstain from sexual misconduct. I commit to conscious sexuality and preserving relationships.
4. Knowing how deeply our lives intertwine, I undertake the mindfulness training to abstain from hurtful or false speech. I commit to speaking what is true and useful.
5. Knowing how deeply our lives intertwine, I undertake the mindfulness training to abstain from the misuse of intoxicants. I commit to care with what I consume in mind, heart, and body.

The vibrancy of heartfelt engagement fuels our exploration. As we practice the precepts, our sensitivity increases. We notice small transgressions and make connections that we may have missed before. An example from the first precept involves a big red watering can I keep outside in the summer for watering the garden. I liked to keep the can full and ready to use. However, one day I found a little chipmunk trapped in the can, swimming in circles. This little dear one, thirsty, had climbed into the can and was going to swim as long as possible in order to live.* Struck in that moment with the urge to live in all beings,

---

* For those of you concerned about the fate of our little chipmunk friend, I can report that I dumped out the can and, after an initial moment of shock, they scampered off.

I made a commitment to keep less than an inch of water in the watering can. Less convenient for me, this decision feels aligned with integrity and kindness.

The precepts are rich explorations that honor our interconnectedness and interdependence. A version developed by Caitriona Reed from Manzanita Village places us squarely in the intergenerational web of life. For example, the first precept from Manzanita Village states,

> Aware of the violence in the world and the power of nonviolent resistance, I stand in the presence of the ancestors, the earth, and future generations, and vow to cultivate the compassion that seeks to protect each living being.

Each precept in this lineage repeats the refrain, "I stand in the presence of the ancestors, the earth, and future generations and vow . . ." We are not a solitary independent person. We are beautifully woven into the web of beings and intimately connected to the earth itself. All are witnesses to our commitment to moral integrity, giving more power to our vow.[3]

Exploring the Precepts with Mindfulness

Exploring the precepts is a down-to-earth daily life practice, inviting mindfulness, compassion, and curiosity into our everyday actions. Let's explore them in more detail from both angles, each precept stated both as "refrain from doing this" and more positively with "do this."

Practicing the first precept, we vow to refrain from killing living beings. In addition, we cultivate the commitment to protect life. The other day I was washing dishes and noticed a bug in the bottom of the sink. Feeling a bit lazy, I didn't want to take the time to rescue the bug. Then I remembered the first precept. This bug wants to live, and so I took the time to move it out of the sink before I proceeded. It felt good to be in alignment with what I knew to be my deepest aspiration.

Sometimes ethical decisions are complicated. In 1984 I served as a cook at the Insight Meditation Society. We followed a strict interpretation of the precepts, which led to cockroaches running on the tables. We tried asking them to leave; unsurprisingly, that didn't work. Finally, somebody on staff said, "Look, I'll take the karma and deal with the cockroaches." We performed a ceremony the night before he put out poison, telling the cockroaches, "Cockroaches, it's time, if you want to leave, leave now."* In ethically challenging situations, we bring the heart into how we "deal" with things. We move forward with care and discernment, trying to cause the least harm possible.

Wider interpretations of this precept can point us toward our collective reality, honoring our embeddedness in our social and natural world. We can explore, for example, our contribution to human-caused climate change and the extinction of entire species. From the perspective of this precept, it is immoral for us humans to continue with human supremacist attitudes and actions that are causing so much loss of life. Our ethical responsibility to protect life may call us to engage in actions that address climate change and its causes. On an individual level many options exist. We may become vegan, take public transportation more often, or buy fewer unnecessary consumer goods. We may also engage in collective action that influences decision-makers. Making choices, however small, that align with our values empowers and grounds us. For example, while the carbon footprint may be minuscule, when I bike into town rather than drive, I feel good because my actions are aligned with my values. This alignment gives us a measure of peace.

The second precept, in its narrowest interpretation, refers to not stealing. However, we can explore more carefully what it means to not take that which is not given. Do we use supplies at work that aren't intended for our personal use? What about borrowing something without asking even if we intend to return it? Or not. On my first long retreat I felt remorse as I remembered "forgetting" to return a shirt that a friend loaned me because I liked it so much. While these examples seem like small

---

* If you plan to visit the Insight Meditation Society, don't worry, times have changed and there are no cockroaches. This incident took place during a more free-form era when, as Sharon Salzberg describes it, "there was no adult supervision."

things, we discover in our meditation practice that even little transgressions create moral dissonance. Our life is woven out of small things.

One day sitting by the marsh, I noticed some lovely fall grasses and wanted to take some home. Since there weren't many, I asked the grasses how many I could take. The answer that came to me was "three." I gathered three grasses, but they didn't look like much in my hand, so I disregarded the answer I had been given and took a fourth. I put all four in my backpack and biked home, yet when I arrived, I only had three. I thought about how, motivated by greed, I had taken more than I had been given and recommitted to respecting this second precept. The next day I found the fourth grass by the side of the road, and it's still unclear how one grass stem extricated itself from the bundle to fall clear from the pack.

The second precept also encourages generosity. Not only do we not take what is not given, we share what we have. As generosity is considered such an important part of the Buddhist path, an entire chapter will be dedicated to exploring this beautiful quality.

The third precept calls on us to refrain from sexual misconduct. At a minimum, this precept asks us to honor our commitments and the commitments of others. Knowing how sexual infidelity can cause enormous pain and sorrow, we commit to not being part of any liaison that breaks our own or others' commitments. When we are in a monogamous relationship, we don't go looking for other partners. If we are attracted to someone in a monogamous relationship, we nonetheless keep our distance. When we are in a more open relationship, we commit to keeping whatever agreements we have with our partners. Honoring this precept, we place respect and commitment to relationships, our own and others', over our individual desires.

A more expanded version calls us to bring awareness to the nuances of how our sexual energy manifests in the world and whether we are causing harm in any way. Respectful dating would apply for those of us who are single and looking. We can explore flirting; do we cause harm if somebody thinks we're seriously interested in them and we're just flirting? We examine the use of power in our sexual relationships. Do we honor others' boundaries? The #MeToo movement brought this precept into mainstream society, highlighting the importance of consent and appropriate boundaries. In addition, we can ask ourselves whether the ways that we are expressing our sexual energy are causing harm to ourselves. Are we listening to our hearts and our true needs? Understanding that sexual energy can be expressed in ways both harmful and loving, this precept encourages responsible and respectful sexuality.

The fourth precept stipulates refraining from lying. This precept is most clear to us when we avoid planned intentional lies. Telling lies messes with the truth. When we tell a lie often enough, we come to believe it ourselves and we get others to believe it too, contributing to delusion in this world. Exploring subtler levels of truth telling refines our sila. Where do we bend or play with the truth? How do we relate to small spontaneous lies, like exaggerating for effect when we're telling a story? Is it okay to say that fifty people attended the party because this sounds juicier when only twenty people were there? When our friend asks if we like their new haircut and we don't, is it okay to say that we do? What about lying to a customer service representative about why our appliance broke? Many opportunities arise to explore this precept.

Honesty is the basis of all healthy relationships. One day I biked into town and stopped at the pizza place to grab a slice. I asked a nine-year-old kid we'll call Tyler if he would watch my bike. When I came out, Tyler and I got into a conversation, and he told me that his bike was broken. When his parents joined the conversation later, I learned that it wasn't. I said to Tyler, "Now I can't believe you and that changes our whole relationship, no? I still like you, but I won't trust you." As he digested this, his parents nodded in support. Telling the truth is the foundation of trust.

In other teachings, the Buddha expanded skillful speech further by recommending that we also avoid harsh speech, divisive speech, and gossip. A short, easy-to-remember guideline is: speak what is true, useful, and timely. When email was first introduced, many of us didn't get how easy it was to send off a harsh message. I posted the Buddha's recommendations next to my computer monitor and devised my own guidelines. I learned to know when the email should go in the draft box to be reviewed in a few hours or the next day. Take out any word in an email that raises even the slightest doubt. When detecting harshness in word choice, find a more neutral way to say the same thing. Texting, of course, has increased the speed and challenge of digital communication. How do we protect ourselves from inappropriate texting? For any social media posting, we can ask ourselves, *Is our sharing true, useful, and timely?* Developing our own guidelines can help us to keep this precept.

Stated positively, the fourth precept encourages sharing words that spread truth, kindness, and goodwill. Yesterday I stopped a member of the IMS kitchen staff to thank her for her work in the last year since reopening after COVID. I praised the flavor of the meals and the kindness of the kitchen staff. Today, I learned that my compliment spread through the whole kitchen and had a very positive impact. My words brought happiness to other people, and that made me happy, too. A lot of goodwill reverberated from a simple compliment. Even the smallest actions can create positive reverberations outward.

The fifth precept involves refraining from the use of intoxicants. Some read this precept as stipulating avoiding all intoxicants that cause heedlessness, and others interpret it to mean avoiding taking intoxicants to the point of heedlessness. Alcohol, street drugs, and plant-based substances fall under this fifth precept. A strict reading of the precepts requires that we refrain from substances that confuse or cloud the heart-mind. At a minimum, we question whether our use of intoxicants hinders us in keeping the other four precepts. In addition, we inquire whether our use of substances supports or interferes with our intention to develop a clear and wise heart-mind.

In exploring our relationship to intoxicants, self-honesty is required. Challenges with addictive use usually call for the strict interpretation; complete abstinence may be the best policy. (Some would argue that harm reduction is a viable alternative.) For others, we might ask, when we have an alcoholic drink or eat a gummy, what is the effect on the state of our heart-mind and our actions? Do we become less heedful? If we have five drinks, what happens then? Are plant-based substances like ayahuasca useful on our spiritual path or a distraction? We explore intimately the effects of ingesting intoxicants and mind-altering substances.

We can expand this fifth precept to include everything we ingest, including food, movies, conversations, social media, and books. This exploration is vast. What are we taking into our mind, heart, and body, and how is it affecting us? Do we consume useless entertainment? What do violent movies do to the state of our heart-mind? The summer before my first long retreat, with too much free time, I watched two soap operas almost daily. The first three weeks of that three-month retreat I found myself repeatedly thinking about the TV shows. *I wonder if she found out what he did? I hope that they're still together.* Not wanting to be thinking about this, I was dismayed, but that was the intoxicant I had been feeding my mind. I learned firsthand a valuable lesson I have never forgotten: what we ingest leaves a karmic imprint. Images, media, and conversations have a lasting impact, so we take care with what we introduce into our heart and mind.

Social media and the internet are powerful intoxicants that require inquiry and mindfulness. While acknowledging the many benefits of modern technology, we also know that the internet is geared toward grabbing our attention and taking it for a ride. It is a distraction machine, activating our nervous systems and potentially robbing us of embodiment and groundedness. Sophisticated psychologists are working full-time to hijack our attention and keep us online so that revenue is generated. Most of us need to explore how this happens, how we get hooked, and how we can set limits so that we aren't constantly distracted. As with many investigations in this book, we can explore this precept actively or in a receptive mode. When our use is compulsive and out of our control, we may need to call forth determination and boundaries. Due to the addictive nature of the internet, we may need concrete limits in order to have anything approaching a sane relationship with our devices. Some people control usage by waiting to turn on their Wi-Fi in the morning. I taught a class at Smith College the other day, and one of the women said, "Every morning when I get up, I go the bathroom and look at myself in the mirror to remember who I am before I go on social media." I put my iPad in airplane mode in the evening so that the extra step needed to access it gives me a chance to reconsider. A technology sabbath—for example, refraining from internet use from Friday sundown to Saturday sundown—can allow us to "remember who we are."

We can also explore in more detail the nature of our relationship to social media, scrolling, and watching the news. Listening or watching the news can seem like a healthy form of internet use, but most news these days, especially from sources that depend on ad revenue, is sensationalized and emotionally impactful, designed to intoxicate, inflame afflictive emotions, and call us back repeatedly. We can investigate our mind state before we reach for our devices or the feeling when we want to log off and can't find the willpower to do so. We can notice the impact on our system after we have spent an hour surfing. We can allow ourselves to feel the stress of answering twenty emails in a row. We can watch the news while tracking our emotions. Then we let the results of our explorations teach us how to proceed with digital communication and internet usage going forward.

We can develop a playful attitude toward deepening our understanding of the nuances of the five precepts. A former partner and I once spent a month exploring the commitment to never speak about a third person. I was amazed how much speech this cut out and what it left for us to talk about. We could take a period of time to focus on not killing any bugs, not even through carelessness. Perhaps we commit to not reading the news for a week—we'll still find out what we need to know about the happenings in the world. During these experiments, we let the impact on our mind and heart, our speech, and our actions teach us about the subtleties of compassionate care. These investigations can strengthen the resolve in our heart to not cause harm or suffering to ourselves nor to others.

Precept practice manifests in responsibility and joy, a heartfelt investigation into how to take care of ourselves and others with compassion and respect. We expand our awareness into seeing clearly the reverberations of our actions within our own heart and mind and with other people, all beings, and the world around us. We make mistakes, forgive ourselves, and recommit to our values. Honoring how intertwined our lives are, our moral integrity is a beautiful offering to ourselves and all those around us. The Buddha called the precepts "five great gifts," explaining that sila "offer[s] freedom from danger, freedom from animosity, and freedom from oppression to countless beings" and that while imparting this, we receive a share of the same.[4]

GENEROSITY

The Joy of Generosity

At the annual retreat for Westerners in the Sagaing Hills of Myanmar, the teaching team not only led the retreat but also engaged in social action. One project supported nuns, who typically get less backing than male monastics. We toured three nunneries and personally handed monetary *dana* (gifts) to each nun. One year, a devout young Burmese woman came with us and brought her ten-month-old daughter. She placed the money in her daughter's hand and then helped her daughter give it to the nuns. She knew that giving is good karma, and she wanted to train her daughter at the youngest age possible to participate in this goodness.

Generosity flows from the paradigm of relationship and interconnectedness. With the practice of giving, we engage the world as a full-hearted citizen. The unobstructed heart is naturally generous. When the barriers causing separation in the heart-mind are dissolved, the connection that remains inspires giving and receiving in an open flow unhindered by self-centeredness. Pema Chödrön says that giving "ventilates the claustrophobia of self-absorption."[1] What a relief to realize it's only one-eight billionth about me. We come out of cramped self-involved cocoons and take our place in the community of living beings, giving and receiving, sharing in abundance. Ethan Nichtern says that offering "transforms our inner hungry ghost into a decent, low maintenance human being."[2] Many of us Westerners are high-maintenance, especially those of us with privilege, which can engender a sense of entitlement. With giving, wanting gets transformed to low-maintenance contentment.

The happiness of generosity awakens the mind and energizes the heart, providing fuel for our journey. Generosity also lightens the heart-mind, making it easier to concentrate. In Buddhist countries, giving is considered a foundational practice that offers protection. People traditionally engage in a lot of foundational practices before meditation, as these practices create a blessed field in which to explore our heart-mind. Giving generously, we live in a field of merit of our own goodness. We inhabit a world of kindness, where we can relax, trust, and travel deeply into the truth of this life. In addition, generosity feels empowering because we align with our values and support what we care about. We enjoy our own integrity and our power to respond to the world. We like ourselves when we are generous, supporting healthy self-esteem. We build the self-confidence needed to practice meditation. Generosity enriches our meditation soil so that seeds will grow.

The Buddha taught that giving brings joy and awakens us to interconnectedness. As back-and-forth exchanges relax our rigid boundaries with other people, we feel less alienated and more part of the whole. When we give something to somebody—whether resources, energy, or time—we strengthen our relationship. The commentaries even suggest that if you are having difficulty with a person, give them a gift. (I've tried this, and you truly feel more connected to this person.) Lastly, practicing generosity teaches us abundance. When we give, we know we have plenty.

Some of us are taught that giving is a duty benefiting other people. We are supposed to give, especially as religious or spiritual people. In Buddhist teachings, giving is considered primarily beneficial for the giver. In Myanmar, people delight in their own and others' acts of generosity. When Burmese donors would offer meals at the monastery for those of us practicing meditation, sometimes saving up all year for the opportunity, they would sit through the meal watching us eat, delighting in their meritorious act. When we give donations to Burmese monasteries, the monks chant with us, wishing for our donation to be beneficial for us, the givers. One time when I returned to our monastery with a Buddha statue, I assuaged the serving women's curiosity by explaining, "Dana ye-ikta America," my version of explaining that I had bought the statue to donate to my meditation center in the United States. The women were so happy for me that they bowed and exclaimed, "Sadhu!" ("well done") as they delighted in my generosity. We the givers are the lucky ones, because giving brings joy to the karmic stream of our hearts.

The entire transmission of the Buddha dharma has taken place in the field of generosity. For 2,600 years the teachings have been transmitted through the generous sharing of resources, time, and energy. In current times, countless practitioners volunteer to run community dharma centers, serve on boards at retreat centers, and carry out myriad other tasks that keep the teachings flourishing. We receive the love expressed in this generosity each time we hear the teachings and practice meditation. Then we, through our own practice and ways of sharing, pass it on, joining in this beautiful stream of giving.

The Practice of Giving

Many years ago I explored giving while drinking my morning tea and watching the birds at the feeder. I found myself thinking, *I've spent a lot of money on bird feeders and bird food. Have I gotten my money's worth? Have I gotten enough enjoyment that it is worth the money I've paid?** As I contemplated this way, noticing tightness and contraction in my heart-mind, I decided to try a different orientation. I thought, *This bird food is my gift to the birds, so that they may be nourished, healthy, and happy.* I felt freer and lighter. Then my heart took one more step, unprompted. The birds and I were each fulfilling our role in the universe in a wonderful, interconnected dance. No giver, no receiver—just the dance. My heart-mind felt open, unburdened by self-concern.

---

* For those of you who are not familiar with bird feeders, they're quite expensive. Every so often the bears run off with the bird feeder and they (the birdfeeders!) need to be replaced.

Giving is a dynamic part of our Buddhist path. For some it comes with ease; others engage in years of inquiry in order to develop it. Because we have a lot of conditioning around resources and sharing, generosity practice involves unpacking any unhelpful conditioning and learning what leads to real happiness. We explore our deepest beliefs around self and other, scarcity and abundance. We practice giving and then we see what the result is: How does it feel to give? How does it impact our relationships? How does it impact the world? We check out the teaching on generosity and learn through our own experience.

Generosity is not just giving financial resources, although that can be part of it. We all possess many generosity assets: our talent, love, kindness, hospitality, time, energy, and resources. Contemplating these ways of giving, we know our own abundance. We may not have much money, but we have love to give. We may be short on energy, yet we can share our talent. The world is ready to receive what we have to offer.

We humans carry an innate wish to give, and we can nurture that urge. One day when I was teaching a retreat, I walked by the side of housing for elders and met an older man sitting in a motorized wheelchair and wearing a hat marked *George*, with feathers sticking out of it. He said, "Hello! Good afternoon. I'm picking the heads off the dandelions." I replied, "That's really nice service." He said, "Well, it gives me something to do and keeps them from blooming and spreading their seeds." By keeping the lawn pretty, he was clearly enjoying giving in a way he was able.

The Buddha recommended consciously cultivating the joy of giving. We should contemplate the joy before we give, while we're giving, and afterward. During one year-end retreat, every night I made a financial donation. Before I wrote the check, I would think of who or what organization I was supporting and contemplate how they would benefit. Writing out the check, I consciously enjoyed the connection. Afterward I took a few minutes to feel the goodness of my generosity, strengthening the joy of giving. The Buddha said, "In the ideal gift the donor before giving is glad; while giving their mind is inspired; and after giving is gratified." Giving provides gladness, inspiration, and gratification.

As we practice generosity, we attune to the flavor of our giving, exploring the motivation, the volitional energy propelling our actions. Depending on the motivation, the same act has a different impact both in our environment and within our own heart-mind. Traditionally, three kinds of giving are spoken of, each reflecting a different level of attachment and nonattachment, of self and not-self. The first kind, called the *beggarly giving*, is flavored by our own agenda. This orientation corresponds to my thinking about whether I had gotten my money's worth with the birds. This giving is very much about me and what I want. Perhaps we give with one hand, still holding on a bit and wondering whether we should give at all. We may give out of guilt or because we want to be liked. This generosity based in wanting something in return is fueled by calculation and bargaining. We inquire within. *Are we expecting something in return? Are we holding back as we give? Are we reluctant to give?* If so, we feel this in mind, body, and heart. *What beliefs underlie our hesitation? How does our heart feel when we give in this manner? What is the manifestation in the heart and body?* There are no right answers, only our own experience teaching us. Although not the purest giving, beggarly giving is still better than not giving at all, because we are beginning to let go and share.

With the second kind of giving, *friendly giving*, we give what we have openhandedly, sharing because we want to help. This type of giving corresponds with my feeling happy to share with the birds. The flavors of metta and compassion are stronger, and we let go more easily. This offering is clearer of our own agenda, so we have more access to the happiness of giving. *When the gift is more freely given, how does this flow manifest? How does the heart feel? What is the manifestation in the body?* Acknowledging these purer motivations and the desire to serve and alleviate suffering helps strengthen them. We feel joy, connection, and lightness in seeing that our giving makes others happy. The pleasantness of the resulting more open heart-mind and relaxed body serves as a homing device for strengthening our innate desire to give.

The third, or purest, kind of giving is traditionally called *kingly giving*. In the interest of gender and class equality let's call it *selfless giving*. We graciously give the best we have, unattached to how it is received and used. Thinking of ourselves as only temporary caretakers of what we are sharing, we allow things to flow where they most appropriately belong. As with my third kind of giving to the birds, we go beyond the idea of giver and receiver and just experience the dance of the universe, resources flowing where they are needed. There's not much self here, just a free heart-mind. We move through these three kinds of giving with mindfulness and curiosity, letting go wherever we find clinging.

In addition to exploring when we give, we also inquire into the times when we were not generous. *How does the heart feel when we pass up an opportunity to share?* Some of my greatest regrets arise remembering when I could've been generous and wasn't. Feeling that remorse retrains the heart, encouraging us to be more giving in the future. It inspires us to examine our conditioning, our beliefs, and our fears, freeing us to act in the future more aligned with our deeper understanding of interbeing.

Of course, generosity requires discernment. We combine the wish to share with discerning wisdom. *What does this situation call for?* The Buddha was very practical about generosity, teaching that it's important to have strong enough finances to take care of ourselves, our families, and our obligations. Maybe we need to pay our rent instead of giving away our rent money. In practicing generosity, we counteract any unhealthy conditioning that limits our freedom to respond wisely and compassionately. Those of us conditioned to give while disregarding our own needs may need to develop a more flexible response, asking first, *In this situation what do I need?* We let these questions lead us into a healthy giving response to all beings, including ourselves.

We should never doubt the power of generosity. The smallest gestures can have unseen far-reaching effects. I end this chapter with a story from the autobiography of Pablo Neruda, the Nobel Prize–winning Chilean poet who inspired many with his poetry and politics, describing how a small act of giving had lifelong consequences.[3]

One time investigating in the back yard of our home in Temuco, the tiny objects and minuscule beings of my world, I came upon a hole in one of the boards of one of my fences. I looked through the hole and saw a landscape behind me like that of our house, uncared for and wild. I moved back a few steps because I sensed that something was about to happen. All of a sudden, a hand appeared, a tiny hand of a boy about my own age. By the time I came close again the hand was gone and in its place was a marvelous white sheep. The sheep's wool was faded, its wheels had escaped. All this only made it more authentic. I had never seen such a wonderful sheep. I looked back through the hole but the boy had disappeared. I went into my house and brought out a treasure of my own, a pine cone, opened, full of odor and resin which I adored. I set it down in the same spot and went off with the sheep. I never saw either the hand or the boy again and I have never again seen a sheep like that either. . . . That exchange brought home for me the precious idea that all of humanity is somehow together. . . . Just as I once left a pine cone by the fence I have since left my words on the doors of so many people who are unknown to me . . . in prison or hunted or alone. This is the great lesson I learned in my childhood, in the backyard of a lonely house. Maybe it was nothing but a game to play between boys. . . . Yet maybe this small and mysterious exchange of gifts remains inside of me also, deep and indestructible, giving my poetry light.

EPILOGUE AND DEDICATION

Walking by the reservoir early in the evening in late October, I see the geese coming in for the night. They swirl and duck as they approach their landing. They honk raucously as each group alights, reestablishing their connection with each other. *Are you there? Yes, I'm here.* The poignancy of the late afternoon twilight reminds me of how much we need each other. We are always calling to each other, "Are you there?" "Yes, I'm here." As the geese slowly quiet and settle down, I imagine them nestling into the comfort of knowing they are not alone and are surrounded by their community. We too quiet and settle down, surrounded by our ancestors, friends, family, and spiritual community.

We have traveled together through the realm of the heart. We have considered the Buddhist teachings from the angle of the feminine paradigm, through receptivity, feeling, embeddedness, nonconceptual understanding, embodiment, intuition, vibrant aliveness, and love. We have considered the contributing balance of the masculine paradigm, of intellect and the mind, conceptual understanding and wisdom, determination, energy, and initiative. Healing ourselves and healing the world ultimately comes down to this combination of wisdom and love, the spacious reality of the emptiness of intrinsic existence imbued with the interconnectedness of all beings.

As we end our journey together, we have two final activities to engage. First, as we part, it's good to clear the air. I recognize that due to the limits of my own conditioning, there are undoubtedly times when I miss seeing how I may cause harm to others. As we humans stumble our way on this spiritual path, it is good to acknowledge that we have further growth to do. In this vein, I apologize for any ways that, through ignorance or carelessness, my writing has caused harm, confusion, or misunderstanding. I commit to continue learning and growing and humbly ask for your forgiveness.

And to conclude, we began our journey by receiving blessings, and we end by offering them back. We cherish everything: cherish our own lives, each other, the earth, and all beings who live upon her. From the paradigm of interconnectedness, we aspire to share our practice with others. We give away all the good energy that we develop, dedicating it to individual beings, groups of beings, and all beings everywhere. We commit to offering this world our care, gentleness, and fierce compassion. May love and wisdom accompany us as we meet the challenges of our individual lives with all their ups and downs. May we be inspired to share our love, talents, time, energy, and resources to free all beings from suffering. May the positive energy of our practice bring healing and the deepest freedom to me and you, our friends and family, our next-door neighbor, our co-worker, our enemies, our animal friends, our plant companions, and our great big beautiful Earth. Invoking the traditional ritual of dedicating the merit, we offer the fruits of our practice outward for the liberation of all beings in the ten directions and the three periods of time.

GRATITUDES

Acknowledging all the people involved in crafting this book lands us directly in the feminine paradigm of interconnectedness. I used to read acknowledgments with long lists and think, *How do they have so many people helping them? I would never have so many.* Until now. Completing this book has shown me that it takes a village (or a universe) to write a book. The support I have received has buoyed and uplifted me, so I want to name as many contributors as I can. Let's enjoy the generosity of so many wonderful beings. This is not *my* book; it's *our* book.

I thank my father, the late Lee Bradshaw, who took me camping from the time I was a toddler and taught me to be comfortable in wild nature. He ingrained in me the belief that I could do whatever I put my mind to. When I was twelve years old, he dropped off me and my two siblings in the middle of the Boundary Waters wilderness of northern Minnesota with a map and a compass and told us he would meet us in his canoe at a distant lake. When I was fourteen, as a pilot by trade he taught me to solo fly a glider. You get the picture.

I thank my mother, Mary Jo Meadow, who bequeathed me intelligence and determination. We have shared the Buddhist path since I returned from my first three-month retreat and told her about my experience. She said, "I'm going to do that," and by golly she did, completing the next twelve three-month retreats. I'm sure I've inherited some of that grit, too.

I bow to my Asian spiritual ancestors through the centuries, beginning with Siddhartha Gotama, known as the Buddha, and proceeding through the generations of benefactors, monastics, and laypeople who studied, practiced, and transmitted the teachings to the next generation. Their legacy first came to me through Joseph Goldstein who moved me along with his pithy one-liners and steady kindness. Sharon Salzberg, also one of my first teachers, met with me daily as a young twenty-four-year-old in the terrifying realms of deconstructive practice. Ron Browning saved me from going home in the middle of this, not likely to return. My core teacher, Michele McDonald, guided me through years of unfolding insight and trauma healing. She taught me to trust my own practice and to relax into the feminine. Sayadaw U Pandita, Sayadaw U Lakkhana, and unnamed (for security reasons) monks and nuns of the Sagaing Hills of Myanmar gave me a sense of place in the lineage as a daughter of the Buddha. A number of amazing (also unnamed) Burmese people supported us on our retreats in Myanmar; their generosity opened my heart. In later years, Kittisaro and Thanissara shared the Kwan Yin dharmas with me, deepening my connection to the heart practices. My qi gong teacher, Kathryn Komidar, helped me to get my feet on the ground and connect with this Earth.

Many people have encouraged me in this journey. Inger Forland would not stop bothering me to write a book, so I finally gave in. She has also provided invaluable advice. Diana Winston kept reassuring me that I had something important to say. Mary Pipes has been a cheerleader and consultant the whole way. Nancy Burnett encouraged me to drop a masculine framework to the book. Many years ago, Joanne Hedrick told me I teach down-to-earth dharma, and the phrase stuck, providing the title for this book. Many colleagues shared conversations about the feminine, including Myoshin Kelley, Dawn Scott, Roxanne Dault, DaRa Williams, Jean Esther, Erin Treat, Devon Hase, Candace Cassin, Gyano Gibson, and Shelly Graf. In addition, Shelly offered invaluable advice related to inclusive language and provided helpful editing that enlightened some of my ignorance. I also have deep gratitude for my coteachers Greg Scharf, Chas DiCapua, Devin Berry, Tempel Smith, and Brian Lesage who have shared beautiful expressions of the feminine paradigm in male-identified bodies.

My paper mentors are many; I can only mention a few. Dr. Robin Wall Kimmerer gave me the courage to speak freely in the midst of patriarchy about a deep connection with the land and the spirits of the woods. Kathleen Dean Moore and Joanna Macy showed me how to let passion shine. I love how Charlotte Joko Beck doesn't pull her punches. Susan Murphy introduced me to the lyrical in Buddhist writing. James Baldwin nails the truth. Ajahn Chah's simple and direct dharma makes me smile. Thich Nhat Hanh shares so much love. The poets Ryokan, Rumi, Wendell Berry, Mary Oliver, Joy Harjo, the early Buddhist nuns, and many others connect me with the heart.

Jacalyn Bennett embodies the joy of generosity. She offered financial support and a beautiful place (complete with food delivery) to practice and write during the pandemic. Her enthusiasm encouraged me to teach from the deep feminine.

Deborah Dwyer, a copy editor by trade, steadily encouraged me to write a book and provided extensive editorial support during the process.

The BuddPsychs (Jean, Lucy, Laura, Tetty, Zeeb, and the late Betsy) for over two decades have given me a place to be a not-teacher, with my foibles and faults in clear view. They seem to love me anyway, which is a great blessing. The Bristlecones (Carla, Peggy, Linda, Kate, Susan, and the other Rebecca) have anchored the teachings down-to-earth with me.

My godchildren, Chanhna, Davi, and Bona Chuong, have softened me through the joys of mothering them. Thank you, Mao and Chuong, for trusting me with them.

Gregory Thorp, with his incredible eye, generously offered to do a photo shoot. Chanhna and Tamsen Merrill as assistants made it a lot of fun.

My gratitude to the trees for their rootedness and openness and to the flowers for their beauty and enthusiasm. The birds for their singing. The other creatures of the woods and the spirits of the land for their companionship and wise advice. To the bears, moose, fox, deer, woodchucks, skunks, porcupines, and turkeys that wander nearby. To Pearl, Sparky, and Iris Bonita who sweeten our home. To the great Earth itself with her lush generosity and stunning beauty of life.

All the people at Shambhala Publications have been so kind and helpful for this first-time author. I am grateful to Tasha Kimmet who believed in this book from the beginning and shepherded it with incredible skill. Sami Ripley brought it to completion with her talent and kindness. Many others at Shambhala whom I have never met contributed time, energy, and talent in its production.

Oh, but I could go on and on! Who and what *haven't* supported me? Living within the vast interconnected web of life, I could continue for pages. My Dhammapala cohort explored the feminine paradigm with me. The Insight Meditation Society has been my spiritual center for forty years and many people have helped make it feel like home, I am grateful to all of them. Let's also include the teachers, board members, and other volunteers at Insight Meditation Community of western Massachusetts, and the sanghas in the Twin Cities, Minnesota, and Yellow Springs, Ohio. Deep bows to the many who have given generously of their time and energy to support our organizations and taken care of me when I come to teach. The students do the hard work of sitting and practicing, sharing their vulnerability with me. All have contributed to this book.

Certainly, we must conclude with my husband, Bob Barba, who takes care of our home as I gallivant around the world practicing and teaching meditation. He gives me a place to return to, complete with a woodstove, purring cats, and a vegetable garden. He's also willing to camp in the wilderness and carry a canoe a third of a mile straight uphill. I am deeply grateful for his steadfast love and loyalty which have grounded me for over a quarter century.

And to all those I couldn't list by name, my deepest thanks.

May the merit arising from this book be shared with all who have helped create it.

NOTES

Introduction: Preparing for Our Journey

1. This is especially true in white culture and less so in some communities of color that have not been entirely colonized, literally or figuratively.
2. While these Insight Meditation communities are called convert communities, not everybody who participates in these communities would consider themselves a Buddhist convert. Some may come from Asian Buddhist families and see studying meditation at these centers as an extension of the religion they practiced as a child. Some may be of Asian heritage and consider themselves converts because their family did not practice Buddhism. Some would not call themselves Buddhists at all but rather relate to Insight Meditation as a secular tradition.
3. We should note that some brave monks and nuns have reestablished the fully ordained nuns' order in the Theravada lineage without the sanction of some senior monks in this lineage.
4. Those who question whether Buddhism is a patriarchal religion need only read the "eight special rules" that clearly establish male monastic dominance over female monastics. These eight rules, which may have been established by the Buddha himself or may have been inserted into the discourses at a later time (for our purposes, which if true is incidental), provide that any nun of any duration of time is still at a lower rank than any monk, regardless of how long they have been

ordained. In other words, a nun of twenty years is of lower seniority than a monk on day one. In addition, the male monastic order exercises control over the ordinations of the female monastic order, but not vice versa. Bhikkhu Analayo makes a convincing argument that these rules were intended to provide protection to the nuns, but they are patriarchal nonetheless. This patriarchal dominance continues even today, manifesting in resistance to the reestablishment of the nuns' order in Southeast Asia, and also in some quarters in the West.

5. Jenny Odell, *How to Do Nothing: Resisting the Attention Economy* (Brooklyn: Melville House, 2019), 143.

Chapter One: Mindfulness

1. *Heart-mind* may be a phrase unfamiliar to many. In the Pali language, the word that we usually translate as "mind," *citta*, can be rendered as "mind" or "heart." While we in the West tend to separate heart and mind, in many Asian languages the words for these are interchangeable. The Chinese and Japanese characters for "mind" can also be translated as "heart." The preference in the West for the word "mind" reflects our tendency toward the masculine paradigm. I often use "heart-mind" in order to bring out fuller expression and choose just the word "heart" or "mind" when more appropriate for the context.

2. This quote originated with author John Barth.

3. Jane Hirshfield, trans., *The Ink Dark Moon: Love Poems by Ono no Kamuchi and Izumi Shikibu* (New York: Penguin Random House, 1990).

4. Paul Shepard, *New Self, New World: Recovering Our Senses in the Twenty-first Century* (Berkeley: North Atlantic Books, 2010), 85.

5. Eihei Dōgen Zenji, from comment on Michael Mullooly, "Contemplation on the New Year," *The Buddha Times*, vol. 23, January 5, 2002, www.thebuddhatimes.com.

6. Li Po, "Zazen on Ching-T'ing Mountain," in *Crossing the Yellow River: Three Hundred Poems from the Chinese*, translated by Sam Hamill (Rochester, NY: Tiger Bark Press, 2013), 94.

7. Elizabeth Kolbert, *Under a White Sky: The Nature of the Future* (New York: Crown/Random House/Penguin Random House LLC, 2021), 86.

8. Thomas Berry, *The Sacred Universe: Earth, Spirituality, and Religion in the Twenty-First Century* (New York: Columbia University Press, 2009), 95.

9. Iris Murdoch, *A Fairly Honorable Defeat* (New York: Penguin Publishing Group, 2001), 170.

10. This version of the quotation is widely circulated, though the exact origin of the translation is unclear. Another translation of this quote is: "Responding to the myriad things from the perspective of the self is delusion. Manifesting the self from the perspective of the myriad things is enlightenment." This translation can be found in Kazuaki Tanahashi, *The True Dharma Eye: Zen Master Dōgen's Three Hundred Koans* (Boulder: Shambhala, 2005), 22.

11. Rainer Maria Rilke, *Ahead of All Parting: The Selected Poetry and Prose of Rainer Maria Rilke* (New York: Modern Library/Random House, 1995).

Chapter Two: The Body

1. Audre Lorde, "Poetry is Not a Luxury," *Chrysalis: A magazine of Women's Culture*, vol. 3 (1977).

2. The Four Noble Truths is the central Buddhist teaching, describing suffering, its cause, its release, and the path to develop. The Noble Eightfold Path is this very path, emphasizing ethics, heart-mind development, and wisdom. The Four Foundations of Mindfulness is the key meditation discourse, covering the body, feeling tone, the mind, and the principles of phenomena.

3. Richard Wagamese, *Embers: One Ojibway's Meditations* (Toronto: Douglas and McIntyre, 2016), 99.

4. Jacques Lusseyran, *And There Was Light: The Extraordinary Memoir of a Blind Hero of the French Resistance in World War II* (Edinburgh, Scotland: Floris Books, 1985), 15–16.

5. Chögyam Trungpa Rinpoche, *The Myth of Freedom and the Way of Meditation* (Boulder: Shambhala Library, 2005), 121.

6. David Chadwick, *To Shine One Corner of the World* (Broadway Books: New York City, 2009), 28.

7. Elizabeth Hutton Turner, *Georgia O'Keeffe, The Poetry of Things* (New Haven, CT: Yale University Press, 1999).

Chapter Three: Effort from the Heart

1. Bhikkhu Bodhi, "1.1. Crossing the Flood," *Sutta Central*, accessed March 12, 2024, https://suttacentral.net/sn1.1/en/bodhi?lang=en&reference=none&highlight=false.
2. Oscar Wilde and Henry Zick, *The Writings of Oscar Wilde* (Lancaster, PA: Wentworth Press, 2016).
3. Rumi, "The Road Home," in *The Essential Rumi*, translated by Coleman Barks (San Francisco: HarperOne, 2004).
4. Some debate has arisen over whether this was a mistranslation of what Sayadaw U Pandita really said, which may have been closer to "Please continue making effort."
5. T. S. Eliot, "Little Gidding," in *Four Quartets* (Boston: Harcourt, 1943), 59.
6. Charlotte Joko Beck, *Ordinary Wonder: Zen Life and Practice* (Boulder, CO: Shambhala Publications, 2021).

Chapter Four: Exploring Our Relationship to Feeling Tone

1. Samyutta Nikaya 22.26, 22.27, 22.28, www.suttacentral.net.
2. Susan Murphy, *Upside Down Zen* (Somerville, MA: Wisdom Publications, 2006), 106.

Chapter Five: Introduction to Emotions

1. Tsoknyi Rinpoche, "How to Make Friends with Your Beautiful Monsters," *Lion's Roar*, February 16, 2023, https://www.lionsroar.com/how-to-make-friends-with-your-monsters.
2. Natalie Goldberg, "Meeting the Chinese in St. Paul: Rhino Hits the Midwest," *Lion's Roar*, September 1, 2007.
3. Sarah Hampson, "He Has Tried in His Way to Be Free," *Lion's Roar*, November 1, 2007.

Chapter Six: Challenging Heart-Mind States

1. Charlotte Joko Beck, *Nothing Special: Living Zen* (New York: Harper-Collins, 1993), 46–47.

2. T. S. Eliot, "Burnt Norton," in *Four Quartets* (Boston: Harcourt, 1943), 14.

3. Pema Chödrön, *When Things Fall Apart: Heart Advice for Difficult Times* (Boulder, CO: Shambhala, Anniversary Edition, 2016).

Chapter Seven: The Heavenly Homes

1. If you haven't practiced these meditations, you may want to take the opportunity to find instructions and guided meditations to lead you. Dharmaseed.org is a great resource.

2. Kathleen Dean Moore, *Earth's Wild Music: Celebrating and Defending the Songs of the Natural World* (Berkeley, CA: Counterpoint, 2021), 59–60.

3. Dr. Martin Luther King Jr., "Where Do We Go from Here?" Speech delivered at the 11th annual SCLC convention, Atlanta, Georgia, August 16, 1967, www.plough.com, posted January 17, 2021.

4. Henry Wadsworth Longfellow, *The Complete Works of Henry Wadsworth Longfellow* (Ann Arbor, MI: Scholarly Publishing Office, University of Michigan Library, 2005).

5. Thich Nhat Hanh, *Being Peace* (San Francisco: Parallax Press, 1987), 111.

6. Thich Nhat Hanh, *Peace Is Every Step: The Path of Mindfulness in Everyday Life* (New York: Random House Publishing Group, 1992).

7. Resistance Revival Chorus, "'This Joy' by the Resistance Revival Chorus," YouTube, September 15, 2020, https://youtu.be/1TbDP-wAo9Bc?si=68Yf5R-ZDf0Zq8FF.

8. This may be one of those instances when my default conditioning as a straight white person becomes clear. It is much easier to feel safe in the world when not faced with the very real dangers of racism, homophobia, and transphobia. As a woman, for example, I am not going to walk alone down an alley at night with only metta to protect me.

9. There is a word for this kind of distress: *solastalgia*, a concept coined by Glenn Albrecht in 2005 to describe the grief we feel seeing environmental destruction of our home, a kind of homesickness while still at home.

10. Ryokan, *One Robe, One Bowl: The Zen Poetry of Ryokan*, translated by John Stevens (Toronto: Weatherhill/Penguin Random House, 2006).

11. Woodland Daily Democrat, "Chico Author Lin Jensen on the Imagery of Words," *Daily Democrat*, October 2, 2008, https://www.dailydemocrat.com/2008/10/02/biblio-file-chico-author-lin-jensen-on-the-imagery-of-words.

12. Shunryu Suzuki in David Chadwick, *To Shine One Corner of the World* (New York: Broadway Books, 2001).

13. Desmond Tutu, *No Future without Forgiveness* (New York: Penguin Random House 2012), 35.

14. The Work of Byron Katie, "Forgiveness," Facebook, September 21, 2022, https://www.facebook.com/theworkofbyronkatie/videos/forgiveness/1807294416281601.

15. Aleksandr Solzhenitsyn, *Gulag Archipelago* (New York: HarperCollins, 2007).

16. Peter Gay, *The Enlightenment: An Interpretation: The Rise of Modern Paganism* (New York: Knoft, 1966).

17. Larry Rosenberg, *Living in the Light of Death: On the Art of Being Truly Alive* (New York: Penguin Random House, 2021), 44.

18. Diane Beresford-Kroeger, *To Speak for the Trees: My Life's Journey from Ancient Celtic Wisdom to a Healing Vision of the Forest* (Toronto: Random House Canada), 264.

19. Joanna Macy, "Healing Begins With Gratitude," *Lion's Roar* online, November 23, 2021.

20. Nhat Hanh, *Being Peace*, 38.

21. I appreciate Abhayagiri Monastery for their contribution to my understanding of this compound phrase.

22. Dr. Robin Wall Kimmerer, *Braiding Sweetgrass* (Minneapolis: Milkweed Editions, 2015).

23. It is important to note that the Buddha taught that the conditions of our lives come together through many causes and conditions, and karma is just one of them. Karma is empowering because it is a cause that we can influence. He also explained that trying to determine the precise workings of karma will cause madness and vexation. Better not to try.

Chapter Eight: Impermanence

1. William Maxwell, *The Chateau* (New York: Alfred A. Knopf, 1961), inscribed on page 393.
2. Ajahn Chah, *Everything Arises, Everything Falls Away*, translated by Paul Breiter (Boston: Shambhala Publications, 2005), 42.

Chapter Nine: Stress and Suffering

1. Kathleen Norris, *The Cloister Walk* (New York: Penguin Random House, 1996), 94.
2. From "Freedom from Suffering," jackkornfield.com, April 23, 2019.

Chapter Ten: Not-Self

1. Matthew Fox, "Aquinas: 'Capable of the Universe'—Humanity's Greatness," *Daily Meditations with Matthew Fox*, July 13, 2022, https://dailymeditationswithmatthewfox.org/2022/07/13/aquinas-capable-of-the-universe-humanitys-greatness.
2. Eihei Dōgen, "Actualizing the Fundamental Point," translated by Robert Aiken and Kazuaki Tanahashi, *The Zen Site*, accessed October 29, 2023, www.thezensite.com.
3. Pablo d'Ors, *Biography of Silence: An Essay on Meditation* (San Francisco: Parallax Press, 2018), 80.
4. Yadonashi Kodo Hokkusan and Uchiyama Kosho Roshi, *The Zen Teaching of "Homeless Kodo"* (Boston: Wisdom Publications, 2014).
5. Richard Rohr, *Falling Upward: A Spirituality for the Two Halves of Life* (San Francisco: Jossey-Bass Publishing, 2011), 82.
6. Ryokan, John Stevens, trans., *One Robe, One Bowl: The Zen Poetry of Ryokan* (Toronto, ON: Weatherhill/Penguin Random House, 1977), 33.

7. Master Hsuan Hua, "Zero: The Great Bright Store of Your Own Nature: Lectures by Venerable Master Hsuan Hua," *City of 10,000 Buddhas*, accessed March 8, 2024, https://www.cttbusa.org/dharmatalks/zero.htm.

Chapter Eleven: Freedom

1. David Foster Wallace, *Infinite Jest* (New York: Bay Back Books, Anniversary Edition, 2006).
2. Issa, translated by R. H. Blyth, *Volume 2: Spring* (Hokuseido Press, 1950), 363.
3. T. S. Eliot, "Little Gidding," 59.
4. Sallie Tisdale, *Women of the Way: Discovering 2500 Years of Buddhist Wisdom* (New York: HarperCollins, 2007), 263.

Chapter Twelve: The Path of Love

1. In later Mahayana Buddhism, more emphasis is placed on both wisdom and compassion as necessary components of the path. In Tibetan Buddhism, wisdom is considered feminine because the deepest practice comes from the feminine archetype, and compassion is considered masculine because of its active component.

Chapter Thirteen: Engaging with Our World

1. Jenny Odell, *How to Do Nothing* (Brooklyn: Melville House Publishing, 2019), 145.
2. Susan Murphy, *Red Thread Zen* (Berkeley: Counterpoint, 2016), 23.
3. To be clear, not all trans people may share this perspective, and Kate Bornstein's thinking may have evolved since this time. We could also consider the privilege we may have of waking up and not having to consider our gender identity at all.
4. Lin Jensen, "Stand By Me," in *Shambhala Sun*, November 2010.
5. The Taoist and the Activist," *Lunch with Bokara* episode 11 with Dr. Benjamin Tong (San Francisco: Cultural and Educational Media Productions, May 22, 2005).

6. Blanche Hartman, *Seeds for a Boundless Life* (Boulder, CO: Shambhala Publications, 2015), 10.

7. Sharon Salzberg, "Love Everyone: A Guide for Spiritual Activists," *Lion's Roar*, November 8, 2022.

8. John Lewis (@repjohnlewis), "Do not get lost in a sea of despair," X, July 16, 2019, https://x.com/repjohnlewis/status/1151155571757867011?s=20.

Chapter Fourteen: Our Ethical Integrity

1. Charlotte Joko Beck, *Everyday Zen* (New York: HarperCollins, 2009).

2. The Ambalatthika Rahulovada Sutta, Instructions to Rahula at Mango Stone, MN 61.

3. These precepts can be accessed at www.fivechanges.com. The more recent version has some changes.

4. Anguttara Nikaya 8.39, the Abhisanda Sutta.

Chapter Fifteen: Generosity

1. Pema Chödrön, *Becoming Bodhisattvas: A Guidebook for Compassionate Action* (Boulder, CO: Shambhala Publications, 2018).

2. Ethan Nichtern, *One City: A Declaration of Interdependence* (Somerville, MA: Wisdom Publications), 87. A hungry ghost is a being with a huge belly and a narrow throat, leading to perpetual hunger and craving for more.

3. Pablo Neruda and Robert Bly, "Childhood and Poetry," from the introduction to *Neruda and Vallejo: Selected Poems* (Boston: Beacon Press, 1973).

CREDITS

Chapter 10 was previously published as "Experience the Truth of No Self" in *Lion's Roar*, July 2023. It has been slightly edited here.

"Watching the moon" from *The Ink Dark Moon: Love Poems by Ono No Komachi and Izumi Shikibu, Women of the Ancient Court of Japan* translated by Jane Hirshfield with Mariko Aratani, translation copyright © 1986, 1987, 1988, 1989, 1990 by Jane Hirshfield. Used by permission of Vintage Books, an imprint of the Knopf Doubleday Publishing Group, a division of Penguin Random House LLC. All rights reserved.

Li Po, "Zazen on Ching-t'ing Mountain" from *Crossing the Yellow River: Three Hundred Poems from the Chinese*, translated by Sam Hamill. Copyright © 2000 by Sam Hamill. Reprinted with the permission of The Permissions Company, LLC on behalf of Tiger Bark Press, tigerbarkpress.com.

"Little Gidding" by T. S. Eliot on p. 79 used with permission from Faber and Faber Ltd.

ABOUT THE AUTHOR

REBECCA BRADSHAW is a Buddhist Insight Meditation teacher living in the hills of western Massachusetts with her husband and their two cats. She has been practicing Buddhist Vipassana meditation since 1983 in the United States and Myanmar (Burma) and teaching since 1993. She completed her dharma teacher training at Insight Meditation Society in Barre, Massachusetts, where she is part of the three-month retreat teacher team, leads retreats for young adults, and has served as a Guiding Teacher. Rebecca has also completed studies in Western psychology and holds a master's degree in counseling psychology. Rebecca's teaching focuses on down-to-earth embodied practice flavored with vibrancy from her years of qi gong practice. Her meditation teaching style is infused with large doses of lovingkindness and compassion in order to strengthen our hearts to touch and be touched deeply by life. The woods, lakes, animals, and plants are also her teachers, and their lessons are embedded in all that she shares. Her hope is that we can free our hearts and minds, learn to connect deeply with life, and be of service to our communities and our planet during these challenging times. For more information, please see her webpage at www.rebeccabradshaw.org.